the

Fasli

to life. I love Delafield's hum

Tuesday, May 2nd

...eak a cord again. Tell ...urie

...y wittily, as I think, that

...ave 4 seasons, Winter, Winter

... Winter.

...y in and attend to the exigencies

... correspondence, but Mrs. Pollar

... the middle tis very garru...

...e tells another xAuntie Nell

... e-solemnity that Work Does...

...ree with Her; at Her Age

...ght to be pensioned off. T...

... versation is very well sust...

... it mildly, x topics ra...

... wide field from the heate...

... the ever. recurrent Political

May 13th. Sat.

Picks with Hilda Tooth.

May 14th Sunday. Day xBest cam

THESE WONDERFUL RUMOURS!

At the outbreak of the Second World War, May Smith was twenty-four and lived with her parents in a small Derbyshire village. Suddenly, the life she had been recording in her diary changed completely. Evacuees arrived at the local school where she taught, and the young men of her circle donned khaki and disappeared to unimaginably distant places to join the fighting; soon, nights would be broken by the wail of the sirens as German bombers flew overhead. But her diary also shows that other things went on as usual, with tennis parties, rugby-club dances and holidays to Llandudno, and that some lesser struggles – such as buying a new hat – were also much on May's mind. And it was over the course of these difficult years that May discovered, to her great surprise, that she was falling in love.

Through May's observant, witty and sometimes acerbic journal, we gain a new insight into how the people of Britain coped with the uncertainty, the fear, the heartbreak and the black comedy of life on the Home Front.

THESE WONDERFUL RUMOURS!

A Young Schoolteacher's
Wartime Diaries 1939–1945

MAY SMITH

Edited by Duncan Marlor
and
Introduced by Juliet Gardiner

virago

Note on the text: Some minor changes have been made to punctuation.
Paragraphing has been adjusted in a few places.
Some names have been changed.

VIRAGO

First published in Great Britain in 2012 by Virago Press

Copyright © Duncan Marlor/The Estate of May Smith 2012

The moral right of the author has been asserted.

A CIP catalogue record for this book
is available from the British Library.

ISBN 978-1-84408-810-2

Typeset in Minion by M Rules
Printed and bound in Great Britain by
Clays Ltd, St Ives plc

Papers used by Virago are from well-managed forests
and other responsible sources.

MIX
Paper from
responsible sources
FSC® C104740

Virago Press
An imprint of
Little, Brown Book Group
100 Victoria Embankment
London EC4Y 0DY

An Hachette UK Company
www.hachette.co.uk

www.virago.co.uk

CONTENTS

INTRODUCTION

Juliet Gardiner

H. G. Wells called the Great War the 'people's war' in 1914. He would later be embarrassed by the epithet, considering it to be a propagandist slogan, a call to arms for the nation. There could be no such reticence about the Second World War. Long before hostilities were declared on 3 September 1939 it was clear that the label had an indisputable veracity. The six long years of war would affect, and in most cases involve, the entire population of Britain (and most of the rest of the world too). Rationing, the blackout, shortages, privations, restrictions and regulations – as well as destruction, loss, injury and death – all impacted on the civilian population. To use a time-worn phrase, civilians were in the front line of war; the Home Front became another battle front – one on which, as Churchill recognised, the war could equally be lost if morale cracked and production ground to a halt.

Nevertheless, wartime was a differently inflected experience: country dwellers were equally as affected as those living in the East End of London, Merseyside, Glasgow and other such continuously targeted areas by strictures such as the blackout (though there had been arguments that only designated 'danger zones' – cities and industrial conurbations – should be so constrained), rationing and other inconveniences. All suffered. Bombs fell sometimes seemingly at random over most of Britain;

almost every city, town or village had their casualties on the battlefield and many on the Home Front too. Those areas that did not dispatch evacuees were usually in receipt of them, and the anxiety, fear and, perhaps above all, the exhaustion of such an interminably long war ground down everyone.

It is because the Second World War was a 'people's war' in myriad ways that the people's experience is so valued. And we are fortunate that, in the knowledge that they were living in extraordinary times, many wrote diaries and long, descriptive letters about how life was then – all of course with different experiences to relate, a different perspective, freighting different peacetime baggage into their wartime lives. There are the diaries that Mass Observation urged its respondents to keep, some of which, most notably those of Nella Last, 'Housewife 49' living in Barrow-in-Furness, have been published. Then there are others – and letters too – deposited in the Imperial War Museum, and in many local record offices and local studies libraries throughout the country. And now there is May Smith's.

May was an elementary school teacher living with her parents in Swadlincote in Derbyshire. She was an intelligent, educated, devastatingly clear-eyed and often wittily acerbic young woman – twenty-four when the war began and thirty when VE Day celebrated the end of the war in Europe on 8 May and hostilities against Japan finally ceased on 15 August 1945. She did not particularly like teaching – she often felt she was more of a lion-tamer than an instructor of her often high-spirited, sometimes unruly charges.

Education undoubtedly suffered during the war: it was a reserved occupation for older men as most of the younger male teachers were conscripted into the forces or directed into war work and schools were obliged to persuade retired teachers to return to the classroom. A town such as Swadlincote was categorised as a reception area receiving evacuees from inner-city

Birmingham and these children had to be fitted into already over-crowded schools – in 1944 May rejoices that she 'only' has forty children in her class for once. Schools dealt with the problem in a variety of ways – running a shift system was one. Local pupils were taught in the morning, say, with incomers getting their education in the afternoon, which is what seems to have happened at May's school with often a frustrating shortage of books, paper and pencils owing to the demands of war. However, her jaundiced view of a teacher's life took a salutary jolt in 1941 when rumours circulated that younger female teachers might be compulsorily directed into munitions or aircraft factories to take over from the increasing number of men needed for the forces, and May decided that instructing children won out over welding.

She looked forward to the holidays – frequently curtailed in wartime when 'inessential' travel was discouraged and 'holidays at home' were promoted instead – and also to pay-day since her fondness for new outfits, underwear, shoes and books invariably left May in debt to her family: 'only 4*d.* to live on for the rest of the month' was a frequent refrain. This proved one place where romance – if that is the word – could step into the breach. May had been jilted by a clergyman, Ron, in the mid-1930s which had clearly caused her some heartache but she was now pursued by two beaux: 'Old Friend Freddie', a fellow teacher, and the solid 'Dougie Dear' who sent regular missives from the Fens – where he was a member of the Home Guard – as well as a fattened cockerel at Christmas and the occasional welcome parcels of eggs and vegetables to eke out her wartime rations. Apparently May didn't suffer too badly – indeed 'lashings of cream' make regular appearances at celebrations and holidays. Her weight (gain, rather than loss) was a constant preoccupation, though her frequently noted skin eruptions suggest a rather carbohydrate-heavy wartime diet lacking in fresh fruit and vegetables. When these two suitors visited (separately – a balancing act May conducted with some adroitness) they would take her to the 'flicks', usually paying, and sometimes treating her to a box of chocolates in the circle rather than a packet of Mintoes in the cheaper seats in the stalls.

But May Smith's wartime diary is not simply a chronicle of films seen, food eaten, clothes bought and altered, hair permed (usually with disastrous results), tennis club doings, atrocious weather, clever-clogs teachers evacuated from Southend anxious to show off their general knowledge at WEA lectures, and would-be lovers kept dangling to make them 'keener'. She listens to Churchill's speeches broadcast by the BBC and finds them uplifting and inspiring, and worries intermittently about the course of the war: 'Awful news. Holland's fallen!' Doug's younger brother is killed in Italy, friends' sons and husbands are posted as missing, May conducts regular gas-mask drills with her class, there are interminable queues for food, the bus to Derby passes through streets of houses sporting windows shattered from air raids, 'bombees' arrive from London and Birmingham seeking temporary billets and May is enlisted to help. And night after night the family repair to Grandma's house nearby where they pass sleepless nights crammed into the cold cellar until the All Clear sounds, and a bone-weary May has to trudge to school the next morning 'feeling like a wet rag'. And while 'Dougie dear' volunteers for the Army Transport service, the 'faithful Fred' (or sometimes the 'faithless' or 'false Fred' when he is suspected of dallying with a comely WAAF) joins the meteorological section of the RAF and is threatened with an overseas posting.

May was an admirer of E. M. Delafield's *Diary of a Provincial Lady* (1930), enjoyed Delafield's regular column in *Time & Tide* and was eager to buy a copy of *The Provincial Lady in Wartime* ('but funds are low', again) and her own diary shares many of the charms and stylistics of Delafield's – albeit a life lived several social notches down. There are similar wry observations and asides, a general puncturing of wartime pretensions and pomposities, and even the same liberal use of capital letters when doing so: 'Warned Against Idle Chatter' or 'Paper Is Going To Be Scarce'; shop assistant informed me that 'Hat Trimming Shouldn't Be The Exact Colour'. May kept a diary before and after the war according to her son Duncan Marlor, who edited this volume. She was a natural diarist – a rarer gift than one might imagine.

The Second World War was an exceptional time – for everyone. But of course it was also part of the history of the twentieth century – its political, economic, social and cultural narrative for six years. The great appeal of May's diary is how it enables us to understand the mundaneness as well as the drama of life in the 1940s: a mélange of dreadful events, freezing winters, endless rain, the occasional boiling-hot summer day, anxiety, bereavements, chilblains, no central heating, not going to church without a hat, the shame of unmarried mothers, borrowed wedding dresses, the contempt for Conscientious Objectors ('Conchies ought to wear skirts') despite the immense bravery of those of them who volunteered for one of the most dangerous jobs on the Home Front – defusing unexploded bombs. Frizzy hair, the constant worry about laddering stockings when new ones were like gold dust, and a fervid rumour factory that seemed to work overtime luridly exaggerating what was already quite bad enough – in her diaries May Smith dilutes the exceptionalism of wartime and provides a compellingly authentic snapshot of life as it was really lived. On 5 September 1942, her mother voiced her two most pressing concerns. 'What should we do if Hitler suddenly walked through the front door? Suppose Freddie asked you to meet him in Derby when Doug was here?'

That, without a doubt, is how it was.

Juliet Gardiner
2012

May Smith, 1940

1938–1939

As 1938 drew to a close, in May Smith's diary bulletins on international politics had given way to accounts of home, friends and school, spiced with the occasional scandal. It is at this point that these extracts begin. We find the Smith family living in two houses in West Street, Swadlincote: at 27 are the diarist and her parents, along with Miss Sanders, their lodger, who is a teacher at the Church School; at 46 live May's paternal grandparents, both in their eighties, May's Aunt Frances (fifties), and their lodger Mr Skerritt (mid-twenties), who works in the accounts department of the local Wraggs' Potteries and is a Baptist lay preacher.

Wednesday, December 21st 1938: Christmas is very near now. Life maintains a very even, very monotonous, uneventful and dull tenor. There are no great ups and no great downs, no highlights and no abysmal depths. But oh, how dull without them! I seem to have no inclination towards diarising now – there is so little of any note to record.

Am the honoured recipient of A Christmas Card today – from His Reverence the Bishop of Brimington!* Feel again many a pang and a little ache. Scrutinise both card and envelope closely, as if to learn as much as I can from them. The card is a small wood-cut with 'Ron' scribbled in very minute letters in one corner inside. The envelope looks as though it were one of so many hundreds – dashed off at an enormous rate, for the writing is so scribbled as to be almost illegible. Place aforesaid card apart from my others, Very Reverently, in my handbag. Oh dear! The past seems very glowing compared with the present.

*This is May's soubriquet for her former suitor, Ron, now a curate in North Derbyshire.

I wish Ron hadn't made himself so incomparable when I knew him.

A Day of Agony at school – it being the occasion of our school parties. And oh! – the noise! Exhort the children feverishly to whisper to each other instead of shouting, but all to no purpose. Somehow manage to crawl home, well-nigh exhausted, on aching feet, at 8.30 p.m.

Friday, December 23rd: Oh day of days! Trot to school amidst the slush and sleet with basket of little gifts for my fellow workers. Find a present already parked on my table – bath cubes etc from Big Miss Smith. Small children trot in during the morn bearing offerings and oblations from Miss Dennis, Miss Harvey, Miss Rees, Miss Ford and Miss Foster. Exercise great self-control – handle and poke but do not unwrap.

Children very hilarious, and my many pleadings, threats and blandishments fall on deaf ears when the nuts, oranges, apples and sweets appear. Half-past eleven soon comes, and with relief we throw the children out and sally forth homewards.

Charge about in the afternoon doing last-minute shopping, then go to the library to choose Christmas reading. Finally emerge with *Four Tales* by Buchan and *T. E. Lawrence By His Friends*. Start reading the latter, and am filled with envy.

Saturday, December 24th: Christmas Eve – oh be joyful! – also the occasion of one of Bella's periodic returns to the hamlet of her birth. Accordingly decide to make an effort and park myself on Burton station to meet her. Turn out in the teeth of an easterly gale, and arrive just as the train has gone out. However, am told by an official that there are three more trains from Derby within as many minutes. See a man in the ticket booth whom I feel sure to be Mr Wood who knows Bella, so ask him if she has passed that way. He says No, and proceeds to ask How my Sister Is. Not time to explain the mistaken identity so I say Getting Better.* Crowded train draws in but still fail to locate Bella, decide to wait no longer and go home still clutching the bath salts which I had taken to present to her. Discover later that she was on the Crowded Train.

Proceed to Bella's after tea and go Xmas shopping to Burton. Bella buys *Peregrine's Progress* to read, in view of the fact that it is about a little man being in love with a tall heroine, and the boy in the office, Chivers, has told her to read it. Incidentally, he is small, and Bella is tall. Bella says that he is Awfully Nice – much nicer than John Scott.

Christmas Day, 1938: Am awakened at the crack of dawn and stretch a toe forth into the freezing outer world. Withdraw it hurriedly, but the deed has to be done, so I hop out and am soon scudding along to church. Am late. Amy comes home afterwards to breakfast. Then begins the delightful job of undoing parcels. Have a very varied and very acceptable assortment – fur gloves and two undersets from Mother, scent (Quelques Fleurs) from Dad, jumper from Auntie Nell, green satin pyjamas from Grandma and Auntie Frances, four pairs of stockings, a box of chocolates, a bracelet, a rolled-gold watch-strap from Amy, bath crystals and soap from Bella, cubes and soap from Miss Smith, a fruit knife from Miss Foster, lavender water from Miss Harvey, bath cubes from Miss Ford, a blue address book from Delia, a Booklovers' Diary from Miss Sanders, an engagement calendar from Miss Dennis, a powder puff, handknitted gloves from Swanee, hankies from Hilda Tooth and a lovely maroon leather handbag from Doug. All this results in Amy's and my being late for church, and I drop my umbrella with a clatter when we get there. Go garbed in blue coat with new gloves, watch-strap and bracelet, and feel very dazzling – but less so when I see Barbara

*May had no sisters or brothers.

Aldridge there in new three-quarter length fur coat and hat with veil, looking very spruce and smart.

The usual Christmas dinner of turkey and plum pudding at Grandma's, followed by fruit, chocolates etc. Continue reading T. E. Lawrence. Then Mother, Dad and I migrate to Midway for tea – usual family party. Tea takes until 6, then play bagatelle. To Grandma's for supper about 10 – the remains of the turkey brought forth. And so to bed.

December 26th, Boxing Day: Yes – and so to bed! What a night. Awaken about 1.30 a.m. with a Most Unpleasant Feeling which speedily resolves itself into the conviction that I am Going To Be Sick. Bleat piteously to myself, and moan several times aloud into the darkness, Oh, I Do Feel Sick, hoping that someone will hear me. Hear the bed creak in the next room, so make my wail rise to a crescendo, and Mother comes in in time for the Awful Agonising Process. Am revived a little by water and a piece of apple afterwards, feel a little better, then fall asleep again.

Oversleep after all this, and arise at 11 with a nagging headache. Crawl to Grandma's and spend the day drowsing over the fire – which makes me feel worse! Ponder dolefully upon how these holiday times seem to fall short always of expectations. Read more of *T. E. Lawrence* but headache prevents my getting very much further. All the same, I am thoroughly enjoying the book. He was a remarkable man.

Play cards and read in the evening – both by the fire – and get very hot thereby. Place the glass firescreen in front of the blaze, and it comes out eventually in curly cracks – about which Grandma makes great moan throughout the rest of the evening.

I wish I had the power of Deep Thought. I don't find myself ever thinking intensively about anything. When I read books, I don't ponder over or criticise them – I merely read them for the story with the passive, unthinking part of my mind. I'm sure my mind used to be more alert than it is now.

Wednesday, December 28th: Wander down at disgraceful hour again, and in a spasm of orderliness and feverish energy dismantle wardrobe and put it straight, after the chaotic state in which it has stood these many moons. Seem to have lots of things to wear but nothing Decent. I wonder why? Sort out two boxes under bed containing scarves, hats and gloves. Proceed then to tidy drawers.

Mother remarks tactlessly but truthfully that I am Getting Older and shall be 25 next. Am appalled; it sounds fantastic and horrible that I should be so old. Feel really moth-eaten and decrepit.

Receive grateful letter of thanks from Doug for the cuff-links – thanking me also and especially 'for the thought behind it'. Oh dear! – the only thought behind it was the realisation that he'd send me a present and that I must perforce make some return. I hope he doesn't think that they were an offering of love or a silent witness to my consuming passion for him. Because they're not. Compose letter to him, thanking him very much for 'the lovely handbag', remarking upon the beautiful colour (which I dubbed 'queer' when I first saw it – but like better now). I am a Hypocrite. Does politeness always entail hypocrisy, I wonder?

Am still engrossed in *T. E. Lawrence* – think he's simply marvellous. When I read books like this it makes me dissatisfied with my own life. I seem to be doing so little with it, and my youth – the most precious part of one's life – is slipping away leaving nothing concrete behind. Life is very complicated. I lack driving power.

Feel more settled now I have re-established contact with my diary.

Saturday, December 31st: The last day of the Old Year. We migrate to a family party at Jack's. Twelve of us there and we play charades, scissors, tip-it, man and his object, bagatelle and cards. Have supper just before midnight, then sing Auld Lang Syne. Joyce wonders whether we'll all be singing it next year. I wonder. I hope so. Listen in to the New Year ushered in, in characteristic style in Scotland (with a wee drappie), Ireland (with dances and folk songs) and Wales (with a horse's head and mummers), and lastly in Cheapside, with 'The Old Bull and Bush' etc. Shortly after this we stream out into the depths of darkness outside. A drenching walk home follows, in torrents of rain and with no protective umbrella or mac. See Mr Skerritt also bound for home, so he comes in with us to let in our New Year. And so to bed at 2 a.m. on this first morning of 1939. Intend to make resolutions but so far have had no time. Goodbye, 1938!

Sunday, January 1st, 1939: Hello, 1939! I wonder what variety of events you have awaiting us? On the whole 1938 wasn't very eventful. It brought no startling changes and no new friends – except Delia perhaps. But one cannot attribute changes – except physical ones – to the years. I suppose it is we ourselves who enact changes. Once ensconced in a nice comfortable groove, there can be no considerable change – from within at any rate. I am beginning to wonder whether I am not in a groove. It needs courage to get out of one. So far I haven't brought any great courage to meet life. I accept the easier, lazier and more comfortable way every time. But why think on such uncomfortable topics on this New Year's Day?

Thursday, January 5th: A late rising! Frost has left its mark in the night, and the roads and pavements are like glass, and there are long, shining icicles dangling from our roof. Father is hopping about in the garage with a friendly robin redbreast, which he feeds until it decides to fly into the open once more. Amy and Swanee both call before I am out of the dressing-gown stage, but neither stays very long.

Friday, January 6th: Despite the severity of the weather, I have to trot out to Miss Barnett's to have my ends curled up. Then migrate to Burton to meet Hilda Tooth. We go to the flicks, and she talks – as usual! All the teachers at her school are jealous of her because she is the youngest, and can teach better than they! Bert still showers attentions upon her, and wants to Settle Down – but she isn't going to yet. All her old beaux seem to hang on to her, in spite of Bert. Mine don't!

Sunday, January 8th: Delia has returned from Wales and accompanies us to church, moaning gloomily about the joys of tomorrow – noxious and thoroughly detestable thought! A spasm of agony passes over my soul. Oh dear! The holidays are like a fleeting moment – gone in a flash.

To Grandma's to supper to find Grandma in the throes of 'a hacking cough' of which we have ample proof in the evening. Mrs Merchant wanders in at supper time, protesting that 'I haven't come for my supper', but partakes nevertheless. She sees me writing my diary and remarks fondly that, 'I see you're getting up your lessons ready for tomorrow ... ' Grandma tells her bluntly that she is 'Getting Fat, yes, really, Quite a Width, noticeably Much Fatter'. Audrey plays a silent game of patience in the corner, while Grandma mutters spasmodically under her breath, 'Sunday'. Grandpa relates a fantastic tale about a bulldog which attacked a pig's ear.

Monday, January 9th: Oh day of gloom! Am wakened at the crack of dawn and am forced from my warm, comfortable bed to get ready for school – loathsome place! Trail wearily thither. Greet the rest of the staff with groans and learn that Miss Ford is engaged! That makes four of our staff on the road to matrimony.

Adopt a fierce attitude towards the children, intending to start afresh this term, but fail to maintain it. Somehow manage to survive, though by teatime I feel as though I had done a week's hard labour. Receive sketchy letter from Bella, containing no mention of her Peregrine. Must ask her about this omission.

At last decide to invest in a new suspender belt, after suffering agonies of torture under the last, so write off to Bourne & Hollingsworth's. Also write – in a spurt of energy – letters to Doug and Vera.

Thursday, January 12th: Oh, what a long week this seems! My suspender belt comes from Bourne & Hollingsworth. I try it on, and it feels vastly superior to my old roll-on. Mean to cherish it – it will be a great boon after hours of agony whilst strangulating round the waist in the other.

Monday, January 16th: Am weary upon awakening. Fear I must be a victim of Horlicks' much-advertised Night Starvation. Wake up a little during the journey to school. Plod through the daily round with fortitude. Joan S trots up to me in the middle of a lesson, bursting to tell me something, but I wave her away, telling her to Tell Me Another Time. She accordingly pops up again at playtime, still bursting, and tells me that her mother was talking about me in her sleep last night! I must be preying on the poor woman's mind.

Swanee comes to tea and after prowling around Salts' (the last day of their sale) we emerge with a 1½*d.* pair of shoelaces. We then go to our weekly lecture, and imbibe knowledge from the lips of the Rees man, who is still lecturing on the Versailles Treaty. He doesn't think much of Mr Chamberlain – compares him with Lord Curzon.

Thursday, January 19th: Miss Foster's romance is progressing. I see dimly another Ring looming on the horizon. Her Man-in-the-Red-Car rides by the school at playtime this afternoon. She is there on the steps, and waves coyly to him. We all poke each other and whisper, 'Did you see!'.

Audrey W tells me with embarrassing bluntness that she Likes Me. Have to receive this declaration in silence, owing to failure to find suitable words to reply. She thinks I did not hear and repeats herself, with added fervour. Have to say something then, so say Oh, and have the feeling that this is a disappointing reply.

Tuesday, January 24th: Miss Foster's Man-in-the-Red-Car glides by again at playtime, but he misses her. Feel convinced however that she was expecting him because she appears after play with rouge-reddened lips and an additional layer of powder on her cheeks. Am just taking games when Doris Dennis beckons me mysteriously into the bike-shed on her way home and tells me with concealed excitement that Miss Foster's Beau is a married man. We exchange shocked comments, then I return to my girls who are still skipping dauntlessly. Well . . . !

To Keep Fit, which goes quite smoothly, and thence to badminton. Have two games and lose both.

Wednesday, January 25th: Scene without resembles Iceland and the Frozen North when I awake, little feathery flakes fluttering softly to the shrouded earth. Hate snowy school days. Garb myself in mac, scarf, hat, snow-boots, woolly cardigan, grit my teeth, grip my umbrella and venture forth. Have a lift from the Clifford boy who says he has skidded once already this morning. Arrive at school to receive message from Miss Harvey urgently summoning me to her room. She says that she knows all – she has discovered the identity of the Man-in-the-Red-Car. He *is* married and has a wife! He is a Glee and a manager of Gresley

Colliery. Oh dear! The news forms the sole topic and includes many surmises when we congregate together after dinner.

Children very hilarious. Snow always seems to fly straight to their heads. Expect two or three snowballs to hit me from unseen vantage points, but manage to get through the day without assault.

Splash home in the slushy snow, and am unearthed against my will to go to the flicks after tea with Delia. We see *St Martin's Lane* which is very good. Chas Laughton, Vivien Leigh and Rex Harrison. Dear little Rex! – he's sweet!

Home to start reading Dorothy Sayers' *Nine Tailors*.

Thursday, January 26th: Children still infected with snow-fever and dance about with hilarity. Raymond P crawls into the class-room at playtime clutching his back and looking woebegone. He tells me that Me Back's Broken, Miss. I raise an alarmed eye. Realise that the ground is indeed in dangerous condition and that he may have sustained some serious injury, when he turns round and adds 'and me trousers are comin' down'. Then I realise that by his 'back' he refers to piece of string holding up his trousers, which has broken, so proceed to fasten his trousers to his jacket with two safety pins. Feel relieved. Expected him to drop in huddled heap every minute and remembered tales of chickens running about with their heads cut off.

Clutch my umbrella all day long. It seems to be in a state of perpetual wetness these days. A weary afternoon. The last hour drags on leaden wings. I speed homeward with relief. My horo-scope tells me that my vitality is low today, and indeed I think it must be.

Friday, January 27th: Confer with Miss Harvey about the Scandal in Our Midst. Miss F's Stan says that nearly all the men at their works talk about it, and Miss H recollects an occasion when Miss

Foster invited us down a coal mine – the Gresley one! We see why, now – obviously to meet her Loved One under our cloak of respectability. What depths! Again meet together in the cloak-room after dinner, and form a conspiratorial group while we resurrect, analyse, and comment upon the scandal. Every step past brings us smartly to attention, with a wary eye on the door and a guilty flush on our cheeks. We decide that there may perhaps even be A Divorce.

Saturday, January 28th: An energetic day! Take an athletic way to Derby with Swanee, Elaine Richards and Edna Clarke to a PT and dancing course given by Miss Hayden, the PT organiser for the county. I shouldn't be going really because I'm not in a senior school. We flit over forms, gallop over ropes, canter round the room, bunny-hop up the walls, and then are Kept Fit to music for an hour by a most supple woman with a lovely figure – scantily draped in a minute turquoise-blue arrangement. All sorts of attire here, ranging from hideous pea-green Grecian drapery on an old teacher of about 50, and very brief knickers and blouses on Young Things. Have lunch at the Midland Drapery and emerge still feeling hungry to catch the bus.

Hastily change, and up to badminton. Play solidly with brief intervals for table tennis, home for tea, and return at night. Some good games. Home by 9.20.

Listen in to a speech by the Prime Minister – in whom, I fear, I have not a great deal of confidence. He relates how marvellously he was received during his last visit to Italy. My father belittles this, saying that they pinned flowers on *him* when he went during the war.

Sunday, January 29th: Oh dear! – perfectly Arctic. I do detest this nasty cold bleak biting depressing vitality-lowering weather. The papers say that this is the severest winter during the last 60 years, and I can well believe it. Cling to the fire with great tenacity and am very distressed when I have to move. Nevertheless, punctiliously perform *all* my Sabbath observances today.

Hear Miss Sutton at Sunday School talking in confidential undertones to her class, and guess that she is once more relating novelettish stories to them about mill-girls and their employers' sons. I righteously confine my remarks to a homily on John the Baptist.

Temperature starts at about zero today and rapidly sinks and sinks until it is about minus 100 at bedtime.

Monday, January 30th: Drop my pen at the history lecture, thus dealing it its death blow, as is seen by these thick, scratchy strokes.

Confidential and very revealing letter from Bella about Chivers. She is very keen, but it will mean (a) looking down on him (in height) and (b) turning Baptist and giving up flicks, dances, theatres and all sorts of blasphemy. But he would give up Anything for Her, she says. They have quite a Position and a large house in Surrey – so on the whole, Bella Could Do Worse. So that is that!

Tuesday, January 31st: The money bags appear, thanks be, and rescue me once more from the brink of a financial precipice. Letter marked 'private' also arrives from the bank, containing a book which now shows a colossal credit of £11 5s. 3d. – with the manager's compliments!

Only 10 at Keep Fit – very very thin. To badminton afterwards and have two games. Still bitterly, icily, Arctically cold.

Thursday, February 2nd: Letter from Dougie yesterday couched in the usual vein and very boring in matter – all about the floods in the Fens and the latest football matches. Admonition also to me to write earlier – but without the interest I suppose I'll be as late as ever.

Receive a lift from the Clifford boy, who tells me that he won't have to join up in the event of war because of his job. Alight like a duchess to be met by a concerned parent who tells me in harassed tones that his little boy has lost his coat. Promise magnificently to Find It.

Friday, February 3rd: Great excitement in the afternoon – the Man-in-the-Red-Car actually comes into school and is closeted with Miss Foster in her room. Miss Dennis sees his car outside as she is seeing the infants home, so dashes back to tell Miss Ford. Miss Ford sends hasty note to Miss Harvey, and Miss Harvey relays the message to me in the form of a Little Note. All agog with excitement. Oh dear – it is getting serious!

Home and up to Miss Barnett's by 5 to have my Ends Permed. Sit and freeze and endure 3 hours of agony and torture while I am washed, baked and set. My soul groans in inward horror as she piles gallons of thick, greasy setting lotion on my locks – assuring me earnestly the while that it is Not Greasy. Emerge with a horrible set look – set waves and horrid little artificial set curls. Speed homewards in horror. Mr Skerritt tells me bluntly that I look Twenty Years Older and repeats it when I make no comment. The others disguise their feelings more or less. Calculate feverishly how long it will take to grow out. Grasp a comb and try to comb it out – but horror of horrors, the first curl I comb becomes a bushy frizz so I give myself up to despair.

Saturday, February 4th: Hardly dare get up, in view of my piteous plight. But it has to be done. I view myself at all angles in the mirror once more. Spend the morn in frenzied efforts to bring order from the chaos. Reset the poor little fragments of hair that are still unpermed, and comb out the curls, frizz or no frizz. Looks a trifle better, but not much. Auntie Frances tells me helpfully that She Knew I Wouldn't Like It. Mother perversely opines that it looks Very Nice . . . at the back.

Auntie Nell and Mother go with me in afternoon to Derby to buy a dance dress. Go to Bracegirdles but they have a somewhat meagre selection. Try on a white strapless one with boned bodice which makes me look fat, then a blue one which is quite nice but not at all startling. I simply continue to look like myself in it. Howbeit, decide to have it, and disburse reluctantly.

Monday, February 6th: After my strenuous day of toil at school, I launch out again in the evening doing Good Works – a house-to-house visitation of Belmont Street, Stanley Street, and Drayton Street about the billeting of children in wartime. Oh dear! A thankless job, though most people very decent. Have to listen to Mrs R's budgerigar saying 'Kiss Billy', while I profess polite wonder. One woman tells her mother that I have come about the Excavation scheme. When I enter the M abode, Mrs M tells me that it is a sign of the Second Coming, while her husband adds Yes, all this has been predicted in the Bible, even what Hitler said in his speech in the Reichstag the other day. Finally make my escape, and the woman in the next house tells me that it isn't safe for me to do this alone, with all these bombs about. Wander wearily from house to house for over 4 hours and finally arrive home exhausted at 9.30.

Tuesday, February 7th: The Clifford boy gives me a lift and tells me handsomely that if I have any far flung and distant billeting to do, he will run me round in his car. Tell him crisply however that that will not be necessary.

Rain falls – and so does our attendance at Keep Fit – only 10 stalwarts turning up.

Friday, February 10th: See Swanee who exclaims, Oh, I've had my

Hair Permed, have I? and adds consolingly, they always look frizzy at first, and that it will look better after the next setting. Oh, oh, oh!

Saturday, February 11th: Finish off my billeting this morn. Then garb myself immediately after lunch in blue frock, coat, hat and shoes, seize hockey stick and go to Gresley to make arch of hockey sticks for Esme after her wedding. She is dressed in white and looks very nice, as do the bridesmaids in apple-green velvet with violet sashes. The groomsmen are in tails, but the groom and best man turn up in grey – with Black Shirts! Oh dear! We all breathe Ohs of horror. There are also some 5 or 6 pals of the groom, also in black shirts, and all looking rather scruffy. After the ceremony we make our pre-arranged arch, and a photograph is taken of Esme underneath it, while the Lads of Lancaster – the Blackshirts – tag themselves on to this and give the Nazi salute. We are disgusted and give loud and long tirades about it all the way home.

Monday, February 13th: Receive letter from Dougiedear inviting me to Ely for Easter and containing snaps of the floods, and I write one to Freddie saying Is He Going to the Dance a week on Wed, but forget to post it. Continue reading biography of Dick Sheppard.

Thursday, February 16th: Oh dearie me! Only the middle of the month and I am on the rocks of impecuniosity. Mother brings me white cami-knicks with blue spots from Birmingham – awfully nice, and I send off for white fur cape to wear with my blue evening frock. I still need shoes.

Friday, February 17th: Am revived by tea sufficiently to undertake the loathsome job of washing my hair. The permed ends feel horrible – just like wet wool.

Forgot to record on Wed a most thrilling and heart-stirring event – a letter from Old Friend Freddo gallantly offering to take me to the Rugger Dance if I had not made other arrangements.

Saturday, February 18th: Receive my White Rabbit – viz fur cape which I have bought to wear with my new evening frock. Attire myself in frock and cape and parade before the family. Mr Skerritt says he wouldn't take me out in it – they'd think he was earning £15 a week. My father says I only need to stand in the garden now, to scare the crows away.

Tuesday, February 21st – Pancake Day: Or to give it its proper title, Shrove Tuesday. Skip blithely home at 12 for half a day's holiday. Receive letter from Bella, who pledges me to secrecy and says that it is All Off with Chivers – they think it will only lead to unhappiness. Bella hints of dreadful scenes – Chivers weeping and what-not, so she has had a hectic time.

Wednesday, February 22nd: The Rugger Dance – and oh my goodness! What a night! Rain simply lashes down, and the wind beats it against the roof and windowpanes with a dreadful sound. Freddie, the mean blighter, decides to leave his car in our entry, whereat I moan, Have We Got to Walk? He mumbles something about his rear light not functioning. Bosh! Accordingly Delia and I pin up our trailing dresses and we plunge into the horrors without. Have not gone far before my petticoat comes sidling down, and I have to go with yards showing, hoping that people will think it is my evening dress. See Swanee there looking quite sober in black and feel very conscious of the newness of my dress and cape, which does not feel quite so staggering or glamorous in the midst of so many. Dance with Stuart in an Excuse Me, and he is excused by Ralph who takes me for refreshments. Freddie hops up as we are going, thinking that I am returning to the fold, but sail by with an airy wave of the hand. He is waiting when we come out, so perforce have to dance with him. Then again with Stuart, and have a premonition that an invitation to the flicks is pending, so hurriedly divert him. Freddie then takes me for more refreshments. Home about 1.15, very, very weary and with agonising feet.

First day of Lent. Fast proclaimed on sweets and chocolate.

Have lift to school and the Clifford Boy tells me he has been at home with the flu. Express lukewarm and vague condolences.

Saturday, February 25th: Hockey – lose to Stapenhill 3–0 on their own ground. Go to WEA lecture on 'The Psychology of Dictators' at night.

Sunday, February 26th: Take a holiday from Sunday school to continue reading *Harvest of Victory* by Wingfield-Stratford and just manage to reach the halfway mark. Ronniedear comes home to visit Mamma, until tomorrow evening.

Monday, February 27th: Am bankrupt and in debt. Woe is me. Pay day tomorrow! Thanks be. Swanee comes to tea but we forswear the intellectual delights of the Lecture and go to the flicks instead.

Wednesday, March 1st: Mrs Tweed and Amy come to supper and Mrs Tweed relates stories about Ron – which only pile on the agony. He is Doing Wonderfully Well, and is Most Popular, etc etc. He went to 14 parties at Xmas and a lot of (foolish) girls tried to get him under the mistletoe. Huh! I bet he wouldn't have needed much pushing! I bet there will be some broken hearts in Brimington – specially the peroxide blonde without the eyelashes, Miss Austen. Still, it's only sour grapes. I think of Ron and write of him now just as though I know him as well as I used, but

I expect if I were to come into contact with him I'd find him a stranger almost. And I expect he'd find me changed quite considerably too.

Saturday, March 4th: Have the Budget* to read over my breakfast. Oh dear! My complexion turns pale green with envy. Lil's letter is written in the rapture of honeymooning. Frank is the assistant Govt Architect of Bengal and gets over a thousand pounds a year. She was married the day she landed and they spent their first night in the train. Now they're back at the service flat in Calcutta. They have natives for servants with a bearer to supervise. Lil looked in his laundry book the other day and saw that he calls her brassiere a 'body'. But she says he speaks very good English. Calcutta, she says, is a very dirty place. Crowds of the natives sleep on the pavements at night. Silk is very cheap in the Indian markets.

Kath is going out to Persia in two years to her engineer Harold. Maretta is going abroad with her French boy for the summer hols. And Joan has returned to our midst. Even she has had her excitement, to wit, two proposals and a new car and a nervous breakdown.

Turn out to hockey v. Burton OG in spite of the liberality with which the heavens send down their rains. Spend the evening writing to Bella, reading and playing Win All with Joyce, Eric, Auntie Nell and Mother.

Wednesday, March 8th: Letter from Bella, which includes mystifying little addition sealed up and inscribed 'Burn This'. I learn from it that John Scott 'wants to be serious' once again, and

---

*May trained to be a teacher at Goldsmiths College, London. 'The Budget' was a circulating packet of letters and photographs of eight ex-Goldsmiths friends.

declares that 'the family will welcome her with open arms', and invites her to go up at Easter. Bella doesn't say whether she is thrilled or not, but I should think she must be. But it has been such a strange affair all along. I don't trust John Scott. He's selfish.

To a political meeting at night. Our Conservative MP Paul Emrys-Evans gives an 'apologia pro mea vita', i.e. explains why he failed to support the Government during the crisis, and I see his point of view and agree with him. I admire a man who will stand his ground and stand for his principles. The meeting very divided. Harold Timms asks if Mr Emrys-Evans considers himself a better man than Mr Chamberlain then?

I am most peeved and most agitated. Mean old Freddie has lived up to his name and reputation. He hasn't paid me yet for the Rugger tickets, not even for his own. Perhaps he thinks *I* took *him* . . . ! Gosh!

Saturday, March 11th: Go to Miss Barnett's to have my hair set and she simply soaks it in horrid setting lotion and makes it look plastered down and skimpy.

Wednesday, March 15th: Oh shocks! A letter from Freddie which I open with anxious and expectant finger, expecting a postal order to flutter forth. But no! I search the envelope. No postal order. I read the letter, but not a mention of it there either, only an invitation to go to the flicks with him tomorrow. My hopes dashed. Very peeved, so sit down in an umbrageous silence and write stiffly and curtly that I am unable to go. Huh!

Thursday, March 16th: Hitler has marched into Czechoslovakia and has taken it – old devil! There's bound to be a clash sooner or later. So that ends the Munich agreement!

Saturday, March 18th: Letter again from Mean Old Fred offering obligingly to take me to the flicks any day next week.

International situation very serious. Hitler has issued ultimatum to Romania demanding monopoly of their export of oils and grain, and the closing of their industries preparatory to becoming an agrarian country, in return for Hitler's guaranteeing the integrity of Romania's frontiers – for whatever that may be worth! Find Joyce and Eric, Auntie Nell and Mother discussing this very seriously. Joyce on the verge of tears at night at the thought of Eric having to go and fight, but Eric looking quite phlegmatic about it.

Monday, March 20th: Write graciously to Old Friend Fred to say that I'll go to the flicks with him on Thursday. Swanee comes to tea and we go to the history lecture. Last one next week.

Thursday, March 23rd: Cold, and I wilt beneath a glamorous cold spot. However, am called for by Old Friend Fredski, and we go to the flicks to see *Suez*. He maintains a cowardly silence about my 2/6. I ponder upon whether to take Bella's advice and ask him sardonically if he enjoyed the dance, when he says suddenly, Oh, he owes me 2/6 doesn't he. I try to say with nonchalance as if I had forgotten, Oh yes, I believe he does. He takes us into the 1/4 seats, and pays for me, so his little purse must be very depleted when he gets home. Poor old Freddie.

Monday, March 27th: Fling on the warmest clothes I can find – long-sleeved frock and blazer. Dive between the snowflakes to school. Children cooped up all day and are extra ebullient while I snarl fiercely at them. The cold has made my peach-bloom skin rough and patchy, I have a cold spot still on my lip and my nose is perpetually pink. Drape myself around the hot-water pipe and morosely contemplate the scene without. This weather brings out the evil in my soul. We are all relieved when 4 o'clock comes.

Swanee breezes in cheerily and we go to the last history lecture. Lecturer said last week that he had a ray of hope to give us about the international situation, but this week gloomily confesses that now he has not, and predicts an inevitable war with Germany.

Swanee and I make excited and ambitious plans for our Easter trip to London.

Wednesday, March 29th: Miss Foster has issued orders, via Trissie, that henceforth and for evermore the staff are not to talk to each other during lines, but merely straighten our respective line and precede it with decorum into school! So now, I suppose, we have to nod curtly to each other and mutely pass on. Huh!

Monday, April 3rd: Little boy asks me ominously if I have my air-raid shelter ready yet. Pooh-pooh the idea with what, I think, is unfounded optimism.

At school we are brought again face to face with the dire necessities of the moment when Miss Foster summons us to her sanctum to ask what we propose doing about Air-Raid Precautions. She doesn't wait for a reply but says that she will write to Mr Austerberry on the council to ask which classes we can attend.

Letter arrives from Doug by the evening post with the usual invitation to Ely at Easter – very pointless because he knows I won't go.

Tuesday, April 4th: Go to the last badminton of the season. Stuart floats in with gloomy forebodings. Poor lad – he seems to be taking the political situation very seriously. Still I suppose one ought. Recruiting campaign held in the Town Hall – lots of uniforms floating about, but my father returns from it to say that the Army of today is 'not what it used to be – no, not by a long way'. This he repeats with emphasis and many times.

Thursday, April 6th: Ha–aa–le–lujah! Oh happy day! Breaking-up day of course, though it is only for a mingy, stingy week. All the same, here it is at last, and a nice sunny day too. Mother, Auntie Nell and I go to Derby in search of a New Coat. Go to Bracegirdles in some despair, having seen nothing at all that I like in the window. However, modish and vastly superior assistant produces nice blue edge-to-edge coat which I try on and like. Then try on frocks to match, though really cannot afford one. Eventually plunge on Gay Flowered thing and emerge broke. Mother has to pay for my tea.

Friday, April 7th. Good Friday: Another crisis – Gosh! We would be lost without a crisis these days – they're dished up to us daily. This time, Hitler's Italian confederate has stepped into the limelight with a surprise march early this morning into Albania, with the intention of snaffling it. Consequent issue of news bulletins throughout the day, creating the usual fearful and nightmarish atmosphere. War and politics today must be quite unlike what they have ever been before. This is a materialistic age, with politics of state-controlled smash-and-grab raids and bandit tactics in the dictator countries. There seems to be only one possible end – war and on a horrible and dreadful scale. Oh dear! One news item seems to be very ominous and significant. Franco has recognised and approved Mussolini's action, implying that he intends to throw in his lot with the Axis Powers. Which will of course make it very difficult for us in the Mediterranean. And we still haven't concluded any pact of mutual assistance with Russia, whose help surely must be of invaluable potential. Oh dear again! Politics today are a veritable nightmare of intricacy and deceit and are fear-impelled.

Saturday, April 8th: Trot off to Burton, alone, unaided and defenceless on that most nauseating of all missions, Buying a Hat. Sally into the shop, and Mrs Mapp, whom I distrust, for she has an oily tongue but a vinegary look, takes charge of me and pushes at me the most vile, noxious and fantastic creations which she calls Models. Try on coarse straw monstrosities, a Modern Beret Shape and an off-the-face Fantasmagoria, and many more. Lastly she produces with the fond look of a mother for a cherished child a thing surmounted by flowers and completely enveloped in gauzy veil, in twists, bows and all sorts of intricate arrangements. I am not impressed but casually ask the price. A howl of horror escapes my lips as I read the ticket she mutely points out – 35/-! In vain she protests that it is new in, a French hat, that it has a flattering line, and that I can have it for 30/-. I escape only by saying that I will take the hat with me to Try On at Home. Mother says Out of All Reason when I get home, and adds Besides it Doesn't Suit You. Which clinches the argument.

After a hurried tea go to Derby to claim my frock and coat. See pretty clover bonnet-shaped hat there on a stand, which looks expensive, but when I timorously ask the price I learn that it is only 12/11. I immediately try it on and immediately decide to have it. Which is the quickest time on record for my ever having bought a hat.

Tuesday, April 11th: Up betimes and to London with Swanee and Bella. Stay at a small hotel in Princes Square – just have bed and breakfast there. Bella has to go to the office this afternoon, so Swanee and I go round the Houses of Parliament and Westminster Abbey, and walk over Westminster Bridge, along by the Thames past Lambeth Palace, over Lambeth Bridge and back to Victoria Street to meet Bella out of the office. We go to Tussaud's cinema to see *Dawn Patrol* – awfully good.

Wednesday, April 12th: Up by 8, out just after 9. Book stools in theatre queues for *Dear Octopus* in the afternoon with John Gielgud and Marie Tempest, a comedy by Dodie Smith about a family reunion.

Thursday, April 13th: Investigate second-hand book shops in Charing Cross Road in the morning. Then wander along Oxford Street and buy a tablet of soap. In the evening we see Ralph Richardson and Edna Best in *Johnson Over Jordan* – a modern miracle play – marvellous acting and awfully good.

Friday, April 14th: We prowl around the National Portrait Gallery where I buy a 2d portrait of T. E. Lawrence by Augustus John, then meet Bella for lunch. Buy a 5/- bag – a pretty blue one from a shop in the Strand. Home by the 6.25 train from St Pancras, arrive at 10. Have thoroughly enjoyed it – lovely time.

Saturday, April 15th: And now am very very Broke.

Monday, April 17th: Am forced by unkind circumstances to put my shoulder beneath the yoke again, so hie me back to school. First day back is always a trial, but it is soon over, thanks be, and Swanee meets me out of school and comes to tea. We go to the flicks to see *Pygmalion* – very good.

Tuesday, April 18th: Play tennis with Delia. Lovely day but am troubled by my skin. It is peeling off my face and the patchy, rough, blotchy result looks perfectly horrible and feels very sore. Am also very, very broke. Have only 3d. on which to subsist until we are paid a fortnight hence.

Thursday, April 20th: Wash my hair after tea and go to Miss Barnett's to have it set. Sit in impatient agony during the drying process, which I loathe, and I keep averting my eyes from my reflection – a creature like a prehistoric monster, with huge bee-hive half covering head, pads of white cotton wool in ears and towel swathed around shoulders.

Friday, April 21st: A nice day, though do not appreciate the weather because it happens to be Waifs and Strays' flag day. Gosh how I loathe selling flags! I would never make a professional beggar. Positively shrink from badgering people into buying. However, it has to be done so I put on a bold face and begin the usual chant – 'will you please buy a flower for the Waifs and Strays?' They sell quite well, so after an hour's arduous toil, come in and count up my takings, 17/9. Delia stays to supper, so I cook some macaroni cheese.

Monday, April 24th: Our staff go to the first ARP lecture, given by Mr Austerberry. To flicks afterwards.

Wednesday, April 26th: Should have gone to Geary* for tennis, but showery weather prevents this, so after having tea at Swanee's, we go to the flicks. Conscription is going to be brought in for the 20–21s. Bill Swan will have to go for 6 months' training.

Friday, April 28th: We Are Paid! Oh be joyful! But have to disburse £4 immediately in debts and what-not.

Monday, May 1st: Go to ARP with Swanee, Delia and Elaine Richards and feel squirmy during eloquent description of War Gases, which inflict all manner of unpleasant sensations upon

*Geary was Geary House, the sports club which May attended in the nearby village of Bretby.

one, from choking to stinging and burning pains. Emerge feeling glad to be out in the fresh air. Freddie-dear there but not so faithful as I would have liked him to be. He pays little attention to me, much to my distress! Can he be cooling in his ardour? How dreadful! Smile quite condescendingly upon him but he does not seek me out. Looks bad!

Sunday, May 14th: Doug and Bert came ...!

Wednesday, May 31st: Driven by the urge to swim, Swanee and I visited the baths and splashed about very gaily.

Friday, June 2nd: I rose at crack of dawn and by 8.30 I was on my way to London. Delia met me at St Pancras, and instead of showing myself completely at ease amongst all the intricacies of Tube, I nearly got her lost, and had to sacrifice my pride and resort to the indignity of consulting the map. Finally we got to the Strand, wallowed in cheese salad and strawberry ices, which were lovely, then sat out in the beautiful, glorious, scorching sun. Passed a cinema advertising *Wuthering Heights* so we succumbed and went in. Lovely – Laurence Olivier marvellous as Heathcliff. Most thrilling love story – made me feel all romantic. Set off to meet Bella, and then to the theatre to see Noel Coward's *Design for Living* (Anton Walbrooke, Rex Harrison and Diana Wynyard). Very cynical and very modern, but not too keen.

Exchanged the latest news with Bella – John Scott has given her up again, she thinks. She didn't see him at Whitsuntide because he was in a Turmoil, he said, and couldn't make up his mind what to do. I'd show him what to do – the cad! He's a mass of selfishness, and I wouldn't trust him an inch.

Sunday, June 4th: Met Bella for lunch and spent the afternoon reclining in the hot and glorious sun in a deck-chair in St James's

Park. Tea, then caught the train home. My books had come – *Letters of T. E. Lawrence*, *Wuthering Heights* and *Goodbye, Mr Chips* – lovely! Gloated over them before going to bed.

Monday, June 5th: Children all very dozy and I simply hadn't the energy to go round poking and prodding them, so they slumbered on. Did gas mask drill in ARP at night. Stood in a semi-circle next to Old Friend Fred and we were instructed by Mr Austerberry on how to Remove the Hat, Place Between the Knees, Withdraw mask smartly from haversack etc, etc. Put them on and off and on for nearly an hour, and felt like a boiled lobster at the end.

Tuesday, June 6th: The last day of my 25th year – ooh horrible thought! How awful and how old! Am beginning to feel moth-eaten. Howbeit – begone, dull care! A most glorious scorching day again, but too hot to teach. Flaunted to school in a brief white coat, and Audrey W told me coyly that I Looked Nice This Morning, Miss. Said 'Oh', very nonchalantly, but was nevertheless pleased.

Tripped to Swanee's auntie at 6.30 and had an evening's tennis on their lovely grass court. Swanee uttered disparaging remarks about the sweet blue-flowered chiffon patterns Bella and I had culled for our bridesmaid dresses.

Retired to rest on this last night of my 25th year feeling Hot, so slept beneath one sheet only. Bella, I learned later, has been sleeping in the nude in view of the heat. How indelicate!

Wednesday, June 7th: 25 years old today, and how I shudder at the thought! Awoke to a glorious sunshiny morning and an interesting post. Cards from Mrs Tweed, Amy, Delia and Mr Skerritt, and as I had hoped a scrappy, non-committal and rather awkward note from Ron, saying 'many happy returns' and then proudly mentioning his forthcoming part in Gerald Lusty's wedding tomorrow, then, 'best wishes, yours very sincerely, Ron'. I didn't want to know about Gerald Lusty's wedding; I never knew the fellow, but he is marrying some desirable society female. Ron *will* like that! He loves exalted spheres and the high life. But that's catty, and I don't want to be catty. Swanee sent me a 3/6 book token, Amy gave me some book-ends, Grandma 2/6, Auntie 5/-, Miss Sanders a box of caramels, and Mother and Dad are giving me a new fountain pen.

Entertained Mrs Hyde, Grandma, Amy, Delia, and Swanee to tea. Bob and Margaret Tweed called at night, and said I didn't look my age, which was pleasant hearing, to me of my advancing years.

Monday, June 12th: Cold, really and truly cold. Vile after the lovely hot sun. To Friend Swan's for tea and we trailed along to ARP dangling our gas masks. Dreadful! Had to enter the most fearsome Gas Chamber containing CAP – chlor-aceto-phenone – and positively dithered with fright. Stood within expecting every breath to be my last, but fortunately emerged unscathed. Old Friend Fred very tickled at our trepidation and braved the Lethal Chamber with the utmost boldness and nonchalance.

Wednesday, June 14th: Discovered a disease on my face at dinnertime, which perturbed me greatly, being a round red spot on the right cheek. Mother suggested that it might be a Ring-worm, and Auntie Frances a Bite, which two diagnoses agitated me so greatly that I tripped over the stool and tore my only wearable pair of stockings. By teatime, it had gone, much to my relief.

Saturday, June 17th: To Geary to play in the Open Tournament in the afternoon. Not a bad day, though showery and dull. Aeroplanes kept buzzing over because it was the opening of the new aerodrome at Burnaston.

A bird had built its nest in the tennis post and the young birds inside were twittering and chirping in great agitation all the afternoon. The mother bird fluttered anxiously around with a grub in her beak. My partner and I lost all our sets except one, and that was against Mrs Smithard and Frank Swindale and she had the cheek to say that They Didn't Bother in that set. Huh! She asked me if I were Courting and said she thought I was, At One Time, then added, Now Don't Colour Up, at which I felt myself going pink but merely remarked curtly and non-committally, Oh Did You?

Monday, June 19th: Assailed by weariness all day. In ARP the dear Eric Austerberry failed to appear but sent Mr Cliff to deputise – *the* Mr Cliff of the Fire Brigade (under whom it makes smart turn-outs according to the local paper). Poor man! He ploughed his way onwards, then suddenly and dramatically lurched forward in a faint. Prompt measures were taken by the local NUT representative, who flung open all the windows, causing a hurricane, nearly choked him with water, mopped his brow, and finally hauled him outside. He returned after a few minutes, nobly resolved to continue, and apologised for fainting, being loudly applauded by everyone. He was then propped up on a desk and wedged in firmly on both sides.

Thursday, June 22nd: To the Majestic at night with the entire family to see a Shirley Temple film, which I did not particularly enjoy. I don't like most children on the films – they're unnatural, and so is she.

Friday, June 23rd: Had my hair done slightly differently last night, taken off my face in two fetching rolls, so ambled to school this morn with ribbons twined about my locks to keep them in their proper place and was told I look Nice with Ribbons Round My Hair Miss.

Monday, July 3rd: Swanee and I spent a feverish hour before ARP swatting up the Gas Chart, getting more and more muddled every moment. At last we wended our way to the Test, and had to be examined two at a time. Swanee and I arranged that if either were to give a foolish answer, the other should give a warning cough, but if correct to give a murmur of approval. This however we did not do. Only had three questions each, so we hope to pass.

Friday, July 7th: Wandered around Salts' after tea with Amy and Delia, in search of a bathing costume. Rayney arrived in her new car, but looking as glum as ever, while I positively oozed envy. She asked morosely about everybody, whether Bella and I were court-ing (the ever-recurring question!) and when I said No, remarked sardonically that There Was Nothing to Look Forward To, was there? Replied skittishly, Yes, the Old Age Pension, but this failed to cheer her.

Thursday, July 20th: Played off one section of the Tournament. Played with Freddie. We were top in our section but lost in the Finals. I won box of linen hankies and friend Freddo won the jam dish.

Sunday, July 23rd: Mooned around the Post Office looking for a birthday card for Ron, but they had nothing to suit my require-ments. Wanted a curt card with a mere 'Birthday Greetings' on, but they all had chants about Flowers of Friendship and Life's Garden etc etc so bought a pseudo-comic one but Mother said it was insulting so decided not to send it. Composed a short note instead but would rather have sent a mere card. He'll think I sent a note because he sent a note.

Thursday, August 3rd: Broke up – thank goodness, oh thank good-ness! Children have been absolutely wild and unmanageable lately.

Thursday, August 24th: Day at Nottingham, at Barbara's with Auntie F and Mrs Gee. Lovely time. Played miniature golf. Awful ominous atmosphere though – everyone expecting war. Hitler – foul old man – threatens to attack Poland, in which case it will mean war. Horrible. Harold Hall sat by me on the bus home from Nottingham and talked about the possibility all the way.

Friday, August 25th: To Bella's for tea, and to Swanee's afterwards with Bella, on the eve of Swanee's wedding. We've decided not to go to the Isle of Wight in view of the unsettled conditions.

Saturday, August 26th: Swanee's wedding. We (i.e. bridesmaids) wore blue chiffon over taffeta, with petunia and blue ribbon velvet sashes and bows. The dresses were sweet. We carried anemones. Swanee wore white taffeta. Nice wedding reception in the Methodist school room at Newhall. Bella and I home to tea. To flicks at night.

Swanee's wedding, Saturday, August 26th

Thursday, August 31st: Oh dear – awful tension again. War seems very near. Evacuation is to be started tomorrow.

Friday, September 1st: Oh horrors! Germany has invaded Poland. Now for hell let loose! Oh dear! Ghastly! Spent the morning from 10 to 2 receiving evacuated children from Birmingham and taking them round to billet them.

Bella came down to tea and I SAW THE BISHOP! Yes, truly! After two years of invisibility I saw him. Most unnerving. Bella suddenly clutched me and gasped, and I knew without being told who was coming. Didn't know what to do. Thought at first I'd pretend not to have seen him, then I thought 'How petty!' so I turned my head just as he was going by. He was in the car with Mamma. Felt my knees and legs go weak and trembly, while my face became suffused with colour, then it went white. Don't think I looked very nice – had only my old white coat and spotted frock on. Wish I were beautiful.

Dreary, depressing, gloomy evening. Went up to Kay's with Bella, and back with them. Everywhere dark. No street lighting, and other lights darkened and shaded. Bombing in Poland. Dreamt about Ron.

Saturday, September 2nd: More billeting. Stuffy old Town Hall – mothers and young children this time. Bella helped – stayed to dinner, then we went back to their place for tea. Back by 5 to do our bit of billeting but only had one mother and baby to billet, so soon finished that.

Sunday, September 3rd: Dreadful day! War declared v Germany. Told by wireless announcer to wait for an Important Announcement at 10.15. We listened accordingly and were told that our ultimatum had been given to Germany, expiring at 11 a.m. If no reply came from Hitler a state of war would be declared. The PM would be speaking at 11.15 a.m. Listened anxiously and with bated breath at 11.15. Heard the worst. No reply – so war. How horrible! At the moment it doesn't convey much – it seems all too remote and unbelievable. But when the fireworks start, oh goodness! Went to meeting of helpers in the Rink with Bella, Delia and Amy this afternoon, but it didn't do much. Airraid signal given in London this morn, when aeroplane sighted over the Channel, but it was a false alarm.

And so to bed, to sleep for some 4 hours. Awakened at 3.30 a.m. by the awful blaring whine of the Air-Raid Sirens. Most terrifying at such an hour. Awoke with a start and a palpitating heart, flung on a dressing gown, shouted to Mother and Dad and dashed downstairs. Mother and I immediately fumbled with our gas masks and soon had them on and sat staring solemnly at each other. When my father came downstairs he viewed us with mocking mirth and told us to take them off. We did and all went dashing up the road to Grandma's to the safety of their cellar and hammered on the door to be let in. A beautiful clear moonlit night. Fully expected to see enemy bombers bearing down on us any minute, while we were still madly battering. At length we were let in. Grandma there, fully dressed including her corsets even, while Grandpa and Auntie F were dashing about closing windows. Couldn't put a light on, not even a candle because the windows weren't effectively screened. Grandma had to be revived with whisky and I curled up in a shivering bundle in a corner of the sofa. A candle was lit two or three times and placed on the cellar steps and under the table, but it still showed so we had to sit in darkness, waiting. Jack and Winnie and the baby then came and Mrs Read, who had tried to get into Sharpe's shelter but had stuck. After half-an-hour's awful suspense, the All Clear signal went. Mother thanked God in a devout tone and we all relaxed and after some minutes dispersed to finish our slumbers very fitfully.

Monday, September 4th: Awoke feeling like a wet rag. Miss Sanders arrived, announcing that they hadn't had an alarm in Brownhills at all. Ours subsequently proved to be a false alarm – not enemy aircraft after all but friendly ones. What agony of mind, and all for nothing!

A very touching and pathetic letter arrived from Doug. He says that all his mates are being called up, and adds gloomily that he will never see most of them again. He expects to go shortly, but says that it isn't himself he's thinking of, but me, and exhorts me to take care of myself. He then declaims: 'It must be pretty obvious to you that I care for you more than any other girl in the world, but I realise that you do not care for me in that way.' He ends in a patriotic flourish 'England for Ever'. I know just how he feels – having felt the same way about Ron, but it doesn't alter my feelings for him.

Went to school to a meeting, but weren't paid because the banks are closed today. The new teacher from Wales turned up and seems very perky, but indicated that it would not take her long to pack up and flee for safety to her Welsh mountains. Made plans for re-opening school, for gas mask drill and whatnot and dispersed about 10.30.

Bella met me at the gates and we all chatted. Doris Dennis says that a lot of the people in Moira hadn't made any preparations or taken any precautions because Cosmo in the *People* (in whom they have implicit faith) told them there would be no war. Now there is, he says that Hitler is a madman because he has gone against his stars. Lots of stories circulating about the refugees from Birmingham – lots of dirty, naughty and mischievous children and fastidious teachers. Trissie Smith had to take in a 4-month-old baby because no one else would have it. It kept them awake by its howls all night and has had to be taken away because it had discharging ears and goodness knows what.

Bella came to tea. Delia came wandering in with her knitting and Auntie Nell and Joyce came, but all left at the approach of dark and our fears began to mount. All sorts of tales are circulating – some that the planes that came over last night were enemy bombers after all.

Tuesday, September 5th: Had very disturbed slumbers. Retired to bed last night about 10 p.m. but didn't feel at all brave or composed. Lay and dithered, awaiting the dreadful sound – kept wakening to listen once more. Awoke quite early, but lay in bed until 9, relieved that there hadn't been a raid after all. Latest rumours report (quoting the American news) that the Germans bombed Paris at 5 a.m. this morn, and that by 6 the All Clear hadn't sounded.

Went to welfare meeting in the Town Hall and to Bella's to tea, but had to return at sunset. Daren't, simply daren't, be out after dark. Oh dear! How on earth are we going to exist if this goes on for long? We were paid, thanks be!

Wednesday, September 6th: German bombers approached the East Coast this morn but were driven back. Col Roberts thinks that Hitler will make one swoop on Eng, with hundreds of aeroplanes. Ooh-er! What a delightful prospect!

Bella went to London to collect all her clothes today. Went to a meeting again. Started knitting a jumper! Plodded laboriously along the rows and didn't enjoy it, but must have something to do. Wrote to Dougie but didn't mention his avowal.

Thursday, September 7th: Reported to school again this morn but nothing to do but exchange the latest tales about the refugees.

Had my hair set, and continued my painful progress with the jumper. Grandpa and my father busy spragging the cellar with logs, destined for our future hidey-hole.

Bella and I trailed up to Amy's to tea. Mamma told Mrs Tweed that Ron wanted to stop and speak to me last Saturday, but that I walked on. Didn't detect any movement on his part to suggest such a possibility.

Friday, September 8th: Enjoyed an undisturbed night's rest, for the first time this week, so awoke feeling very thankful. We never appreciate these blessings until they're threatened.

Usual morning jaunt to school where we gossiped but did nothing. Have decided that if we don't start on Monday we're going to learn first aid and ambulance. The new teacher, Miss Evans, was itching to be off, as usual, much to our annoyed condemnation. We predict that She Will Shirk.

We played tennis until 8 o'clock by which time it was too dark to see a thing. Had to dash home then – on a darkened bus along dark streets and into a deserted, dark Swadlincote. Still, managed to forget the war for two hours. To bed and slept soundly – thanks be!

Saturday, September 9th: Continued the jumper, which I now view with a doubtful eye.

Hitler is continuing his advance through Poland, while we're harassing him a little on the Western Front. For every bomb we drop on Germany, he has promised us 10.

Went to Tweeds' to tea via Bella's and home about 6. Bought sal volatile with an eye to the future and parked it in the bathroom. Jack and Ivy called, with tales about last Sunday's raid and we all managed to laugh heartily.

To Grandma's for an hour before bedtime. Jack, Winnie and the baby are staying there at nights for the duration of the war. How long?

Monday, September 11th: Reported at school, but still don't know when we're to start properly. Stayed there all the morning again, wasting time, which annoyed me greatly, while AMF led a mournful, monotonous and dispirited conversation.

Was walking to the library about 2.30 with Amy when I was vaguely aware of a man driving a car politely raising his hat to me as he drove by. Didn't realise until he'd gone by almost that it was Ron. Huh! What was there to prevent him stopping the car then, if he'd wanted to speak to me? Alas, one conclusion only to be deduced. Still, why worry? I know by now what to think of him.

Delia and Miss Green parked themselves here at suppertime.

Tuesday, September 12th: Shattering blow! Toddled serenely and brightly to school, to be told that we start tomorrow. Oh hang! Don't want to. We're going to work 9–12.30 and 2–3 for one week, and 10–11, 1.30–4.30 the next. Morn and afternoon spent at school footling around. Wasted time. Auntie Nell to tea.

Wednesday, September 13th: Had to resume the shackles once more and apply myself to the care and nurture of The Young after six weeks' respite. Have 48 in my class this year, but have hopes that they'll be brighter than the last lot, who were dull and dozy. One new Birmingham child warmed my heart with her intelligent answers – let her entertain the class by reciting for half the morn.

The shift system has begun. We are sharing our school with the Birmingham Bloomsbury Street one, so we had to stay for lunch after our morning session of 3½ hours, to meet the incoming teachers and show them round. Nine of them arrived, including the startling phenomenon of two males! – but there are only about 90 children between them. Have a man named Robinson in my room – big and dark with horn-rimmed spectacles, but didn't like him very much. Should have taken the children for games from 3–4 this afternoon but it rained so we sent them home. Latest rumour says Hitler intends to bring 3000 aeroplanes over to poor little England. Nasty old man!

Thursday, September 14th: Another morning's toil and then the rest of the day free – whoopee! The shift system isn't at all bad – though goodness knows what the children's intelligence will be like at the end of it. Mr Belfield says that as soon as we hear an air-raid warning we're to say brightly and jovially to the children, 'Hello, children! Time to lie down,' whereat they will all creep under their desks like little mice. Huh! As soon as the sirens go, there will be pandemonium and panic, excitement and much leaping about.

Saturday, September 16th: Embarked on a search for a winter coat. Accordingly, Mother, and Auntie Nell and I caught the 1.40 bus, bound for Derby, all replete with gas masks and hoping that Adolf wouldn't pick on this particular day to shower his bombs on Derby. Delia and Miss Green were on the same bus, also bound for a shopping expedition. Had an awful journey, steeped in Stygian gloom. Outside, it was a lovely golden sunny after-noon, sun shining, green fields, blue sky and golden light etc, but viewed from the bus, through its newly tinted blue windows, it all looked cold and wintry. Very dreary – except for the sun, that even the blue windows couldn't dim. Looked out eagerly for the famous Balloon Barrage when we neared Derby, but was very disappointed. Had expected to see the sky covered with a ring of massive balloons, but instead saw only two tiny little sausages far away in the blue. Can't see that they can do much.

Mother, Auntie N and I went coat-hunting to Bracegirdles. Usual very inferior feeling as we entered the magnificent portals. Asked to see, 'Coats, please', and we were shown into a cubicle with large mirror and antique chairs, also a magnet for picking up pins. Immediately my blue coat, which before had seemed to me the height of perfection, dwindled into a creased and shabby covering. Woman shimmered in with two or three models and an endless stream of small talk and trite comments. Tried on black – which made me look like a hag and which had a brownish hue, then a green with grey collar – also awful. Then a pretty smoky-blue with two fur pockets. Liked this but M and Auntie N immediately said, 'Huh! No change from your summer coat,' and cast their eyes upon a purple edifice hanging on the wall. Tried it on and they said it looked nice, so stifled a few misgivings and decided to Have It. It had black lamb's wool pockets. It was then fitted and I disbursed a reluctant £6 10s. Hope I'll like it.

Finished my jumper – praise be!

Monday, September 18th: Had to amuse the children this morn, so we took them to the games field and pranced about there with them. Afternoon shift this week – most wearying. Didn't finish till 4.30, so staggered exhaustedly up to Bella's to tea. Felt quite worn out and limp. The last half-hour seems to drag, and the children just sit and doze.

Tuesday, September 19th: Bella to tea today, but left before dark as usual. Am getting quite used to lurching about in darkness now. Have my bedroom window draped with a rug and have to furl it up in the dark. Do this with great ingenuity by starting at one corner and tossing on the top of the wardrobe when finished.

Wednesday, September 20th: Bella to tea with us again. Both she and Joyce have got jobs under the Food and Fuel Control sections of the Council Offices.

Called in to Swan's to see the wedding photographs, which proved to be quite good. All except one, on which the best man seems to be leering out of the corner of his eye at Bella, who has her lips compressed in a firm and unyielding line.

Thursday, September 21st: Oh dear! This shift system likes me not. Too much toil and stress involved. Feel as though I've finished my day's work at 12, instead of not having started. This morn we misguidedly took the 4 classes for a ramble over Storey's Nob and up Bridle Lane. We had an unending and noisy crocodile of some 200 little dears and staggered up Springfield Road with them while faces poked out of every window and doorway and dogs leapt yapping at the gates. Grimly, we plodded on, trying to look unconcerned, until we got to the fields, where we relaxed a little. Halfway through we halted and Miss Smith conducted them in song, then off we set again. Trailed exhaustedly in home at 11.30.

Pored over numerous patterns for winter dresses from Austin's, and although I'd have liked a ready-made frock, have decided to have some made instead, for economy's sake. Chose and ordered three materials:

1) rose-pink liberty silk with coloured flowers
2) blue all-over liberty crepe
3) plain blue wool georgette

Swanee wrote, saying that she had hardly returned from her honeymoon before 'a hag' arrived at her door and requested her to accommodate a mother and child. Whereat Swanee persuasively outlined the impossibility and sent the woman unsatisfied away.

Freddie has once more jilted me, methinks. Not a sign of him since last term except a card from the Isle of Man. Think he must have found Another. Ah me! These faithless men! I am a disillusioned woman.

Russia invaded Poland last Sunday and the poor Poles are hopelessly outnumbered, but Warsaw is still holding grimly on. The Czechs have revolted against Germany and are being executed in hundreds.

Saturday, September 23rd: My new coat came yesterday, so am still at the stage of trying it on umpteen times a day. Everyone likes it – it's a pretty colour, not purple, more blackberry. Shall not feel satisfied now until I have a hat, scarf and shoes to wear with it, but fear that will have to wait until I am reimbursed.

Letter from Dougiedear, who has volunteered for the Army Transport, he says. Rick is in the Tank Corps. He says that they have had 3 Air-Raid warnings and affirms that 70 bombers came over once, and 36 were shot down. He says too that some of the planes return in such condition to Mildenhall, with bullet holes through them and bits dangling down, that it is marvellous they ever get back again. Letter on the whole very morose and gloomy, but typical. He supposes he'll end up in the front line, but has heard that it is a glorious death to die fighting for one's country. He hopes vindictively to have the pleasure of seeing the Germans smashed to blazes. Poor old Doug!

Doug (centre)

Sunday, September 24th: Suffered most grim and gruesome dreams of corpses and catafalques during the night, so awoke with some relief from my uneasy slumbers. Oh dear! 8 a.m. Communion every Sunday now. The Territorials came to Church again this morn, so when Delia and I arrived we had to trail right to the front pew before we found an empty seat. Most awful and embarrassing position! Mrs B* was sitting immediately behind, and I could feel her gimlet eye fixed upon my every movement.

Warsaw subjected to almost continuous aerial bombardment today. Thousands of civilians killed. Horrible!

Mother perfectly convinced that Hitler is coming straight to Swadlincote next with 3000 bombers at dead of night. She sits over the wireless all day with a brooding expression, giving vent to groans.

Monday, September 25th: Ping-ponged with Delia after tea until dusk fell. Then adjourned indoors and finished reading Cronin's *Three Loves.* Usual recrudescence of war talk as the night wore on. We're all quite cheerful and optimistic during the day, but as darkness falls our imagination works and our fears increase.

Tuesday, September 26th: Honoured by a visit from the nobility this morn, viz. Sir Roger Curtis, His Majesty's Inspector. Fortunately he remained closeted with madam and left without deigning to visit us.

Wednesday, September 27th: Oh dear! These afternoons of merry sport and game tire me out! Staggered once more with the Tribes of Manasseh and Gad to the Sandholes and there frisked around in circles with them. Staggered exhaustedly home afterwards and thence to Tweeds' to tea, to help Amy fill in her Goldsmiths College

*The vicar's wife.

entrance forms, though why she couldn't do it herself beats me. Can't remember taking it so seriously myself. Brought back many a memory of College days – very pathetic now because they're so long ago and so definitely over. Oh dear! How these joys speed by!

Monday, October 2nd: Afternoon toil this week – noxious and loathsome. Played about with the children in the Sandhole fields this morn.

Went to the first WEA History lecture but mistook the time and arrived half an hour early. Very uncomfortable. Delia and Miss Green rolled in later and the noisy crowd from Newhall. Became Librarian, though reluctantly. New lecturer, Knowles, seems quite good, though is badly in need of a haircut. Very interesting lecture – about the war.

Thursday, October 5th: Pouring wet day – oh, dreadful! Freddie very kindly agreed to take me to Goad's Nurseries to buy flowers for the Harvest Festival. Felt very conscience-stricken, using him thus for my own ends. Still, he didn't seem to mind. He wandered around with me and carried the flowers. Bought 3/- worth of red dahlias and white chrysanthemums. Let him go, after he'd brought me home.

Went to the Eng lecture. Mr Addison discussed Walpole's *The Cathedral* which I have never read, so had to sit oyster-like in a corner. Still, if I had read it I don't suppose I'd have vouchsafed my opinion.

Saturday, October 7th: Dashed to Mrs W's to consult with her about making up my 2 lots of material, and as usual she vowed she was Very Busy, and couldn't possibly do it for a fortnight, though I know for a fact that she's done nothing for weeks. Her daughter giggled from the background at intervals, though I don't recall saying anything funny.

Sunday, October 8th: Ploughed the fields and scattered 3 times today, it being the occasion of our Harvest Festival. After a preliminary sally to early Communion in my blue summer coat, prepared for the great éclat, viz garbed myself in my new autumn attire – blackberry coat, black hat with petunia ribbon, petunia scarf, black gloves, shoes and handbag – and, thus attired, swaggered forth feeling like Solomon in all his glory to the 10.30 and 3 p.m. services. Surreptitiously fingered my lamb's wool pockets during the sermon and felt very gratified by their touch.

Monday, October 9th: To the History lec. But have decided that they're a red-hot bed of socialists, and they annoy me. Mr G changed the discussion into a dialogue between himself and Knowles. The latter gentleman appeared after an obvious haircut looking considerably less hirsute. He has rather an obsequious and placatory manner, but when he gets going is interesting and expressive.

Thursday, October 12th: To Mrs W's to have silk dress fitted. Home by 6 and to the Eng Lec at 6.45. Discussed *The Cathedral* again. Man who had most to say was the only one who hadn't read the book. Have a sore throat.

Friday, October 13th: Friday the 13th with a vengeance. Awoke with spots on the throat but struggled to school. Had to go to bed at dinnertime however. Usual trouble – tonsillitis. Ached all over, throat awful.

Tuesday, October 17th: Got up about 1 p.m. today, feeling rather weak, but my throat is lots better.

Thursday, October 19th: Was just about to depart after dinner, when exclamations of surprise came from Mother as the door opened, and in walked – Swanee! Had no idea she was coming over. She came yesterday to see Bill, who is on leave for 4 days before going out to France. Bella and I went there for tea. Had letter from Doug this morn. Doug says primly and righteously that he can't tell me any war news because large posters have been put up advising people not to spread news and rumours. What does he think I am? A German spy?

Saturday, October 21st: Oh dear! A belated postman arrived bearing Income Tax Assessments, and I reeled to find that I have to pay £2 10s. each half year, as well as an additional 8/4 tax on my night school earnings. However, I went through the forms with an eagle eye to find that I had been charged twice for night school. Full of righteous indignation, I put pen to paper and composed a dignified protest to HM Inspector of Taxes, getting rather involved, however, in the repeated use of the word 'assessment' that popped up in every sentence.

Bella and I went to Burton with Esme to buy a coat. Dreadful trying to get on a bus these days; they are all crammed and it's the hardest pusher who gets the best seat. Waited patiently for a bus at the Chesterfield, only to see it whiz triumphantly by in its usual crowded state. To add to our chagrin, Kay and J sailed serenely by in their car on their way back from Burton, which caused Bella and Esme to brood deeply, with a sense of wrong and unjust dealing.

To Herrat's for the coat. Silly woman there talked incessantly and in a high-pitched London voice, while the subservient sales assistant almost grovelled at her feet. She tried lots of things on, declaring, 'Naow, Ai daon't think Ai laike thet!' and 'Ah! Thet is jast lavly.' Esme tried on a coat and turned to ask Bella if she liked it, whereon Bella said with awful distinctiveness, 'Naow, Ai daon't think Ai laike thet!' There was a dreadful silence. I'm sure the woman heard.

Monday, October 23rd: Mrs W finished my rosy-coloured flowered dress on Sat, but found to my horror when trying it on that it is Much Too Short. Silly woman! Don't know what I'll do with it.

Thursday, October 26th: My mother is most fond of bursting in with dramatic statements. She ponders, then she bursts. The door was flung open at dinnertime today and in she charged exclaiming, 'He's going to *rain* bombs on us.' No preliminaries but the stark unvarnished statement for dramatic effect.

Wended a reluctant way to my first (shame!) National Union of Teachers meeting, accompanied by Trissie (and under compulsion). Staggered, on arriving, to see a magnificent repast – a most sumptuous board, so felt very peeved to think I'd had my tea before coming.

Came out before the end to go to Magister Addison. He talked about Forster's *Passage to India* (through which I've not yet succeeded in wading). Tucked myself away in a corner during the discussions and held my peace. I wonder what he thinks about us all. I bet he thinks I'm most dull and wooden – I don't think I've uttered a syllable yet. The earnest cadaverous-looking woman was there, with her usual intelligent remarks. She always finds something bright to say.

Friday, October 27th: A visit from the nobility again today, Sir Roger, His Majesty's Inspector, intimating that we are to go on full time instead of the shift system.

Another dramatic disclosure from Mother. She flung herself headlong into the house exclaiming that they Had Had the Red Light at the Rolls-Royce works last night.*

---

*Rolls-Royce at Derby made aircraft engines.

Saturday, October 28th: Maurice, who used to work for us, is now on the *Ark Royal* that the Germans are so anxious to destroy. Until Feb of this year he was on the *Courageous* that was sunk recently. I bet he will have some hair-raising tales to tell!

Oh dear! This dreadful war! Nothing is secure any longer. It's like living on the edge of a precipice. Auntie Nell says that Hitler is going to drop thousands of men over England in parachutes. Oh how awful! For them, I mean.

Wednesday, November 1st: Had a voluminous mail this morn – 3 letters, from Dougie, Vera and Hilda Tooth. Dougie says viciously that he wants to have A Real Good Bust at some sort of a German, and thinks he will enlist as a carpenter. How he will have his bust that way, I know not. He is now 12 st 3! How coarse and obese! He has picked a cockerel from his stock for me for Christmas, but says that it is still wilting under the strain of present circumstances. Fancy being wooed with a cockerel!

Miss Tooth's effusion was very stilted and precise, as usual, but quite friendly and very typical. She is annoyed, in a ladylike way, about our one day's holiday instead of the promised week, but has decided philosophically to Grin and Bear It like a True Briton, fortifying ourselves with the knowledge that Christmas is not far away. She says that the Birmingham teachers are bemoaning the cold and asking what it will be like in the winter. She adds grimly Perhaps It is Better that they should Not Know.

Thursday, November 2nd: End of term today. Broke up for our marvellously long holiday. After promising us very grandly a week, they fling a scrap of a day at us.

Yanked myself to the English lecture. The emaciated young lady there again, very earnestly making apt remarks, leaning forwards as she did so to Mr Addison, while the rest of us sat back and looked dumb. Mr Addison's nostrils contract as he speaks, but I think he has a nice face – shrewd and intelligent and clean.

My blue wool georgette arrived from Mrs W, and is awfully sweet and has the general approval. Paraded in same.

Sunday, November 5th: Bonfire Night, whiz bang! Or rather pitter-patter, lash, lash, howl, howl. It was a really dreadful night, wild storms and as dark as the proverbial bag. The wind rose and moaned around the house, and we groped our way blindly to Grandma's. No degrees of darkness tonight – just one thick blanket without shape, colour or dimension. Usually one can distinguish a dark grey object here or a moving shape there, but not tonight. The darkness seemed to have seeped into everything.

Monday, November 6th: Our first day on full time again. Goodness! Felt as if I'd done a week's toil and grind at the end of it. Escaped with relief.

Our weekly inroad into International Relations this evening. Mr G made his usual involved and high-sounding outbursts. Every sentence either began or ended with 'In hard practice' and we all had to stifle hysterical giggles. Could hear Charlie Fairbrother asking Where Hard Practice is – is it in the Balkans? whereat all in his row giggled, and I was afraid the man G would hear them.

Mr H was enquiring very earnestly about The Red Menace, and seems to have a positive complex about it. He asked in a sinister way, 'What about Russia and Japan? What if Germany Goes Red?; What about Communism among the English Intellectuals?' And so forth.

Tuesday, November 7th: Mrs Tweed and Amy to tea. Mrs Tweed and Auntie Frances carried on a gruesome and confidential

May, Mrs Tweed and Delia

conversation about cancer, and quoted examples from all their friends. Enter Ethel then, with latest details about her mother's colitis, which developed into a general discussion of illness and sore throats, then Uncle Will came to phone Derby Royal to see how Auntie Sarah is. In fact, an interlude of sickness, diet, operations, haemorrhages and what not. Thence to bed, to dream of being in an air raid. Found it most unpleasant.

Wednesday, November 8th: Was proceeding in my usual hurried manner to school this afternoon when Mr H stopped me and asked if I had Been Following the Situation. Said uncertainly Well

No, to which he declared that All Things Point the Same Way – the Small Countries are going to be Wiped Out. With that he solemnly departed, and I resumed my way to school very uneasily.

Seemed to spend the afternoon snarling. Children shouldn't be made with such chatty natures. They should make excellent conversationalists when they grow up – they have a perpetual and never-ending flow of small talk.

Thursday, November 9th: Mother awakened me with the dramatic statement that They've Tried to Bomb Hitler. Further elucidation revealed that a bomb exploded in a beer hall 15 minutes after he left it last night. 8 people were killed and 60 injured and Hess of odious repute is supposed to have been among the victims. Old man Hitler seems to bear a charmed life! It will take more than a puny bomb to remove him from the face of the earth.

The usual little gathering congregated in the Miners' Offices for our weekly English lecture. Mr Addison very good tonight on Robert Lynd, on whom he spoke in his usual calm and unhurried manner, and with typical urbanity. Can't imagine him ever getting excited about anything – he just glows when he is speaking of anything he particularly likes. He discussed the first four of Robert Lynd's essays, together with his humour, sympathetic tolerance, his attitude as an interested spectator, and his style which is easy, flowing and readable. Mr Edwards listened intently in a Napoleonic posture and with a studious frown. Mr Thick smiled gently and dreamily, as though half asleep. Jessie Gilliver sat rigidly upright and looked as matronly as usual. Vera Dennis slouched ungracefully, surmounted by her most startling headgear to date – a shallow plate placed precariously over the left ear, and the cadaverous Miss Wales sat expectantly forward, lips slightly parted ready to be intelligent at the first opportunity. Time passed very quickly and enjoyably.

Friday, November 10th: In the middle of a political discussion wherein we were elaborating upon the world's economic problems, Mother, who was beginning to look very worried, burst in concernedly with, 'I say!' We looked expectantly ready to hear her solution to the world's problems or fresh insight on them, when she continued impressively, The Fish Man who lost his wife a few months ago Is Married Again – to somebody's wife's sister.

An invasion of the Low Countries prophesied to be imminent.

Bella and I ventured forth in the quickly creeping dusk to sell poppies. Suffered the usual slights and elaborate excuses – most of these generous people apparently having rows and rows of poppies adorning their mantelpieces at home, and those who had not had Promised to have one from So-and-so.

Saturday, November 11th: Armistice Day, but a very strange and different Armistice Day without the hooters and the general cessation of all activity at 11 a.m. Mother and I sat still at 11, but everyone else seemed to be carrying on with their activities. But it does seem farcical to be celebrating the end of the last war while we're just at the beginning of a new one, which according to prophecy is going to make even the old one pale before it.

Sunday, November 12th: Only 6 weeks today until Christmas Eve. Whoopee (though it seems rather wicked and tempting Providence to look joyously so far ahead these days). I hope they don't cut down our Christmas holidays. If they do, I really shall ask for an interview and wave a banner. Listened in to entertainment for the troops from France – Maurice Chevalier and Noel Coward there. Then out into the Stygian gloom, and after walking into the palings, reached light once more, at Grandma's. Dispiriting and not very entertaining conversation about bacon. Grandpa related a tale of a pig that was blind with fat and compared it with a local man.

After we had expounded upon every Aspect of the Pig, conversation turned to Mrs Cartwright's new blue curtains, which each in turn condemned roundly, then on to Conscientious Objectors, with the entrance of CO Skerritt.*

My father was inspired to delve into his last war experiences and remembered fondly a Gun named Betty and his Dug-out in Italy. The latter was apparently very dear to him, after he had laboured over it for a fortnight, and he waxed most indignant as he recalled how a Bloomin' Hound tried to take it from him. Rats then featured in the conversation, also inhabitants of the dug-out, and we were told how a rat walked along a wire. Mr Skerritt, not to be outdone, joined in here with the fantastic assertion that the ants will decoy an unsuspecting greenfly underground, there to milk it!

Tuesday, November 14th: Usual sort of day. Rampaged about Unlearnt Tables and Blots but promptly forgot all about them at 4 p.m. Tramped home with Bella – she has a simple faith about the Future and thinks Ron and I will be reconciled. Nothing seems now more improbable. Our paths have diverged irreconcilably and if we were to meet we'd be strangers, below the surface acquaintance. Besides, I don't think about him now. The present Ron is unknown to me – for all practical purposes, the Ron I knew is dead and beyond all resurrection. It is strange to

---

*Mr Skerritt had declared his intention to apply for conscientious objector status. Exemption from military service on the grounds of conscience, provided that it was approved by a tribunal, was first introduced in the First World War. A person wishing to claim conscientious objection had to make a declaration to this effect when he registered for service. In due course he would be called before a tribunal to justify his claim.

think that what was once so alive can fade so irretrievably. I wouldn't have thought it possible for one human being to love another for years and years without reciprocity. But perhaps I'm getting hard and cynical.

Thursday, November 16th: Letter from Dougie – a replica of every other he has sent – badminton, football, dances and the Fens all feature in it as usual. Went to English. The intelligent Miss Wales has returned to Birmingham, so our discussion descended to a lower level.

Friday, November 17th: Wailings and lamentations. I uplift my voice in Anger, Indignation and Protest. I place an immediate order for a Banner. We have been Swindled. The Education Committee have decreed with majestic and impassive loftiness that we receive exactly One-Half of our Christmas holidays. That's all! Just one week and a day! Held a little indignation meeting at school, at which I raised my voice with some vehemence. If I have a breakdown as a result, I shall Claim Compensation.

Pleasant-voiced announcer stated conversationally over the wireless that a German reconnaissance plane had flown over England this morn – over the Manchester region. Sounds quite ordinary but if it had come over here I'd have quivered and shaken like a jelly. I don't think I have a great amount of courage in my make-up. I expect Swanee got the warning – I wonder how she reacted. I expect she took the usual precautions in her usual matter-of-fact way and then thought no more about it. She isn't easily stirred, not even on her wedding day.

Wednesday, November 22nd: Six aeroplanes flew frightfully low over school this dinnertime. We all popped out of our rooms and gaped at the spectacle like mooncalves. Storms and tempests. Miss Foster had a purge, and whisked round the school with her cane like Hitler himself, chastising the law-breakers. A grisly proceeding – Miss Foster's mouth was shut like a rat-trap as she swish-swished. Her purge left behind a very chastened school.

Bella double-crossed me. After urging me to rake in Freddie as our Combined Partner for tonight's little dance, she backed out. Very peeved and very reluctant to go. Would much rather have gone to the flicks with Delia. The escort arrived in due course and we perambulated forth through a rainy night to the Rink. Nobody dancing when we arrived. However, one or two tentative couples took the floor, and by 8.30 there was a seething, shuffling mass. Noticed the girls' faces in the cloakroom. Nearly every one had a theatrically powdered look, as though they were ready for the footlights instead of a dance floor. Surreptitiously rubbed my own face and vowed mentally never to daub it like that.

Had a dreadful experience. I was just stepping delicately across the floor when my feet shot from under me and I fell prostrate, wildly clawing the air. Felt most humiliated. If it had been anyone else, I would have been most tickled.

Thursday, November 23rd: Applied myself assiduously and dutifully to my 'English homework' – an essay on Robert Lynd's style, more from curiosity than zeal. Curious to know whether I could, and found to my horror that it was the hardest job in the world to produce what once used to come quite easily. Could have done better when I was at school. Oh dear! However, finished it off in a fashion, then migrated to the flicks with my father to see *The Hound of the Baskervilles.* Very good, thoroughly enjoyed it. Basil Rathbone was exceptionally good as Sherlock Holmes, I thought. I love his lean, fastidious, sensitive nose and his mobile mouth. Dr Watson very good too.

Friday, November 24th: Bomb dropped on the Smith ménage this morn, by Audrey. She's going to be married next week! In secret, unknown to Ben's parents, strict Jews, or Audrey's father, a strict Gentile. They're going to the Registry Office in Staines.

Sunday, November 26th: We are going to win the war, says our neighbour because one of the Big Men From London has told her so. He says that we have 'one of the most deadliest poisons ever'.

Tuesday, November 28th: A new wartime diary, so goodness knows what dark and dreadful doings will fill these pages yet unwritten. Wartime – and yet so far not so very different from peacetime, except for the blackout, earlier closing of school, wireless bulletins and the appearance of uniform in almost every public place. Burton seems more prolific of uniform than the other places round about us. Almost every other girl and woman is swaggering about the streets in her khaki stockings and costume, and soldiers are nipping about here and there, with or without stripes. I expect we shall begin to feel the pinch a little more when rationing begins on January 8th. Thank goodness our Christmas dinner won't be stinted! What a hoggish thought!

Mrs Tweed bustled in at teatime loudly affirming that She Hadn't Come for Her Tea. She then proceeded to eat a hearty meal, nevertheless. She was vicariously thrilled when Old Friend Frederic rang up to invite me to the flicks. She giggled like a young flapper and fondly imagined I felt the same. But oh no! I agreed to go merely for a free trip to the flicks. How selfish! Quite the wrong spirit, I fear, quite wrong!

The faithful Fred arrived at 6, very punctually, and bore me off. We had to crawl like a tortoise through the darkness, and I sat bolt upright all the way, with my nose almost on the windscreen and my eyes glued on the darkness before us, anxiously scanning it and trying to penetrate it and locate Dangerous Obstacles,

Turns, Twists and Prowlers. But the road to Burton seemed almost deserted, and we arrived without catastrophe.

We went to the Ritz to see *A Spy in Black* – which was very topical, being all about German spies and submarines in Scapa Flow. Two girls sitting behind us kept telling each other in loud and penetrating whispers that they Couldn't Follow It Yet, but at the end decided that it had been Ever So Nice.

Thursday, November 30th: Quite a motley throng at the Eng lec tonight. Mrs Baker junior, with a hat like an inverted mushroom and masses of fair hair, Mrs Clulow and Betty Measures. Mr Buck, the Miners' Agent, frowned intelligently from one corner, with a hand covering the lower half of his face as though he had toothache and his eyes fixed keenly on Mr Addison, as though the subject of Robert Lynd were the most serious and important problem in the universe.

Friday, December 1st: Teatime, and in sailed Mrs Tweed, talking as she came, and sustaining the flow as long as she remained. She thinks that Frederic is such a Nice Boy, and asked vaguely – What Could Be Nicer? And did I Have a Nice Time? – she's sure I did. Mrs Tweed is to be in high society tomorrow, having been summoned to a meeting presided over by the Duchess of Devonshire. Delia came sauntering in. The Present Situation came into the limelight – she thinks that it is getting Serious now that the 20s to 23s have been called up today, and that we Really Aren't Doing Very Well, what with these Mines and Everything.

Saturday, December 2nd: Placed myself in the deft hands of Miss B, who moulded my errant locks into sleek waves and luscious curls. Then home to make a ginger cake and nine mince pies.

Travelling in this here war is just about the last word in Refined Torture. To get to Burton, once so simple, is now a

Herculean task, and one must combine the patience of Job with the frame of a prize fighter and the tenacity of a bulldog. To be timid, polite and unselfish is fatal. One must either park oneself in front of the hardest and most savage-looking pusher, or else assume the tactics of the rest and jostle, elbow, poke, manoeuvre and otherwise propel oneself forcibly forward until the goal is reached, viz the first step of the bus. This done, one can reassume one's better nature, eye the jostling throng with surprise and horror, and proceed with dignity down the bus, aloof and detached from the pushers. Bella and I made our way to the flicks. *Goodbye Mr Chips* was marvellous – a lovely flick.

Sunday, December 3rd: Delia came to tea. A dreadful night – wet, and very black. We all sat round the fire in comfort – Delia reading *7 Pillars of Wisdom,* my father reading the *News of the World,* Mother snoring gently and rhythmically from the depths of an armchair – while I read *Time & Tide,* containing another Provincial Lady series.

Discussed – in his absence – Mr Skerritt and his fastidious peculiarities, the Robinsons, now evacuated to Sidmouth, Aunt Emma's dug-out – an architectural wonder with a stove, and whether Aunt Emma is to be wheeled in a wheelbarrow if and when necessary.

Monday, December 4th: Experienced the profoundest sympathy and fellow-feeling for the dwellers of Greenland and the Arctic wastes. The weather suddenly laid an icy hand upon everyone today, and assumed a most wintry aspect – not a nice Christmas-card aspect, but a miserable, damp, raw, icy cold that penetrated everything. Shivered and dithered all day, and moaned continuously. Expected to have to be wheeled home on a barrow, but instead managed to propel my benumbed limbs through the icy rain and arrived home with relief. Thawed slowly but methodically by standing in the hearth and refusing to move until I felt the blood circulating in my extremities once more.

Uprooted myself with the greatest reluctance to imbibe knowledge from the lips of Mr Knowles. Delia and Miss Green equally reluctant, but we struggled there, clattered up the bare wooden stairs, along the echoing passage, and into the room – felt as though I were attending some secret and nefarious conclave, liable to be interrupted by Gestapo men at any moment. Parked ourselves as near the fire as possible, behind Charlie Fairbrother with his pimpled neck, and I tried to listen and take notes, but was so bored and cold that I wrote nonsense, viz an oration addressed to Mr Knowles as follows:

I am So Bored. What do I care about the Combines or the Profits of Vickers Armstrong? You have some figures have you? Well you can keep your figures. If they were a hot-water bottle I would accept them gladly. How agonising – to be cold and bored at the same time. So it is Quite Obvious, you say? Maybe – but not to me. Icicles are forming all over me, like barnacles on a rock. My chair is no longer passively hard – it is actively hard and unyielding. I shall never be warm again. The Arms Manufacturers are Full of Abuse? So am I. Silent and concentrated abuse. Need you be so eloquent and for so long? I am Extremely Bored. Ha! you make your little joke. Your cronies laugh obediently. But not I. You will now give us statistics? You may keep your statistics. If they were a warming-pan, I would grasp them with eagerness. There is a close connection, you say, between Big Business and the Peerage? There would be a closer connection between the fire and me if Pimpled Fairbrother didn't bar the way. Alas! The man G is upon his feet. He is telling us to accept something or other in Hard Practice. If it were a foot warmer I would not only accept it – I would fight for it. Even die for it. There are some causes worth dying for. My numbed fingers refuse to function. I can write no more. My mind has collapsed. Oh, Mr Knowles!

Tuesday, December 5th: Snowed about two flakes this morn, whereby the dear children went into raptures – noisy raptures – and had to be subdued.

Amy descended like a locust upon us for tea, but left early to go to *Wuthering Heights*. She had just gone when, oh dear! – palpitations and heart-throbs – the Voice of My Beloved came floating over the telephone. No, it was only Dear Freddie, so my heart remained untouched. He invited me to the flicks, so having nothing to do, and making use of him, his pocket and his car again, I went. Saw a mediocre programme and promised to go to the dance with him next Wed. He smoked a pipe, but he puffed furiously at it as though he wanted to get it over quickly, so I'm sure he only did it to appear the Strong Silent Type and not because he really enjoyed it. His faults seem to strike me much more readily than his virtues. I must be more forbearing.

Wednesday, December 6th: Shocks again! Vera wrote – the most sad and pathetic, but still practical, letter – announcing that she had Broken Off Her Engagement to Rick. Sat back and gasped, though I'm not frightfully surprised, because she said once before that when she suggested getting married he refused. Anyhow, she had resurrected the thorny topic of a date for the wedding, and he confessed that he didn't want any responsibilities, then followed the usual blah-blah about her being Too Good For Him. She says mournfully that I Know What It Feels Like to be Thus Disillusioned. I do! I still remember that Agony of Agonies, that Dreadful and Harrowing Time. She shall have my full and unreserved sympathy. The Spurned must Cling Together.

Miss Sanders asks if these diaries are intended for ultimate publication. Tell her grandly that they shall be bequeathed to the British Nation.

Thursday, December 7th: The temperature of this noxious clime is well below zero, I'm sure. Rolled to school through banks of white fog to find the playground a network of slides and gliding figures.

Sped hastily indoors. My classroom was like some gangsters' den, having collected a machine gun and two fierce-looking rifles which adorned the table for the rest of the day. We are also resplendent with two artificial Christmas trees, but they seem most unseasonal. I can't think that Christmas is so near, although I had a Christmas card from Lilian in India this morn. It is just like our English ones.

Article by Ellen Wilkinson in *Time & Tide* accuses us of taking this war too easily, and predicts that the struggle will be graver and more fierce than we are led to believe. Oh dear!

Friday, December 8th: Spent the afternoon scrambling upon desks and performing intricate acrobatic feats in an effort to make the room gay and Christmassy. Draped festoons, garlands and lanterns from every conceivable object and grew more and more irate as I did so because the little dears *would* work themselves up into a frenzy of excitement. Threatened ferociously to tear all the decorations down, but didn't. Instead hurled threats right and left and continued to charge over the desks and drape. The result was a mess, and most inartistic, but the children were delighted.

Saturday, December 9th: Up betimes and on my way shopping to Derby. Fairly large middle-aged woman with powdered wrinkles and reeking with sickly scent lunged into the seat beside me and tut-tutted to herself every time the already full bus stopped to pick up more passengers. Her son has been in France almost since the beginning of the war, and she hasn't heard of him for six weeks. Sympathised and said lamely, What a Worry! She stated grimly that the Germans will Make For Him because he patches up the Aeroplanes. When we reached Derby she trotted off leaving a trail of her perfume behind. Felt sorry for her.

Sunday, December 10th: The usual migration to Grandma's after tea. Mr Skerritt again discussed in his absence. We busied ourselves drawing 3 white promotion stripes on the sleeves of his black mackintosh. Sergeant Skerritt, what, what!

Monday, December 11th: Did a Mean Act – tore up a boy's cigarette cards with malice aforethought, but when he laid his pathetic little head upon the desk and with shaking shoulders began to cry silently, felt as Herod must have done on Innocents' Day, or the Man who Murdered the Princes in the Tower, or any other Oppressor of the Young.

At home we have acquired mural decorations of a lavish and original kind, viz a ham and a large expanse of bacon, upon which my father's eye rests lovingly many a time and oft.

Prowled forth into the blackout with generosity of spirit to buy Dougie a Christmas present. Really I wasn't actuated by anything more exalted than the conviction that he'll shower a gift upon me, and that it will look mean if I don't retaliate. Anyhow dallied amongst the Men's wear at the Co-op and emerged at length with razor, which I exhibited to all at home. My father said Huh, rather rudely, and said Why Not a Silk Handkerchief, and everyone else had an alternative to offer, although when I asked for suggestions before going out they were all struck dumb.

When Rowena and Delia called to go to the lecture, I made

excuses and let them go without me, preferring to be a Backslider tonight.

Tuesday, December 12th: Repeated demands for extortionate amounts of income tax by this morning's post. Also request from the Council for donation for the evacuees. Also facing me long list of still un-bought Christmas presents. Have selfish desire of my own for new dress with which to improve the festive season. Oh dear! All incompatible with the contents of my purse.

The ritual of the Locks performed again after tea, in preparation for the dance tomorrow. Sat in front of garrulous woman on the bus. She declared that Old People have No Right to Be Out in the Blackout – they are a danger to themselves and others. And did her companion know that Stella is to be married on Boxing Day? After all she has been engaged for two years and should know her own mind. Speculated idly upon who this Stella was and then it dawned on me it must be the star of our hockey firmament – Stella Clarke. Good gracious! Everyone's getting married. Had a nightmare last night. Dreamt that I had just got married to Freddie in a green dress, and woke up in stark horror. Thank goodness it was only a dream!

Miss B decided that it would be better if I kept my grips in all night. For once I was thankful for the blackout to hide my degradation, feeling like an out-of-work charwoman. I am also afflicted with a row of bulbous cold spots along my lower lip. I am a most piteous spectacle of Humanity.

Spent the evening by the fire. Mr Skerritt goes around muttering about Retaliation – for his 3 stripes – so I think it wise to secrete this confidential document, or it may be defaced or outraged.

Wednesday, December 13th: Mr Wheat our caretaker loomed suddenly before me and told me soothingly to Never Mind, I Look

Better Today. Gazed with mystification, and he added that I Didn't Look Very Gay Yesterday. Oh dear! In future I must dash about the school with sprightly step or else Mr Wheat will be Worried. Had no idea he was so concerned about my health.

Read chunks from *The Wind in the Willows* to the class, and added still more units to the general scheme of decoration. The room now looks like a Christmas nightmare, with chains of every hue and description. Shudder each time I enter and feel responsible.

Parcel of books arrived from The Phoenix – *A Room with a View*, *Some English Diarists*, *Uncle Fred in the Springtime* and *Barchester Towers*. I love new books, and the arrangement of them in my bookcase. Also present myself punctually at Jebbett's each day to ask whether *Time & Tide* has arrived, but now she says No before I ask. There seems to be a conspiracy to withhold it.

Bella and I adorned ourselves in our Models, groaning all the time, in preparation for the dance, and induced Delia to go too, clad in an old bridesmaid's dress of mine. So when the punctual Fred arrived on the dot, he found Three Dashing Females waiting. Manoeuvred in the blackout so that Bella walked next to him on the way there, and she kept prodding me indignantly, but I ignored her.

Danced with unknown man who asked if I'd noticed Santa Claus hopping about earlier in the evening. Said yes and was just going to add It's a pity he didn't have his dirty robe washed before coming, when he confided bashfully that He Was Santa Claus.

The faithful Fred of course very attentive.

Thursday, December 14th: Ow! I hate late nights. Awoke this morn feeling weary and quite unfit for work. Took lesson on A Coal Mine, whereupon all the class had some grim and gruesome tale to relate about uncles, fathers and brothers who had had their toes, ears and fingers severed in the pit.

Many tales in circulation about Attacks made by Prowling Men in the blackout. Dreadful! Bella has several stories and Auntie Nell and my father added more, all very terrifying.

Friday, December 15th: Miss S reminded us that presents for France must be posted by Tuesday next and added that she has 'at least eight to send'. Said, 'My goodness', and looked greatly impressed but mentally allowed for great exaggeration.

Mrs Tweed ambled in at teatime. She has been signally honoured with a Christmas card from Ron – containing Such Nice Words. She went on to recollect the time when we all visited Summerfield for the Sunday School Teachers' Party, when he told Mrs T not to ask me to go home with them because he wanted to take me ...! Mrs T concluded with a solemn look and the profound words You Know What I've Always Told You. Mrs T is an incurable optimist, and always tells people what she thinks they want to hear.

Saturday, December 16th: The *Graf Spee* is now very much in the news. It was followed by some of our light cruisers in the South Atlantic, which opened fire. In the firing it was badly damaged and had to retreat to Montevideo Harbour for repairs. It is still there, with a 36-hour time limit expiring at 11.30 p.m. tomorrow, and our ships are waiting for it to emerge.

Sunday, December 17th: To Grandma's as usual – lighter tonight – a new moon, bright stars, some clouds, and the searchlights playing around the sky. Speculated upon what the *Graf Spee* is going to do. Concluded that its days are numbered because Maurice, our apprentice, is now there on the *Ark Royal.* My father said profoundly that there are Clever Men On Both Vessels and then

May's parents (back row, right) and May (middle row, left)

embarked upon a long discourse upon How Minesweepers Work. Mother who had apparently been pondering on other matters, remarked irrelevantly that she hopes Doug sends the chicken before the weekend, then we can have it for dinner on Sunday.

Monday, December 18th: The *Graf Spee* left the harbour about 7.30 last night and shortly afterwards its crew scuttled her! Jubilate! That's evened matters out a little.

I have omitted to relate One Important Thing which I received on Sat morn – a Christmas card from Ron! A nativity silhouette as usual with an ashamed little 'Ron' penned in one corner. Scanned the words critically, but they don't seem like the Nice Ones that went to Mrs Tweed.

A visitor at teatime – the Gallant Fred. He sat down comfortably and looked hopefully at the tea-pot, but didn't ask him to partake. That would have been much too encouraging. He hasn't given me the 2/6 for the dance yet.

Went to the History lecture with Rowena and Delia. The man G as eloquent as ever but I had a seat almost in the hearth, so sat in a somnolent posture and dozed. Heard fragments about the Ruling Classes (the lecturer), the Big Combines (Mr G) and the Red Menace (Mr H) but too dozy to concentrate.

Tuesday, December 19th: News from Dougiedear. He *is* going to send me A Cockerel for Christmas. I think I'll send him a hundredweight of potatoes. Volunteered very generously to sell it, but Mother wouldn't respond. I think I'll stuff it and keep it in his memory.

Wednesday, December 20th: Received my post at dinnertime – cards and a large carrier bag containing the Promised Bird from Doug – though it was addressed to Mother. Very thrilled – a proper 'Dougie' touch. He doesn't say it with flowers, oh no! Dougie has to shower birds. Howbeit, it looks very succulent, and I like poultry.

Thursday, December 21st: It still doesn't seem at all festive or Christmassy – I expect it's the blackout and the war that have made things different. We all reluctantly changed into Our Best at dinnertime in readiness for the cacophonous medley, the deafening din – viz the children's party. Miss Ford in a very sour temper and remarked that I looked as if I were Going To A Wedding. No games this year but a conjuror who delighted the children's hearts, and then lemonade and buns and home at 3.30.

Friday, December 22nd: A horrible fog shrouded everywhere today, but despite its pall, I tripped to school on nimble feet – first because it was the last day of term, and second because the shekels awaited us. Children still very hilarious, but at last we packed them all off home for their Christmas holidays – with unbounded relief I exchanged the usual little packages with the rest of the staff but religiously kept my acquisitions sealed until the great day of revelation.

Had a Christmas card from Freddie yesterday, which everyone thought Very Funny. It was read out numerous times by wits and humorists simply because the lengthy verse within ended with 'All joy and peace be yours, my dear'. Think he must have over-looked that choice phrase when he sent it.

Saturday, December 23rd: Bushels of Xmas cards. Had my hair moulded into Xmas waves. Poor Admiral Langsdorff of the *Graf Spee* has committed suicide.

Sunday, December 24th: Card – very luscious-looking mother-of-pearl-y with 9*d.* on the back – from Doug. The verse inside was very touching. Poor old Dougie. He's a very faithful and loyal soul.

Have suffered from pimples down the left side of my face for the last two days. Shall look truly wonderful for Christmas.

Christmas Day: Hoofed along to 8 o'clock Communion. The vicar picked two of the highest carols he could find, and we all screeched on the top notes. Home again by 9 and then the Great Unpacking. Very thrilling. Had some lovely presents – I'm sure my gifts must look very mean beside some. After my grudging and half-hearted letters to Doug, he magnificently sent me the most lovely pearl and diamanté bracelet. Audrey, to whom I sent nothing, sent a luxurious midnight-blue powder puff. Vera, who only received two little hankies from me, sent a sequined evening bag. I had a crêpe-de-chine nightdress and white satin set from Mother, box of hankies and a 4/11 pair of stockings from Dad, 5/- from Grandma, a white underset from Auntie F, a Yardleys box of bath crystals and soap from Auntie Nell, as well as stockings, a box of Golden Glory soap, writing paper, 'Pink Lilac' scent, 'Devon Violet' scent, a white Swiss linen handkerchief sachet, silk hankies, blue slippers, a leather stamp case, lovely chromium lantern-lamp, chocolates, a calendar and a box of shoulder strap ribbons. I think I'm very lucky. Yanked all these in a box to Grandma's to exhibit them, and they all exclaimed in awe over Dougie's bracelet.

The usual Christmas dinner of turkey and plum pud at Grandma's. Afterwards I changed into my new black frock, put on Dougie's bracelet, and we migrated to Auntie Nell's. Their first question – 'What has Dougie sent?'

After eating the usual large tea of ham and tongue, trifle, fruit, jellies, pork pie, mince pies, Xmas cake and other cakes, we played cards, Lotto and darts, and then listened to Gracie Fields broadcasting to the troops in France.

Friday, December 29th: Late getting up. In the middle of making mince pies, Tom descended upon us in his Air Force uniform and looking very pale. He is an air gunner and was on his way back again to S Wales, where he is stationed. He wasn't too enthusiastic but said sombrely that life was 'all right'. Talked about aeroplanes and riggers and fitters etc for over an hour, and we fed him on chocolates and promised him a parcel.

1940

Staff of Springfield Road School, summer 1940; May is front left

Monday, January 1st 1940 – New Year's Day: It doesn't do to spec-ulate too much upon the potentialities of 1940 – too many bad ones. Better to accept each day as it comes. Our *Burton Mail* makes the startling and (I am sure) entirely unfoundedly opti-mistic statement that Hitler has A Cancer In The Throat and has only 18 months to live. Wishful thinking! If everything happened to him that has been predicted, his end would take a variety of forms and it would be both imminent and violent.

Tuesday, January 2nd: Simply Arctic, and freezing hard. My room at school felt as frigid as the coldest igloo in the further-most part of Greenland. Vainly clutched the hot-water pipe and twined myself miserably round it. Occasionally detached myself for long enough to prowl round and exhort the class to do Best Printing and No Blots, and No Dirty Finger-marks. Then made a frenzied beeline for my pipe again. 3.30 came at last, and I dithered home.

Friday, January 5th: My father is in great demand – out 'burst-ing' all day, this being the season of burst pipes. Room at school beginning to be a little less frigid.

Adjourned to the Majestic with Delia after tea to see *Confessions of a Nazi Spy*, which I didn't care for very much. I think we want to get away from Nazi spies and suchlike at the present time, and have something lighter for entertainment. Played draughts and listened to wireless play by J. B. Priestley called *Dangerous Corner*.

Saturday, January 6th: Spent most of the morn writing my little bit for that literary masterpiece, the Budget. Had no amorous incidents to relate, to my chagrin, except odd outings with Freddie, and the permanent incompatibility of Dougie's temperament and my own, despite his lavishness with cockerels and bracelets. Had to enclose a snap. Would love to have flung in a careless holiday snap of myself surrounded by a bevy of admiring males, but had to admit that no such snap existed, so included a picture of myself sitting solitary and alone in the Lake District.

Changes in the Cabinet announced in the *Telegraph* – Hore Belisha and Lord Macmillan have resigned. I'd love to know why. I'm sure Chamberlain doesn't pick the best men.

Man on wireless prayed solemnly and devoutly for the Children, and the blessings of innocence. Could have made acid and caustic comment, but refrained.

Sunday, January 7th: Am utterly – or almost utterly – broke, though it's only the beginning of the month. Went to Grandma's in time for supper while my father carried on long discourse about Bursts and Stop-Taps with references to Past and Present Cases from his Casebook.

Monday, January 8th: Circular informing me that I figure among the Prominent People of the District and have therefore been invited to the posh Chairman's Dance causes me to revise my Mental Estimate of Myself.

Had a letter from Poor Old Vera, who stirs a sympathetic chord in my heart. Rick didn't even send her a Christmas card. Re-read again tonight my tragic experiences of 1936, the year of the Great Schism. Ron was jolly mean – not in giving me up, but in the nasty, sly way that he did it. If I hadn't written and asked him, he never would have told me properly. He caused me months of unhappiness, through hoping, and then being disappointed, and hoping again, and in general not knowing what to think. It was horrible, and I don't think now that it was worth it.

Must organise a search soon for my gas mask. No idea where it is. At first I daren't venture a yard without it, but now I seem lulled into such a false sense of normality that I never dream of yanking it out with me.

Tuesday, January 9th: Had just entered the bath before tea when Freddie phoned to ask if I'd like to go to the flicks with him tonight. Had to be brief, as I was dripping copiously all over the hearth, so I hurriedly said Yes and Goodbye. He accordingly presented himself all wound up in college muffler at 5.20, and we hoofed along to Burton to see *Jamaica Inn* with Chas Laughton. Very enjoyable. Consumed coffee and biscuits afterwards and talked about the war and Finland. We retired home and arrived about 9. Thanked him dutifully, and he said Oh That was All Right, and added as an afterthought that he had Enjoyed It. He hasn't refunded my 2/6! How I harp on about it. Miss S said Well he sent me a Christmas Card with My Dear on, but tell her I'd rather have one with my half-crown on.

Thursday, January 11th: Went to the Sunday School Prize Giving. Evacuees there too, and they ate like ravening wolves. One boy poked me in the back and said imperiously, 'Tea please,' at which I gave a spontaneous and severe speech on Manners. Ron's Mamma there too. Her tongue is smoother than butter, but I know she has war in her heart, even now. We shall never be friends, because we regard each other with profoundest suspicion. Mamma says that Ron doesn't like these modern girls with waved hair, lipstick and cigarettes. My word, he's still hard to please! Mamma gave him a little talk and asked him if it wasn't time he thought of getting married, to which he retorted that there was plenty of time. I've always said that he'll marry some sweet young thing when he's in his thirties. Never mind!

Auntie F is leaving me her engagement ring in her will! So I *shall* have one ring, at any rate.

Friday, January 12th: Mrs Tweed told me some disquieting news – Mamma thinks I'm Getting Bonny. Huh! I know what her 'bonny' implies – it implies 'fat', pure and simple. Oh dear!

Monday, January 15th: Played draughts with Amy after tea, but only pushed a moderate draught tonight, losing more games than I won. Played cards then until suppertime. Mrs Tweed enlarged upon Mamma's 'bonny' remark, and commented sorrowfully upon my only wearing a jumper and skirt on that occasion, when I have So Many Nice Dresses.

Tuesday, January 16th: Auntie F came in announcing dramatically that Hitler is coming tomorrow, at which my father remarked that He Would, now that he's Just Finished Papering Upstairs.

Wednesday, January 17th: Interesting article in today's *Telegraph* on 'Where Mankind Takes Shelter'. Discusses the philosophy of Stoicism which was particularly interesting in the light of T. E. Lawrence's attitude towards pain and hardship. Article says that our best shelter is in our fortitude of mind and ability to withstand, and concludes, 'To the friendly sandbag, mutely sustaining the buffets of wind and weather with intent to screen us from the enemy's screaming messengers of hate, homage and thanks; to the cold austerities of the concrete shelter, which may one day witness the inspiring triumph of the unknown citizen's cheerfulness and courage, homage and respect. But each of us should find his best shelter in himself.' Feel this to be very true.

Thursday, January 18th: Activity at school today – workmen arrived and put up a little hut outside, ready to start work on our air-raid shelters. The children's noses kept gravitating towards the window. They were far more interested in the doings of the workmen than my wonderful talk on Buds. Felt very peeved and reproved them sharply.

Monday, January 22nd: The Cold Spell still holds out, and maintains its place in conversation – talk revolved around frozen pipes, burst pipes and dangerous pipes, and the general inability to keep warm, accompanied by moans and groans. My moans exceed everyone else's because I loathe the cold more bitterly than anyone else. And still we survive!

I think Dougie must have got frozen in his Fens – he hasn't written since Christmas! Goodness, I'm beginning to be alarmed! Possibly he's fed up with doing all the giving, with nothing in return, and has decided to throw in the sponge. So be it!

Our two workmen at school – Walrus Moustache and his Mate – joined today by others with barrows and spades, a lorry, and an 'American Devil', so we've had a continual source of entertainment outside the windows all day long. They've dug out some of the earth towards our 6 trenches.

Tuesday, January 23rd: The frost continues its iron grip. Work on our trenches also continues at an unhurried pace, but couldn't see Walrus floating about anywhere today. Hope he hasn't succumbed to a cold or a germ. No wonder they didn't do much without him. The other workmen – hardy souls – clumped about without coats but with red faces and smoking breath and most of the time they seemed to be congregated in a little knot about the lorry, engaged in amiable conversation. Spent many intrigued moments viewing their activities. Recalled myself hastily when I saw the children watching me watching them.

Still no sign, sound, or other indication from Dear Little

Dougie. This is really Most Irregular, Most Irregular! Perhaps he's a German prisoner of war! Or even in a Concentration Camp. Or perhaps he really has Jilted me – and is even now hitting the high spots with his local blonde, and painting the Fens a lurid red. I can just imagine Dougie suddenly wearying of the role of faithful but rejected follower, stamping his foot and going berserk.

Thursday, January 25th: Still a bit nippy, but it is actually thawing at last, praise be! Staggered by a letter from Dougie, who apparently has not jilted me but explains his silence by stating simply that he's been skating every night, as the river is frozen and they can skate from Ely as far as Cambridge. So all my conjectures were wrong! I was not supplanted by either a local blonde, or the Army, but by a Pair of Skates. Well, well, what an anticlimax! He is very reticent on the subject of Rick's Broken Engagement, merely saying Poor Old Vera, which I know to be hypocritical because he's never liked her.

Walrus has reappeared at school but none of them do much work. They still either lean on their spades smoking a reflective pipe or cigarette, or else congregate cordially around the lorry.

Air-raid sirens tested at dinnertime, and we all recollect the first occasion at the beginning of the war, when we thought bombers were upon us. My father recalls with mirth how Mother and I sat in our gas masks when he got downstairs. All giggle at this distant recollection of what appeared so awful at the time, but I suppose we'd do the same again.

Went to Burton to meet Hilda Tooth and see Will Fyffe in *Rulers of the Sea*, which was very good. Thought I heard the sirens halfway through and said so, with many palpitations, at which a couple sitting in front promptly turned round and said So Did They, at which we all giggled with relief. On the way back to the bus, Hilda coyly withdrew her glove to show me Bert's

Christmas present – an Engagement Ring! Was duly surprised and impressed, and she seemed very pleased when I said so.

Saturday, January 27th: It has been snowing all night and we're covered in about a foot of snow. Everywhere looks very beautiful – like the icing on an uncut Christmas cake. Went to Miss Barnett's to have my ends permed and when the bus stopped at the park gates it had to be dug out with spades before it could start again. The snow ploughs were out later in the day. My perm took from 9.30 to 12.30, but don't think I quite like the way she's done it – she's given me a sort of halo of little curls and they don't look quite right round my moon-like countenance. Felt very dubious about it, and still do.

Mr Skerritt rubbed my face in the snow – mean blighter – because we pushed snow through the window into the bathroom when he was inside.

Sunday, January 28th: And still snowing when we got up. I've never seen so much snow in my life! It's piled high and lies in great smooth drifts like sand dunes in a desert.

Monday, January 29th: More snow. Tons of it. This must be Hitler's 'Secret Weapon'. The roads were feet deep in it this morn, but gangs of men were out with spades and soon the roads were lined with mountains and steep snow escarpments. Couldn't walk on the pavement – snow about 3 feet deep. Stacks of people about on their way to work, walking because no buses about. Grimly ploughed through the drifts to school, feeling like Scott on his voyage to the South Pole. Was the first to arrive, and had only 12 children out of 46.

Had a letter from Swanee. Bill is having a rough time – he's been out on manoeuvres to isolated spots in French cattle trucks and has been sleeping in an almost roofless loft with no warmth except a fire in the distant village hall. Oh dear, my woes seem very small compared with some.

Wednesday, January 31st: Only 7 children out of my 46 turned up this morn, but wasn't at all sorry or disturbed thereby.

At last, after aeons of waiting and an agony of dreadful suspense, We Were Paid! Had to dish out quite a lot of it immediately for one cause and another, but still have sufficient balance to bring relief to my soul and the provision of certain necessities for my welfare – stockings, for example, and vests. Shall be able to take off my wellingtons in school now. Haven't dared to before, because of ladders in my stockings.

Thursday, February 1st: My father has made me a most beautiful blue and white toboggan with black lines and steel runners, so Delia and I sailed forth in search of a hill. Found one in the football field, so after ploughing through two feet of snow to get there, and dragging each other down the track several times, we made a track and had a lovely time. Came back about 5.30, after tearing my stockings to shreds and hacking a grain of flesh out of my leg which bled copiously. Mother said I Told You So.

Saturday, February 3rd: Up quite early, dressed in my old mac, wellingtons, scarf and hood, and Delia and I pulled the toboggan up to Tweeds, where we gathered in Amy and went to the fields at the back of their house where there were some marvellous hills. Soon we had a good track and went down marvellously, only we kept coming off and rolling headlong in the snow, but it was good fun. Delia made a solo flight, careered into the hedge, then nearly fainted when she got back to the top of the hill with the cold and the effort, so we decided to pack up. By 3 o'clock we were back again. We had a lovely time,

and the sledge simply zipped down. Walked home about 6.
We played Lexicon and ate Delia's oranges and Black Magic
chocolates.

Sunday, February 4th: It's thawing! And we'd arranged to go
tobogganing on Tuesday – oh blow! Snow sliding from roofs
and spoutings everywhere, and the ground a slushy, soppy
mess.

Mrs Tweed, Amy and Delia came to tea. Mrs T says that
Mamma said once that Ronnie wouldn't get married while I'm
single . . . ! Huh! He'll have a long time to wait for his wedded
bliss then. He probably wants to have me off his conscience
before he can feel free to take the plunge. What bitterness and
rancour flows from my pen!

Tuesday, February 13th: Words between Miss Harvey and Miss
Smith today. Miss H says that Miss Smith's boys bully her girls,
and Miss S retorts that the girls are Mardy. Miss Smith became,
as Miss H related graphically, as White as the Snow with temper,
and Miss H says ominously, 'Wait, just wait – I'll have my own
back!'

I think we're doomed to Perpetual Winter. Cold days, freezing
nights, biting winds and whirling snow – we seem to have had
nothing else for months. Started snowing this afternoon and
continued for hours.

Spent the evening indoors again. My father held forth about
the Destructiveness of Wood Pigeons.

Wednesday, February 14th: St Valentine's Day, so naturally have
been kept busy receiving cards from all my numerous admirers,
secret and otherwise. I had to hire a sorting clerk for the day.
What a thing it is to be such a source of admiration.

Have never had a Valentine in my life!

Went with Mother to Mrs W's after tea to take material for my white coat, but as usual she can't make it for Weeks and Weeks.

Thursday, February 15th: Oh dear! More snow! Am reduced to despair by this continued cold spell. My face is becoming horrible, rough and patchy, despite my nightly ministrations with cold cream.

Miss Ford had half the afternoon off to go on a last little outing with her dear Stan, who has to join up tomorrow. He'll be in the Signals Corps and is to train in London.

Went to the English lecture – quite a crowd there. Mr A talked about *Eminent Victorians.* Hitherto I have kept my own silence, remaining mute and impassive in my corner, through sheer fear and lack of confidence but tonight when he couldn't remember the title of a book, I was aghast to hear myself supplying it. Immediately I had spoken I felt myself blushing.

Friday, February 16th: Awoke in fear and trembling in the depths of the night after a horrible dream – most vivid. Dreamt I went on some sort of day trip to Helsinki and as soon as I got there I was scared stiff of air raids and wanted to come home. So I proceeded to the station, but there wasn't a single train for Swadlincote, only for other unknown places. Decided to go to one of these – anywhere to get out of that hateful place – but missed the train and had to wait five hours for the next, expecting bombs every minute. Then a train drew in, and lots of German soldiers brandishing long curved knives alighted, and drove us all into the train as prisoners. Then I awoke with the greatest relief. Glory, it was awful! It was quite a pleasure to go to school as usual, after such horrors.

Bought some green angora material from Austin's for a dress – quite nice. A dull shade of green – sage.

Lots of aeroplanes buzzing up aloft today, and Mr J and other knowing people say that one was a black German bomber, hotly pursued by two Spitfires. Oh dear! Now it will carry an important little photograph back to Hitler showing all Swadlincote's impregnable defences.

About 9 o'clock the snow began to pelt down again in a driving sheet. This has been the worst winter for about 60 or more years. No one can remember anything like it.

Saturday, February 17th: Tea at Bella's. Great excitement when Esme walked bashfully in after a new and very glamorous perm. She didn't know how to have it done, so she wrote to the coiffure expert in *Woman* enclosing a description of her face. She accordingly took *Woman*'s advice and returned with three fetching curls on the top of her head and curls all round. Bella thought it emphasised the size of her nose. I'm getting a bit weary of curls. I think I'd like my hair plain again and natural. But it feels old-fashioned to have it done like that now. Bella's mother remarked that I Don't Change the Style of My Hair, Do I? But I couldn't gather whether this was meant as a criticism or not.

Sunday, February 18th: We went to Grandma's for supper and talked about German bombers, the latest product of Rolls-Royce – a bomber that can fly over 500 miles an hour – sore throats and Operations. Told that my tonsils ought to come out.

Monday, February 19th: Miss H hissed in my ear in prayers this morn Not to tell Miss Ford, but My Cousin says they call the Signals Corps the Suicide Corps. Gazed back at Miss H in alarm and we both clicked our tongues in concern. Miss F was meanwhile playing for the hymn in happy ignorance.

Listened in to Lord Haw Haw at 9.15, getting very bitter about the rescue of our 400 English prisoners from the *Altmark*, pouring forth sarcasm upon our exploit – 'not the act of a gen-tleman,' he said. Then he proceeded to call Mr Churchill 'a cad and a brute', in his most nasal and contemptuous tone.

Tuesday, February 20th: Two of our children were at school by 7 o'clock this morn. They'll be bringing their beds next.

Freddie rang up at teatime to inveigle me into a jaunt to the flicks with him, so having nothing better to do I obligingly said I'd go. He presented himself at 5.45 all swathed up in college scarf and plus fours and we tootled off to Burton to see *The Four Just Men.* Had coffee afterwards and Freddie announced that he was contemplating joining up as a Weather Forecaster – with a max-imum salary of £320 a year – after 9 weeks' training. Told him I thought it sounded better than lying in the trenches shooting Germans, to which he replied callously that that wouldn't worry him and that in any case Shooting was One Thing He *Could* Do! Very shocked and horrified at this and said that I thought it was horrible to have to shoot even Germans. He retorted, with a jin-goistic generalisation that There Were No Good Germans. Which is silly. So I disagreed hotly. So we came home. Didn't offer to pay for myself – I'm sure the pleasure of my company is worth more than money to him. But he asked me to go to the Dance on Thursday and I felt obliged to say I would after this, even though I don't want to.

Thursday, February 22nd: Miss Ford and Miss Evans asked each other mournfully how they were Getting On. Both their boyfriends have had to join up and both mooch about with sad and absent expressions.

Reluctantly faced the prospect of the dance this evening. Attired myself in my blue chiffon, and with a flower in my hair sat waiting for the dear sweet little Freddie. Delia duly presented herself in her purple that she had hacked and slashed last night, but it looked quite nice, so I inserted a flower in her hair too. Eventually the Dear Fred arrived about 10, after Trouble With His Car, and we hoofed off. Had to wear Bella's shoes because my chilblain was causing me excruciating agony. Quite a nice crowd there – just enough to dance comfortably, without jostling. Freddie kept mooching off, but didn't dance with anyone else. Don't know why he went or where he went to. We left about 1. Pushed Freddie off very hurriedly when we got home in case he should become amorous. And so to bed, very weary.

Saturday, February 24th: Letter from Dear Doug, who has been laid low with the flu, and is consequently – like all men with an ailment – feeling sorry for himself. But he devotes a page to his pre-flu activities and would have me believe that he has been a Butterfly and has been making whoopee in Ely. As he's going to be in the Army soon, he declares bitterly, he's Going to Spend What He's Got first and go with nothing on his mind. He also abuses the Lousy Conchies and says they ought to wear skirts. Have visions of Mr Skerritt prancing down High Street in one of my frocks.

Journeyed to Mrs W's in the morn to take my green angora and confer with her about the style.

To Burton with Bella and Esme and saw Lots of Babies and Fleets of Prams. Saw Ethel W and had to admire the occupant of her pram, but it was a very old-looking child of about 6 weeks. Then Joan loomed, looking fat and matronly, so she yanked us along to see her baby Christine. Oh dear! Christine not a pretty baby at all – glum and morose and we couldn't see her chin because of her pout. Meanwhile another baby – a fat lusty boy – leered at us Knowingly and said 'Dada'. Bella and I were shocked by this orgy of Ugly Babies, so we made a hurried retreat. Decided that we weren't in the least envious.

Tuesday, February 27th: Balmy, so flounced forth in silk frock and short-sleeved cardigan. Miss H told me I looked Spring-like. Workmen reappeared at school after a long absence and continued to delve and dig and have their frequent conferences. Great excitement caused by their activities. One child observed excitedly that They'd Taken a Tank into the Trench, Miss. Had visions of a tank being parked there for some grim reason, ready to lumber forth to mow down parachuting Germans, then realised with relief that the child must have meant a cistern tank, used in the water system. Breathed again.

Wednesday, February 28th: Straight from school to have my green dress fitted, but could get only very inadequate views of the creation through Mrs W's sketchy little mirrors. Had an argument with her about Leaves – wanted her to appliqué some on the collar, but she thought it was too much trouble. But I think she will.

Thursday, February 29th: Snow in the night – and Arctic conditions restored again. Icy wind and bitterly cold. Scholarship exam at school but have no hope of any of my 4 entrants shining. They seemed optimistic – but nothing would daunt them.

Friday, March 1st: A day's holiday! Ate a gloating breakfast then washed my hair, failed to set it properly, waxed irate and finally popped off to Miss B where she gave me the usual stiff and unyielding curls. Endured them like this until after dinner and then relievedly combed them out more naturally. My green angora frock arrived and looks quite nice – but I immediately wrenched off a horrible great brown bow and put a little bunch of felt flowers in its place. Attired myself in all this glory ready for our visit to Swanee in Wilmslow, and Mr Skerritt told me that it Suited Me. Then Bella arrived in her Black, and we set forth at 10 to 6. Only just caught the 6.25 train at Burton. When we got on the Manchester train at Derby, it was nearly full of soldiers. Three who sat across the gangway were energetically discussing a sergeant named Walker. He had told the men that in All the Messes that he'd been in, he'd always Rigidly Observed the Rules of Etikwettie. The three finally observed that He'd Never Come Back from the War Alive. Couldn't see any of the scenery because the blinds were all drawn, so read my *Time & Tide* while Bella more frivolously dipped into *Woman & Beauty*.

Caught the train to Wilmslow, arriving at 10 o'clock. After supper fell thankfully into bed. Awoke in the night chilled to the bone. A gale was blowing through the window and lashing round my neck. The next minute, Bella rolled out of bed, put on the light and proceeded firmly and grimly to close the window. Thereupon I disclosed the fact that I was awake and cold also, so we moaned and giggled in duet. Put on my knickers and stockings and Bella did the same. Still cold, so swathed my scarf round my neck, but had a very cold sleep. Cramped and chilly when I awoke, as was Bella, so we groaned in unison and felt a little better in spirit. Swanee arrived then with tea, so hastily and surreptitiously removed the scarf so that she shouldn't know of our nocturnal trials.

Saturday, March 2nd: Oh dear! I wish I'd known I was going to the North Pole this weekend. Never been so cold in my life. Bella, Swanee and I made an icy journey into Manchester this morn. Saw some wonderful shops, but frightfully expensive. Evening bags were 5 guineas and upwards in one. Made our way with great relief into the warmth of Lewis's where we had lunch while we listened to Jack McCormick and his Orchestra. They played 'Scatterbrain', to Bella's delight. After lunch, we wandered among the materials. Bella and I bought some shantung for dresses. We were back in Wilmslow in time for tea. Bella and I hung frigidly over the fire and thawed gradually. We had hoped for a show or the flicks at night but dear Geoffie had other plans – A Walk round Wilmslow, ending in a Tour of the Council Offices, where he works. Back by 8, when it was dark, with the searchlights playing in broad bright beams over the sky. Had supper and retired to bed about 12.30. Bella and I closed the window, draped things over the bed and finally clambered in half dressed and with giggles. Got on a little better, but even so felt a little chilled when I awoke.

Sunday, March 3rd: Swanee entered with tea and exclaimed with horror to see Bella reclining in bed in her cardigan. Said she surely wasn't cold, was she, and why hadn't Bella told her? Wondered sardonically if Swanee knew that Bella had on also a bed-wrap, pyjamas, vest and knickers. Bella said Oh No, she wasn't cold, and added vaguely she just liked to feel A Weight on her.

Set off for Manchester and home at 12.30. Still bitterly cold, but we found a seat in the dining-car on the train and ordered coffee, toast and biscuits. When we got to Derby we found we had two-and-a-half hours to wait for a connection, so we hiked to the bus park for a bus to Burton. Misfortune overtook us again – we were sat behind a fresh-air fiend, who asked politely if we'd object to his opening a window. Said graciously No, then repented all the rest of the way when a gale swirled round our necks. Had tea at Bella's, then came home about 8. Proceeded to get thoroughly warm. Next time we visit Wilmslow, we'll take care to go in the summer.

Friday, March 8th: Am told in warning tones by a serious assistant when I go to buy this book that Paper is Going To Be Scarce, and that it is Going Up a Hundred Per Cent. Apparently everything is going to be either unobtainable or outrageously dear within the next month or so. Had better get in a stock of potential diaries and keep them under lock and key, or be forced to resort to rolls of wallpaper. Am dying to buy *The Provincial Lady in Wartime*, but funds are too low.

Saturday, March 9th: Decided to renovate my face this morn so bought a face-pack and applied same, on Miss B's recommendation. Felt my mouth being drawn into a furious grimace. The instructions said Leave Until Dry, but couldn't endure it for so long, and washed it off after about five minutes. Looked hopefully for a new and blooming face and thought it looked a little better, but when I asked Mother she said No, she couldn't see Much Difference.

Bella, Mother, Auntie Nell and I went by bus to Derby to buy a spring outfit. Invaded by a group of soldiers who tumbled on to the bus at Melbourne and proceeded to chatter and joke and yell at each other all the way. Auntie Nell very touched by one who said he wished he could go home, as we passed the station.

Went straight to Bracegirdles. Served by the girl who served me with my blue coat last year. After many hesitations and deliberations, decided upon a blue two-piece – a frock with a petunia suede belt, and short blue coat. Left it to be altered – and incidentally until I have enough money to pay for it.

We had not long emerged before I received a frantic tug on the arm from Bella. 'John!' she yelped, 'Look! John Scott!' Turned, and there across the road we saw the leprous Scott carrying that most humiliating of things, a Paper Carrier, while by his side strode the future and unfortunate Mrs Scott. Bella grabbed my arm and propelled me along in pursuit of them, but after stalking them to the top of the street we gave up the chase. Whereupon Bella spent the next hour enumerating What She Wished She'd Done, or Actions She Might Have Taken.

Proceeded to the Midland Drapery for tea. Nice little notice –

lovely little thing – at our table (and all the others) warned us about Idle Chatter and giving away information to the enemy. Mother moaned lugubriously because she was only allowed three tiny lumps of sugar for her two cups of tea. She put them all in the first cup and morosely sipped her second sugarless, wondering whether she could bribe the waitress.

Eric had his papers today and has to go in the infantry to Lincoln next Friday. Auntie Nell and Joyce wept. Poor old Eric! And Mr Skerritt had to register today, among the 24s. He registered as a CO.

Sunday, March 10th: Have gained 3 lbs this week so decided to eat less.

Monday, March 11th: Wireless announcer said that we have offered unrestricted help to Finland – not at all surprised. Think it should have been done before, in our own interests.

Tuesday, March 12th: Letter from Dougie but merely a replica of all his other letters with a different date at the top. He refers with melancholy to his imminent joining up but tells me encouragingly that he will pop over to see me before he goes. He needn't bother! He always tries on the pathetic attitude, in order to arouse my sympathy. Every time he writes he hints that soon he will be at the front, but he hasn't gone yet. Incidentally, Mr Skerritt was the only CO to register on Saturday in the district. What notoriety!

Eric came with Perce, Renie and Brenda, to tea to say goodbye to us all before entering the Army on Friday. Poor old Eric! It must be an awful change for boys from decent, comfortable homes to be transplanted suddenly to Army conditions and environment.

Wednesday, March 13th: My petunia shantung with the white spot arrived from the Midland Drapery – quite pleased with it.

The Finns have come to terms with the Russians and have signed an armistice. Oh dear! Sounds ominous!

Thursday, March 14th: Feverish activity on the Home Front today – Mother embedded in a sea of account books and ledgers, frantically cramming in a year's accounts, ready for the auditors who have said they're coming next week.

Went to the last but one English lecture and discussed smatterings of poetry from work of the younger moderns – Auden, Day Lewis, Spender and R. E. Warner. Mr Addison opined that among the post-war poets there are 'several singers but no great voice'. Vera Dennis sat enigmatically in a corner, with one of her plate-like creations adorning her head. Jane Wilson lounged nonchalantly in a luxurious fur coat, while Pamela Jones leaned confidentially towards her. She always seems to me to cultivate the friendship either of Those in Authority or Those with Position or Those Likely to be of Help Socially. But I may be prejudiced and probably am. She was once a rival of mine. Beryl and Mr Skerritt sat huddled together in silence, occasionally exchanging a tender sidelong glance. The man from the bookshop gave several weighty opinions, as usual.

Sunday, March 15th: The Ides of March, but no Blitzkrieg.

Saturday, March 16th: Delia and her landlady had their Blitzkrieg yesterday after all. They had just retired for the night when there was a tremendous explosion. Some disused gas pipe had burst, and the smell of gas soon filled the house. They dashed frantically about and finally got a man from the gas works to come and attend to the leakage.

Went to Mrs W's for my white coat this morn, but had to

return without it because the lining wasn't in.

Joyce and Auntie Nell here for the weekend – to help with the cleaning ready for the auditors' visit next week. Mr Skerritt stayed till about 11.30. The usual argument about pacifism and conscientious objectors.

Sunday, March 17th: All toiled and worked until nearly teatime. I made two rich cakes and tarts also. News came that 14 German planes had been over and bombed Whitechapel, but we later discovered that it was Scapa Flow, not Whitechapel, that had been bombed. And only one plane was brought down.

Monday, March 18th: Mrs W sent my white coat – which looks Very Nice. I like it. Exhibited it many times and paraded proudly.

Tuesday, March 19th: Cold and showery day with a roaring March wind and vicious squalls of rain. Still oppressed with weariness and the children are quite mad, quite mad. Talked their heads off, while I bellowed furiously. Thanked heaven very fervently when 4 o'clock came.

Wrote to Doug in reply to his pathetic effusion. Bella says – amidst giggles – that she knows that I'll be Inconsolable when he goes to the Front, and our combined and extravagant imaginations produce a wonderful picture of my suffering agonies of loneliness and anxiety. Ha!

Wednesday, March 20th: On the verge of breaking up at long last – Oh joy! Thank goodness this long-drawn-out term is nearly over! I'm thoroughly weary of it, and this week the children have been like demons. I've snarled like a hyena, roared like a lion and bellowed like a bull, and still have failed to curb their spirits.

Met Bill Swan on the way home from school at dinnertime.

He's home on leave from France and looks very fit and brown and is as cheerful as ever. His spirits don't seem to have suffered at all.

Thursday, March 21st: The day at last, the longed-for day! After struggling with the end-of-term register Totals and a mass of Figures, emerged to be rewarded – We Were Paid!

Friday, March 22nd: Good Friday opened with a letter from Vera, proclaiming that Maretta is engaged to be married this Easter to her Frank, the stockbroker. Goodness! Very confounded by this piece of news, and also unexpectedly rather jealous. Everyone is either engaged or married these days.

Glad I didn't go to the service this morn. Miss Tunnicliffe died as soon as she came into the church, so it was abandoned. Poor Vicar. Mother whispered ominously to me during his sermon at night that He'll Be Next.

Easter Sunday, March 24th: Fed up with all my winter clothes so went to morning service gaily attired in my blue summer coat (cleaned), flowered dress and clover hat and scarf, and felt much better for the change. Noel Perks and Howard Tooth there in khaki.

Easter Monday, March 25th: A lovely sunny day again. Wish we could have gone away this Easter – it's been so nice. Saw Mamma sailing along in a car – evidently after spending Easter with Her Boy at Brimington. My father reminisced at some length before going to bed on Italy, Grape Vines, Venice, Silk-Worms and Gondolas.

Tuesday, March 26th: Mother and Auntie Nell went to Miss Tunnicliffe's funeral service and returned discussing the wreaths and the mourners with lively interest. Joyce came to tea – jubilant because Eric is coming home this weekend from Friday until Monday.

Curiosity led me to unearth the last six of Ron's letters to solve the riddle that has always been at the back of my mind – i.e. why he gave me up. At the time it seemed both incredible and unreasonable, but I couldn't see it in perspective then, and so naturally couldn't judge. It seemed impossible that his love could die so quickly and so thoroughly after so many years. Haven't read these letters for ages and ages, so read with curiosity. Until his ordination his letters were scrappy but affectionate, and hinted at no change at all either in our relationship or his feelings. The scrappiness I understood – owing to exams and what-not. But immediately after his ordination – what a change! Quite cool and impersonal as though he felt he ought to write but would merely fling me a few crumbs to satisfy my eager appetite. He didn't bother to answer my letters for weeks, and then finally after about eight months he wrote to say that before he had been at Brimington long he knew that there could be 'no advance in our relationship'. I wish I hadn't taken it so calmly and forgivingly. Not a word of explanation, excuse or regret – just the mere statement of fact that must suffice. Huh! All these years I've made excuses for him and even tried to understand his position! I think he is a Pig and a Brute and a Selfish Beast. I bet he hasn't been troubled with a single regret or pang of conscience. Joyce thinks that it wasn't I who wasn't good enough for him, but the family – but I'm not so sure. I believe he actually thought I wouldn't fit in with his circle of friends. Intellectually at least I consider myself his equal.

Started *Barchester Towers* and read some 50 pages but must confess that I found it a little ponderous in style and so far am not frightfully keen. But I know I ought to like it, so optimistically tell myself that it is Too Soon to judge.

Wednesday, March 27th: Tramped to Mrs W's to see about my spotted frock.

My horoscope told me I would receive Surprising News today, by word or letter. And I did! By word – I received a stunning blow – my heart has been smashed, broken to little pieces a second time. I am numb with despair and suffused with silent misery. Freddie, the faithful Fred of so many years, is False To Me! Yes, false and perfidious. He has spurned me and found solace in Another – a Birmingham teacher, 22 years old. I am sorely grieved. Gone for ever – my faithful Freddie!

Thursday, March 28th: Arrayed myself in my best and tripped off to Nottingham with Mother and Auntie Nell. A bitterly cold day again with an icy wind. An influx of fur coats on the bus – but nearly all were the straggly, scraggy, moth-eaten type, so not envious. I bought suede-backed gloves (dark clover) from Griffin & Spalding (8/11) and shoes to match from Barratt's (23/9).

Friday, March 29th: Decided to pop off in search of a hat and clover trimming for my spotted frock, so caught the 10 to 10 bus to Burton, but had a fruitless mission. The only trimming produced by Stockbridges was a hectic clover, not at all the right shade, but when I said so the girl said she thought it was a Perfect Match and added threateningly that I Wouldn't Get a Better. She gave me a lecture on Trimming, its Uses and its Selection, proclaiming profoundly that Trimming is Only a Decoration and shouldn't be The Exact Colour. Disagreed, but said nothing except to ask to see White. Chose the white eventually. Had no intention of humouring her.

Went then to Elizabeth Wright to view the hats. Tried on one and then another, growing more and more depressed and despairing as I did so. Had imagined when leaving home that I looked fairly respectable, but viewed through the mirror of

Elizabeth Wright I looked a mess. No one else in the shop, so I received her undivided attention. She presented a whole series, with undiminished hope, until I began to look wildly round for escape. Finally said madly that I'd have That One – indicating awful thing like an elevated beret and costing 8/11, and emerged knowing that I should never wear it. Came despondently home. Mother took one look and said she didn't like That Thing. When my father saw me in it he declared bluntly that I Wanted Locking Up if I Wore That Thing, while Bella giggled. Mr Skerritt told me consolingly not to take any notice of Those Others, he liked it and thought it looked Smart. By now I loathed the sight of it.

Then I saw the very hat that I would have liked – a navy one with blue and clover chiffon round – but it was part of Joyce Ward's trousseau. I gazed enviously at the Hat of My Dreams, contrasting it mentally with That Thing. Saw some lovely wedding presents and felt ashamed of my meagre little serviettes displayed amongst all the gleaming silver and glass etc.

Saturday, March 30th: Letter from Dougie. Opened it, fully expecting either (a) another moan about soon being in the front lines, or (b) the news that he had joined up. Letter contained neither, except the casual statement that on Easter Saturday he volunteered at Cambridge to Join The Boys, but was rejected because he's in a reserved occupation. But he adds with firm and noble purpose that he's going to have Another Shot before long. Anyhow that cancels his promised visit, and I experience a feeling more like relief than regret.

Clutching the despised hat I retraced my steps to Burton this afternoon. A lovely day and quite warm so I donned my spotted shantung and blue coat. Met Kath Hull waiting for the bus, and she observed that Here I Was Looking Sweet and Dainty in My Silk Frock while she Doesn't Dream of wearing Such Attire until

July. Noted that she was arrayed in tweed costume and woollen jumper.

My heart sank as I neared the fatal hat shop, but summoned up a bold smile as I crossed the threshold. Told Elizabeth Wright bluntly that They Didn't Like Me In It and asked her to change it. She was very obliging, but I didn't risk another hat, preferring to play safe and choose stockings.

My new spotted frock has arrived – not bad, but no one seems frightfully keen.

Monday, April 1st: Went to the Picturedrome with False Fred where we saw a mediocre programme. He said nothing about the Young Birmingham Teacher, but I decided that she could have him. Noticed a smudge of red ink on his finger, and though I must have gone out often with a smudge, it annoyed me in him, and I condemned him silently as Slovenly. Besides, he plays hockey nearly every Sunday and I'm sure he never goes to church. (How virtuous and righteous I sound!) Still – our souls would never harmonise, I'm sure. And all this after letting him take me to the pictures and pay for me! I'm mean.

Tuesday, April 2nd: Letter from Hilda Tooth suggesting meeting in Burton next week, and stating simply that These COs make her See Red. Her Bert has registered and has applied for the Royal Marines but so far hasn't received The Great Call. So she and the aforesaid Bert spent a lovely Easter at Weston. Lucky things!

Finished *Barchester Towers* which I have enjoyed very much. Love the characters in it – Mrs Proudie, Quiverful and Mrs Q, Mr Slope etc etc.

Saturday, April 6th: Am compelled by penury and destitution almost to be Very Mean. Have spent nearly all my month's money already.

Bella

After about ¾ of an hour's wait, Bella and I managed to scramble on a bus to Burton. Bella indignantly confided en route the latest news she had of John Scott, who apparently mixes with a doubtful character named Bungalow Bess

Informed on reaching home that Ronniedear has got another Church – a big one at Buxton. And a fashionable one too, I'll bet. Formulated a very telling sentence to myself before going to sleep. He gave me up because I Am What I Am, and Live Where I Do, and he Is What He Is – a Practical but Socialite Parson with High Ideals but also High Ambition and No Illusions. In short, he intends to Get On, and to utilise all means of so doing, rejecting as he progresses those things, persons, interests or ideas likely to hamper his progress. This being so, he did the best thing when he gave me up because our ideas don't tally.

Monday, April 8th: I have been assailed by a Cold, which has induced a feeling of lethargy and fed-upness. Another cause for self-pity too – an unexpurgated account of a conversation between Mrs Dean and Mrs Gee, in which I figured. Apparently Mrs D mentioned that she had seen Ron last Sat afternoon. The spectre of my Poor Little Affair was resuscitated, Mrs D remarking cattily that I never meant any more to Ron than any other girl and that Mrs M never meant Ron to Have Me (sounds as though I'm in a Shop Window), nor did she ever mean him to marry into Our Family, and that Ron never even thought of marriage. (People do know a lot about other people's affairs.)

The conversation was related afresh for Grandma's, Bella's and Auntie Nell's benefits at three successive stages throughout the rest of the day. Mother exclaims truculently that she's As Good as Ron's family, and resurrects various historic catty remarks made by Mamma about me, fulminating greatly about same. Quite a to-do about what is now Past History.

Listened in to a short talk by the new Food Minister Lord

Woolton. He seems very competent and very practical, and has a very pleasant personality and voice. I like him.

Tuesday, April 9th: News! Wireless buzzing with short news bulletins all day. Germany has invaded Denmark and Norway simultaneously this morn and Denmark offered little resistance but Norway is fighting. We have of course offered Norway all our help. Hitler has 'taken those countries under his protection' after our mine laying. Ha, ha! (Sardonic mirth.)

Mr Wheat is doing his bit, Digging for Victory at school – being busily engaged in digging up the lawn to plant potatoes there. The painters are Doing Their Bit, making our school all nice and clean ready for the bombs and the workmen are Doing Their Bit, providing us with shelters for when that happens. So altogether we are well provided for.

Garbed myself in gym tunic but with a great dearth of enthusiasm and sniffed to Hastings Rd at 5 o'clock with Delia and Miss Sanders. Miss Kemp there and a motley array of female teachers, ready for the Juniors PT course. About three-quarters of the assembly lined the walls in their hats, mufflers and dignity, while the rest of us – poor souls! – slipped about minus stockings or dignity. We had to be infants, dogs, little boys and all sorts of odd things.

Retired wearily to bed full of my cold and sniffs. A naval battle is reported to be raging off the coast of Norway, but no details available.

Wednesday, April 10th: Mr Wheat is still grimly Digging for Victory and has now converted nearly half the lawn into what looks like a ploughed field. Great aerial and naval activity round and about Norway and report has it that Norway is prepared to negotiate with Germany. Oh lor'! If Germany snaffles a few nice little ports and air bases there we may be dished.

Thank goodness our shelters are nearing completion – though

my father says they're no good and this verdict is endorsed by Miss Harvey's cousin. Anyhow, the Norway developments have certainly given a fillip to the news. 'After many months of smouldering inactivity, the fire of war has burst into flames,' says a man on the wireless dramatically.

Thursday, April 11th: All eyes are still trained on Norway, but we aren't allowed to know very much authentic news. About 1600 aircraft are engaged, and lots of ships from both sides have been sunk. Oh dear! In spite of all this, Mr Wheat is still doggedly digging for victory, so perhaps he'll be rewarded. Mr Churchill is very optimistic about it and refers casually to all the destroyers, supply ships and cruisers etc that we have sunk, but reticent about our losses. Miss Harvey asked me if I thought Hitler would commit suicide before the weekend, but had to tell her in all honesty No. At which she looked considerably dashed.

Sunday, April 14th: Judging by official comment we're winning all before us. And judging by German comment, they're meeting with equal success. Strange! I suppose that an unbiased account will be let loose in about 50 years' time, if the war is over by then! By which time we shall have ceased to care. Didn't go to church at night because Grandpa so ill, so we sat up there with Grandma and Auntie. Mother and Auntie Frances were up all night with Grandpa, so Bella stayed the night with me in case my father had to go hurriedly. The doctor says Grandpa is very ill, and won't get better. Oh dear!

Monday, April 15th: A very ominous, oppressive sort of evening. The doctor came twice to see Grandpa and said he might go at any minute, so Mother spent the evening journeying backwards and forwards between our house and Grandma's and I went once. Grandma looking very miserable sat with her head in her hands and Auntie Frances looked very solemn and formed the words 'death sweat' with her lips to me when Grandma said how hot Grandpa was. Oh dear! I do hate deaths and changes – I wish people needn't die but that sounds rather a heathen wish. Everything very quiet and still at Grandma's except for Grandpa's breathing and his ramblings from the front room. Uncles Harry and Charlie came to see him. Huh! The only time they do visit is when they think he's going to die. Life seems puzzling, with death as its inevitable goal. Times like this seem to slow up the normal feverish pace of life, when one is faced with truths and inevitabilities instead of events and happenings. The temporal gives place to the eternal for a brief space of time, and then one is caught up in the normal stream of life again and the truths fade away. I fear death and all its trappings – coffins and tombstones and funereal clothes. But most old people don't seem to fear it. Perhaps they have grown reconciled to the idea, or are tired of life and anxious for a rest. But I don't think Grandpa knows he's going to die. Oh dear! It will be horrid. But even if he were to get better it would only be for a little time and he would have it all to go through again. When it does happen, it will be Grandma I'll be most sorry for, because of us all she will feel it most, after 60 years. There is so much mystery and so much speculation about death. I wish I were more certain.

Gruesome conversation about deaths before retiring to bed and my father declared that he had seen some Awful Deaths and showed us in a truly terrifying manner how his Auntie Addie looked when deceased. Thought I shouldn't be able to sleep after it but I did.

Tuesday, April 16th: Mrs Merchant, who sat up last night with Auntie Frances, came for my father at 4.45 this morn to keep Grandpa in bed because he'd been trying to get out all night. He's still very ill and the Doctor said he wouldn't last the day, but he seemed a little stronger at night.

Had the painters at my windows at school all day to my disgust, and had to stay till 12.30 to dole out the free dinners, which have begun this week. Think it's rather a waste of govt money at such a time.

Had letters from Dougie and Audrey, Dougie still moaning about not being able to join up, but stating bravely and simply that he has Signed The Forms, so is ready to be called upon at any time. He feels it is his duty, he remarks viciously, to kill a few Rotten Germans off. Audrey's Ben has chosen the RAF when registering – it being Just A Question of Uniform, says Audrey. Naval uniform came first in their preference, but the dear did not fancy the idea of a battleship, so he chose the RAF as next for smartness. Audrey prefers the idea of knitting in blue to knitting in khaki – which incidentally she can't spell (to my malicious joy).

Wednesday, April 17th: Grandpa died at 11 o'clock this morn, after an awful night, but he was unconscious from about 9 a.m. onwards. A general quiet and depressed sort of atmosphere everywhere. Everything seems unnatural. All the machinery of burial now in progress – certificates, ground, coffin, clothes, wreaths and so on. Went to Grandma's at night with a Mars Bar for solace.

Thursday, April 18th: Can't think of much to note beyond a general atmosphere of gloom. Question about whether I shall go into black. Don't think so – it is only bowing to public opinion to do so and doesn't seem necessary to me.

Saturday, April 20th: A gloomy day. Spent the morning receiving wreaths etc and preparing for Grandpa's funeral. Had the service at Grandma's about two – all the family came. Mr Grange was a typical undertaker – most funereal and efficient with his silk hat and bucolic face. Awful. Hated the sight of the coffin deep in the earth. It looked so lonely as we all turned away to come home and left it. Poor Grandpa! I do hope he's happy somewhere. Back to the Victorian ham tea. The men all sat round the table and attacked plates of ham etc but the ladies had sandwiches and talked about cooking, jam-making and clothes. The men talked about the coming Budget, the war, and tiles and slates for roofing. All trickled away after tea and the house was left with only Grandma and Auntie in by 7 o'clock. Depressing evening. Started to read *Jane Eyre*.

Sunday, April 21st: Mother, Dad and I went to Auntie Nell's for tea and I wore my white coat over my black dress. Eric over on leave, so Joyce not at home. They got engaged yesterday. I spent the evening engrossed in *Jane Eyre*. Most absorbing – one of the most interesting books I've read for ages.

Monday, April 22nd: Finished *Jane Eyre*. Lovely book. Story is melodramatic in parts, especially the abrupt arrest of the marriage service and the antics of the mad Bertha, and the children in it are very wise and have a marvellous range of vocabulary for their tender years. The story is very moral too, in parts, but the characters are vivid and alive. Mr Rochester is very masculine and passionate, and Jane very plain-spoken and direct but capable of deep-rooted feelings and rigid standards. The moral retribution that descends upon poor Mr Rochester, when he is blinded and crippled, betrays the Victorian flavour. I'm glad I didn't read the book at school as a set book. I enjoyed it much more as I have just read it – for pleasure, even though I shan't perhaps know so much about it as if I'd swotted it.

Tuesday, April 23rd, St George's Day and Budget Day: At dinner time Barbara Gee burst in, demanding excitedly, 'Have you heard the news – that Germany has invaded Holland?' We all gasped in horror and consternation and frenziedly turned on the 1 o'clock news. All we heard was the peaceful voice of the announcer stating in even tones the progress of the war in Norway. So we all calmed down again, saying disgustedly, 'Huh, rumours!'

Wednesday, April 24th: Dragged to the library. Finally selected *Lorna Doone*. Also a Dorothy L. Sayers – *Unnatural Death*, but have a feeling that I've read it before.

Thursday, April 25th: Received a certificate this morning stating majestically that I had received an Anti-Gas Course. My knowledge, however, is nil, so what avail will my certificate be?

Saturday, April 27th: A lovely afternoon – spring-like and warm. Took a jaunt to Derby – a lovely ride on the bus. Most of the blossom is out, looking very frothy and gay, and the hedges and trees seem to have burst into leaf all at once.

I bought some cream shantung for a tennis dress, while the refrain from the assistants was the same as ever – Prices Going Up, Material Getting Scarce, Buy Now, etc etc. I tried various models of headgear on but looked like a comic turn. Wore my blue summer coat and dashing petunia frock and felt very smart.

Tuesday, April 30th: Pay-day! Also had a most welcome rise, so received £15.4s, but had to disburse a debt of £2 immediately to my father. Tracked to Mrs W to ask when she intended to make my dresses. She told me tartly Not Yet, and I felt very umbraged. She unbent a little and said she would do my tennis frock for Whit.

Wednesday, May 1st: May Day, tra la la! Not very balmy, however – a dull day with quite a nip in the air still. The trenches at school appear to be finished and look like so many barrows or tumuli. Unpleasant train of thought arises: Hope they don't serve the same purpose!

Friday, May 3rd: My father remarked that They do have Some Bloomin' Stuff on the wireless today. They're either Cackling Like Fowls, or Laughing Like Hyenas (with great scorn). He thinks that The Nation is Going Potty.

Our staff made a solemn expedition to view the trenches from the interior today – just in case! We found them dank, dark and ominous, an inch deep in water. Felt the beginnings of claustrophobia before we emerged.

Mrs Tweed came down with news that our choir has gone on strike. The Vicar ordered one of the female members to push her curls under her hat as they looked 'common and not fitting for church'. Accordingly she no longer comes, and two or three others have gone on strike in sympathy.

Saturday, May 4th: A letter from Stuart, now in the forces, thanking me for the chocolates I sent by his mother to lighten his lot and saying rather pathetically, 'It makes the burden lighter to bear when we know that friends at home are mindful of us.' Poor old Stuart! He'll never make a soldier. He isn't the type. They're due to go overseas any day, he says, but hopes it won't be to Norway. We've had to abandon South Norway, so the Germans are now in possession of the south and centre. Oh dear! Very black news!

Decided to give my face a face-pack while I was having my bath, expecting to emerge with beautiful pink-and-white complexion. After I washed it all off I gazed expectantly into the mirror. Nearly expired on the spot – a purplish-red horrified visage stared back at me. Frantically dashed cold water at it, but the purple blotches remained. Dressed in deep dejection and remorse. Gazed again when dressed but careful scanning and a morbid inspection with a complicated system of mirrors could discern no improvement. Began to wax agitated, which made the blotches worse. Repaired to the window to let the cool morning air fan my cheeks. Contemplated assuming a yashmak, but fortunately my face reverted to normal during the course of the morning. Never again. Boncilla can keep their beauty preparations.

Garbed myself in white coat and tennis dress and went with Delia to tennis. Had tea at Geary, then had a good evening's play. Glorious, hot day. Biffed a very vigorous ball and won most of my sets. Very enjoyable, but felt exhausted by the end of the evening. Taken home in an ambulance. Mabel D had to take it to the ARP centre, so she gave us a lift home in it.

Sunday, May 5th: Delia is in tribulation. She has received notice from her landlady to pack her bags. Delia cannot understand why – she's sure she is easy to get on with, and has never caused any trouble. So she is now scanning the horizon for another possible billet. Her landlady has been mean – she's never made Delia feel comfortable and at home because she's never wanted her. She only took her to avoid having evacuees billeted on her.

Monday, May 6th: Had to bestir myself after tea to go to tennis at Geary with John Ollerenshaw. His pal Colin Latham met us there – had to play with him against the Oller. Lost every set, but gritted my teeth. I hate people who always play to win.

Did some subterfuge beforehand and got caught up in the coils of deception. Dear Freddie rang up to say would I like to go to the flicks tonight. Said Er-um, well, I had promised to stay in and help Delia look for digs. So he said hastily, Oh well, never mind, so I murmured weakly Sorry etc and hoped fervently that he wouldn't discover I'd promised to go to Geary with Friend Oller. However, promised to go to tennis with the dear Fred tomorrow.

Tuesday, May 7th: Went to the PT class and saw model children straining every muscle and behaving like clockwork. Contrasted them unfavourably with my own small hooligans. Felt an unholy joy when any of the clockwork children made a mistake.

When Freddie called to take me to tennis, I presented Delia to him too, all attired for the sport. He looked a little taken aback but politely mastered his feelings and said nothing. On the way, Freddie remarked that a teacher at their place, Latham by name, had joined Geary. Felt a guilty blush. He must know that I went last night. Hurriedly changed the subject. George made up a set and he and Delia beat us badly. Fred took us home, saying casually that if he went to tennis on Thursday, he'd call for me – but if wet, he might perhaps take me to the pictures. But he couldn't promise, so I mustn't rely on it ...!!! What condescension. I nearly made a Tart Rejoinder, but told myself that I had No Room to Talk.

Wednesday, May 8th: Spent the first part of the evening embroidering circles on an old blue frock, with intent to beautify. Then strode forth with Delia in search of digs. We visited a bed-sitting room in Highfield Road – not really bad, but wouldn't like to think of spending my days there. But Delia thought it might do.

Mrs Tweed paid us two visits during the evening. She says that she and Amy lay in bed counting how many dresses I have. What an absorbing occupation!

Thursday, May 9th: My father wonders if they pay These People on the Wireless much because some of them Aren't Worth Threepence.

Considered whether to attire myself for tennis and wait with patient expectation in case Freddie decided to call for me. But thought with outraged independence and dignity, No! At 6.30 he poked his affable head round the doorway saying genially Was I Ready? Ready? No! But I said in an offhand way that I wouldn't mind a Game of Tennis. So we went to Geary and found ourselves the only two players there. We played two sets, and I lost both (to his inward satisfaction I'm sure, because he Played To Win).

And so home. Not too bad – but not frightfully exciting. I could never grow obsessed with Fred. Find myself saying Nasty Things to him. If he misses a ball, I hear myself saying in Sarcastic Tones, 'Oh, good,' or 'Marvellous!'

Friday, May 10th: Awakened by the 7 o'clock news booming below that Germany has invaded Belgium and Holland. Gasped in a half-awake manner and tried to catch fragments of what was being announced – German parachutists dressed in Dutch and British uniforms – attacks occurred simultaneously – fierce fighting – flooding in Holland, etc. Listened in more fully to the 8 o'clock news. The Germans used Dutch prisoners as shields – dirty dogs! – and have bombed lots of places and aerodromes in France to prevent French fighters taking off. The war, it seems, has actually started, after these months of uncertainty and waiting.

Arrived at school to find Miss H and Miss Smith closeted together discussing The Situation. They said Didn't I Think It Was Serious, and What Were We Going To Do Now? etc, etc, and we reproduced to each other what we had all heard on the 8 o'clock news. We dispersed to our classrooms feeling most disinclined for work, and quite expectant of an air-raid alarm and the sight and sound of enemy bombers, but luckily none came and we broke up in peace – but not without many heart-failings and misgivings because the announcer declared at 1 o'clock that Whitsun Bank Holiday was to be annulled and business was to go on as usual. So we half expected our holiday being rudely wrenched away from us. It was with considerable relief that we departed at 4 o'clock without hearing the fateful order to remain at our posts. All the shops are to be kept open, holiday trains cancelled and Bella and Joyce aren't having a holiday at the Council Offices – poor creatures!

Delia, Amy and Mrs Tweed came to supper and Mrs Tweed said Wasn't it Dreadful and What Did We Think of it Now? She thought it was Simply Awful. We all congregated round, plus Mr Skerritt, to hear the 9 o'clock news, which began with a broadcast from Mr Chamberlain, in which he announced that on Tuesday he realised in the debate of the H of C that 'some new and drastic action had to be taken, if confidence was to be restored' (i.e. after the Norway fiasco), so he has therefore tendered his resignation as PM to the King, and Winston Churchill has been appointed in his place. He himself is going to continue as a member of the War Cabinet, and the Socialists are going to come into coalition with the Government to give it a broader basis. Felt frightfully sorry for the PM when he was speaking, although I have long felt that it would be best for him to go, and for us to have a change. His tones were really emotional as he said that we must rally round our new leader 'and with unshakeable courage fight and work until this wild beast that has sprung out of his lair upon us is finally disarmed and overthrown'.

The Dutch and Belgian ambassadors also broadcast during the day – felt particularly sorry for the Belgian one – the Belgians are only just finishing the work of reconstructing their country after the last war and now it is upon them again. I think it's wicked of Hitler. Mr Chamberlain said quite truly, 'In all history no other man has been responsible for such a hideous toll of human suffering as he … My words have proved to be insufficient to describe the vileness of those who have now staked everything on the great battle just beginning.'

Retired to bed, quite expecting the sirens again, but slept peacefully through the night. Warned on the wireless to keep a look out for parachutists in the hours of darkness. Oh glory! If I saw one of them I'd run. Renie says that the Germans have got the Mason's Arms spotted – Haw Haw gave it out on the wireless that that was where the troops in the Midlands turned to go to Bretby, etc.

Saturday, May 11th: Nothing much more in the way of news yet. Mounted my new bike very precariously and wobbled carefully to Mrs W's to collect the tennis dress she promised to finish for me. She greeted me with the brazen What Had I Come For? and when I said My Tennis Dress she laughed sarcastically and said She Hadn't Touched It. Dumbfounded, so made an abrupt departure after she promised to send it down today.

Walked to the Library, where the assistant told me bluntly that I ought to be at school – it wasn't fair for everyone else to have their holiday snatched away and us to be left in undisputed possession of ours. Continued on my way home in the joyous anticipation of a week's holiday. Then lo! How are the mighty fallen! A heartless announcer declared in indifferent tones at 10 a.m. that schools were to reopen – those in evacuation areas on Monday and those in reception areas (that's us!) on Tuesday.

Monday, May 13th, Whit Monday: Miss R came round exclaiming dramatically Had We Heard the Latest News, and when we said No, she said, Oh Well, she Daren't Tell Us and thereon departed, leaving us to surmise all sorts of grisly possibilities.

Tuesday, May 14th: Barbara G said Had we heard that a parachutist dressed as a hiker has been dropped at Packington –

together with his collapsible bicycle and firearms etc? Amy T also says that a spy has been arrested at Blackfordby. Oh dear! These wonderful rumours!

Had to resume the irksome shackles. Miss Evans returned without a smile, looking as glum as a disinherited Scotsman, avowing that her Alan had had no leave and she was sure that he would Get Killed Just to Spite Her. Our Miss Foster has not arrived. She has shirked her duty and joined the lotus eaters, preferring to carouse upon the sunny strand of Bournemouth, instead of applying her nose to the grindstone of Springfield Rd. The newly married Miss Ford is back with us looking little different, but being forced to serve this last week of her notice, instead of having it as a holiday. We philosophically decided that it would have to be borne, but mutinously had a long play[time] and finished school at 20 to 4.

Decided to gambol about at tennis, so Delia and I wended our way there at 5.30, in the calm of a lovely evening. I played with John O. During our first set, Freddie strolled in, and yelled to me quite peevedly, 'I called for you but you'd gone!' He melted a little at the end and asked if I'd like a lift home, so on behalf of Delia and myself I deigned to accept, and so we were whisked home. When I aired my views very authoritatively on The Situation, he told me I was a Defeatist. Then he asked blandly Did We Know whom the Germans Always Shot First in the Defeated Countries? The Teachers! Yelped with horror and declared my affrighted intention of Going on the Land.

Mrs T says that Lord Haw Haw has declared Bretby Park to be an admirable place for landing parachute troops. That man has the most incredible sayings attributed to him.

Mr Eden, the new Secretary for War, broadcast in the 9 o'clock news and asked men from about 17 to 65 to volunteer to form a Home Defence Corps to combat the danger of parachutists. They are to wear badges and carry firearms and do it as part-time work. Mother immediately alarmed in case my father should offer his services.

Wednesday, May 15th: Oh dear! Awful news again. Mother called dramatically upstairs at 7 a.m., 'Holland's given in!' and sure enough the Dutch have laid down their arms. Oh glory! When are we going to start and let into 'em? They seem to be having it all their own way.

Our errant headmistress turned her recalcitrant footsteps towards Springfield Road during the course of this morning, proclaiming feebly that she didn't know until yesterday that we'd had to come back. Huh! A good excuse! Barb G came at dinnertime and asked Had We Heard the News? – Italy Has Declared War On Us. All aghast, and congregated round the wireless for the 1 o'clock news, but Italy not mentioned, so this is presumably Another Rumour.

Started reading *The Provincial Lady in Wartime.*

Thursday, May 16th: Miss Harvey asked me dramatically if I'd heard aeroplanes in the night, but had to confess No, whereat she was astounded, and went on to relate highly confidential tale – told to her under an oath of secrecy but she knows she can Trust Me – about bombers over Derby last Saturday, and Hitler's new nerve gas in Holland. She has also heard that the news of the Packington parachutist is Authentic.

The Budget arrived from Lil in India, containing the usual literary gems and snaps of our octet. Joan is gaily frivoling with a bishop and his curate, Peg is engaged, Maretta married and Kath doubtful whether to go out to Persia to marry her Harold now, or wait until after the war. Woodie is engulfed with work, as usual, and Vera is prepared to Go Gay now that her engagement is off. As for me – I am leading a wildly exciting life. School, tennis, school, flicks, and school again, with a dash of Freddie to relieve the femininity of my companions. How stirring!

Washed my hair in a Stablond shampoo, in order to induce a flaxen sheen. Gratified therefore when Miss Barnett observed that my hair looked Lighter than Usual – and had an Autumn Sheen! Would have preferred the epithet Golden, but one mustn't expect too much. She said Had I heard about Lord Haw Haw's reference to Gresley? He announced that the park there would soon be a Graveyard!

The greatest battle in the history of the world is now in progress, says Mr Duff Cooper, the new Minister for Information, and we must expect Bad News as well as Good. The wireless announcer also issued a warning to motorists re parachutists, and advised them to lock their garage doors at night and put their car out of action before leaving it. Oh dear! I must deflate my bicycle tyres before retiring – they would probably welcome a bicycle!

Friday, May 17th: After hearing a woman on the wireless trilling, 'Wake up, wake up', with a warbling note like the sirens, my father remarked curtly No Wonder We're Not Winning the War. Couldn't quite see the connection, but my father looked very definite.

Delia, Mrs Tweed, Amy, Auntie N, Joyce, etc, came at night and John Ollerenshaw called for me to go to the Group. Undecided whether to go, but thought it would look mean after promising and after he'd called, so went. Then wished I hadn't! He took the group and wasn't good and wasn't bad – but afterwards! Oh glory! Felt my blood beginning to boil and bubble and my spleen arising. The discussion turned to pacifism etc, and they all righteously declared how wrong we were to be fighting Germany. The wrong method to use altogether. Huh! I suppose we should send a humble little note asking Hitler to please stop bombing and invading smaller countries. And Hitler would be so touched that he'd at once cease. After enduring their indictment of their country for as long as I could, I excused myself and walked out. Unleashed my simmering indignation when I got home.

Saturday, May 18th: Biked to Mrs W's at 9.15 to have my voile dress fitted. She was in Narky and Independent Vein, and said Had I worn my tennis dress yet? Said No, whereat she was consumed with indignation, saying Huh! After she'd stayed in all last Saturday, feverishly sewing. Reminded her that she had promised it to me for Sat, and that I wanted to wear it last Sat. This produced a long monologue – she'd had visitors, she'd had to put off everyone else, poor little Beryl had nothing to wear, she couldn't do more than she was able to, etc. It's like entering the lion's den to cross the Whitehead threshold to ask for a frock to be made.

The Germans have broken through and made a bulge in the French line and Gen Gamelin has told his troops to Win or Die. Stacks of aeroplanes about. Saw one circling Bretby Park and expected to see parachutists drop but they didn't.

Sunday, May 19th: Woman on the wireless asking What She's Gonna Do When You're Gone induces my father to leap to his feet in a frenzy to shut it off, declaring dramatically that if he listens to That Noise any longer, it will Drive Him Silly.

After tea, Delia, Amy, Joan G, Miss Green and I went for a ramble round Bretby to gather bluebells. Glorious evening and a glorious walk. Picked an armful of bluebells each, then began to stagger wearily homewards. Was just slinking guiltily by Mrs Swan's when I saw her waving, so had to go in and apologise for my neglect. She's worried about Bill – she hasn't heard from him for over a week and doesn't know where he is or what he's doing.

Had supper at Grandma's, then we trekked homewards to hear Winston Churchill speak (as Premier) about the War Situation on the wireless. He didn't attempt to disguise its seriousness, but said that the Germans have broken through the French line and that we must be ready for any sacrifice. After that great battle that is now raging in France, we shall have to fight for our islands, he declared. Oh dear! Sends shivers down my spine.

Miss R came to Grandma's and opined that Churchill sounded Serious but Hopeful and went on to relate that at one place the German dead were piled five feet high, and that the tanks went over them. Mother declares that she was born in the wrong century, and adds piously that we must endure our trials with Courage and Fortitude.

Monday, May 20th: Another glorious day – except for the news which is still serious – still violent fighting going on – the Germans pushing forward. Had another air-raid practice and had to shunt all the children out into the street once more.

Delia and I jaunted along to tennis. Had a set with Freddie and lost, and Freddie got me a lemonade while he drank a glass of beer, to my open disgust. Told him bluntly that lemonade would do him far more good. Played again with the Oller and won. Freddie then loomed over the court and bawled Was I Ready, so after the set, proceeded forth and was joined by Delia, who took it for granted that she was included in the offer of a lift (to my relief), and Esme, who was Sure Freddie Would Give Her a Lift. Accordingly, Freddie looked rather taken aback, but I said sweetly He Didn't Mind, Did He? and he replied blankly Er, No, a Pleasure. So we all bundled into the car.

The latest rumour professes to have solved the identity of Lord Haw Haw. He is the black sheep of the Joyce family, which explains why he knows so much about the Midlands.

Tuesday, May 21st: Letter from the neglectful Dougie, late obviously to pay me out for keeping him waiting. He has now joined the Local Defence Volunteers and goes on to declare that when our counter attack starts, we shall Slaughter Thousands of the Lousy Blighters (presumably Germans). He offers to play me at tennis for a pint of beer when the war is finished and adds recklessly, 'Dashed if I wouldn't let you win if you would drink it.' He needn't hope. Why my male friends would like to see me behind a pot of ale puzzles me. They never will.

Circular from the Education Committee, stressing the need for Gallophilism in our schools – must have pictures of France, portraits of Frenchmen, accounts of French doings etc displayed. AMF is therefore preparing to teach the French *Marseillaise* (in English) for Empire Day.

Biked to Mrs Whitehead's to take mauve buttons for my voile dress and arrived just in time to hear the six o'clock news. Very grave. The Germans have taken Amiens and Arras – so are very near the Channel ports now. M Reynard has spoken to the French Chamber of Deputies, stressing the gravity of the situation. Mr W had his map spread studiously on his knee as he listened and showed me Amiens. Nearly died of horror when I saw how near to the coast it was, and Mrs W said Didn't I Think it was Awful. Agreed that I certainly did.

Ivy and Joyce called on their way to tennis in the park, so I went and played with them from 7 until 8.30. Home in time for the news at 9 – still the same, still grave – everyone ordered to carry identification cards around.

Wednesday, May 22nd: I started reading Charlotte Bronte's *Villette* but didn't progress far – only far enough to learn that Villette is not the heroine's name, but the place in France where she went to look for work.

Listened in to speech made by Herbert Morrison, present Minister of Supply. A thoroughly stirring and fine speech – well written, well delivered and, I should think, well received. He seems to be a thoroughly capable man, with a capacity for inspiring others, if that is typical of his speeches. He urges the need for increased labour, increased output, increased drive, for we are fighting with our backs to the wall, for liberty and all these islands stand for.

Mrs W has finished my voile frock, in which I duly paraded. It's very sweet, I think. It's trimmed with blue velvet ribbon and little mauve pearl buttons. Mother took one look and remarked without enthusiasm that That Sort of Dress Looks Nothing without A Lot of Sun. Very dampened by this remark, but still like it very much.

Friday, May 24th: Empire Day. Accordingly wafted about school flaunting a red, white and blue ribbon, while the children did likewise, and some strode proudly into school bearing flags and banners. After play we migrated en masse into the Hall, where we chanted 'Rule Britannia', with gusto, 'God Save Our Gracious King', with feeling, 'What Can I do For England', with despair, and then we broke up – with enthusiasm. Last year we droned the patriotic old chants with indifference, little thinking what feelings they would arouse this year. They all seemed specially significant.

To Bella's for tea and to tennis again afterwards. Congregated in the Pavilion afterwards, heard part of the King's Speech and the news (Germans have taken Boulogne), and drank orangeade and ate crisps and chocolate.

Saturday, May 25th: My financial status is deplorable. Am now over 10/- in debt to different sources – and still a week to go.

Sunday, May 26th: A day of National Prayer – which we need, judging by the mess we're in. The news now is very vague and general, and talks of violent fighting, slow German advances and so on, but tells us nothing tangible in case it helps the enemy thereby.

Monday, May 27th: Miss D related alarming tales of Spies in the District. The curate of Twycross and the manager of Netherseal Colliery have been arrested, the Captain of the soldiers at Stretton, a spy, has been shot and a dentist at Tamworth has been discovered with a transmitting set up his chimney. At this juncture Miss Smith tells us of a couple of arrests at Ashby – people with a broadcasting set in the house. Miss Harvey then diverted the topic by a scandalous story of their parson, who was drunk in the service last night, before a church packed full of people. He got the service all mixed up, had to grope his way to the lectern, and couldn't read the prayers. He kept asking Miss H's father in the choir how he was doing. When the church council went round to dress him down, he sank down in a drunken slumber on the vestry floor.

Delia and I arrived at tennis round 7, so only got in two sets. After this we sustained a most Shattering Blow. Freddie had arrived, so Delia and I were smugly expectant of a lift home. Accordingly we didn't hurry ourselves and played ping-pong in the pavilion afterwards. But by 9.30 he hadn't mentioned a lift, and had more or less ignored us, so we became uneasy and I said we ought to make a move to go. We accordingly got slowly to our feet, making ostentatious preparations for departure. Nothing was said. We quavered Goodnight. Still nothing said. So we departed – and he let us! We had to walk, and didn't we fume!

Tuesday, May 28th: A dreadful piece of news – King Leopold of Belgium has surrendered to Germany and our BEF is now encircled. Oh dear! How awful! The news gets worse. Everyone talking about it – they say we've been sold again etc, etc. Discussed it with Miss B when I went to have my hair done. Should have had it permed, but too much perm still in, so had it cut and set.

Wednesday, May 29th: Situation still very grave. Discussed it in detail with Mrs Swan when I went there for tea. Bill is out there in the Arras region. Barbara, Bill's fiancée, there to tea too. My father says we'll have a bottle of champagne when West Street is retaken.

Had to go round billeting again, in readiness for an expected 400 evacuees. Everyone I approached refused, on some pretext – Mrs R because she has Attacks, Mrs C because she is Old, someone else because of Her Heart, etc, etc, but they all hoped that I wouldn't think them unpatriotic. The only one who volunteered to have a child was a boy whose mother was out – and I don't think he dared refuse me. But I bet his mother will have something to say when she returns.

We practised going in the air-raid shelters for the first time. I'm to have some evacuees with my class. Awful feeling when we're inside. Awful little places. Had an air-raid practice at night along with our street – everyone turned out to witness with great mirth (though there won't be any when it actually happens!). Efficient and officious wardens and constables were dashing around two prostrate men on stretchers, and two ambulances arrived – one of which had to be pushed because it wouldn't go.

Have no money to buy a new diary until we're paid. Very hard up.

Thursday, May 30th: We're to be evacuated to Australia from this country, says the latest report. And Lord Haw Haw has announced that the Rolls-Royce works have had their last pay day!

Attired myself for tennis and was just waiting for the 6.35 bus when a vision loomed – the False Fred, an affable smile on his face. 'Hello,' he trilled, 'Going to tennis?' Responded tartly that I was. Whereat he said he had called to take me and added that he didn't know we were going the other night – that there would have been room for us in his car! Made no answer to this.

Friday, May 31st: Friday, and a pay-day – tra la la, tra la la! All sign posts are being taken down – in preparation for the expected German invasion. Oh dear! How ominous that sounds. Destination boards are being removed from the buses too.

Adorned myself in white frock with clover scarf, blue coat, clover shoes, gloves and bag, ready for tennis, and fancied myself very much. However, Delia, having just bought a new bike, insisted on going to Geary on it, so had to take off my finery and put on old clothes.

Saturday, June 1st: Up betimes because I had arranged to bike to Burton with Delia to do some shopping. I think she wobbles worse than I do. Flung my money about very rashly – as I always do when I have any – and bought soap, face cloth, shoes, tooth-brush, powder puff, braid, cakes, etc etc.

Have to report at the Town Hall at 2 p.m. tomorrow to billet children who are coming from the SE coast. Oh blow!

Sunday, June 2nd: Had to go in the boiling sunshine to the Town Hall at 2 p.m. to receive evacuees from Southend. All Swadlincote turned out to view them, and the Town Hall was buzzing with teachers all clad in their Sunday best. The children arrived in due course, but after waiting until 4.30 doing nothing, found that there were none for me to take out, so went with Amy to tea.

Tuesday, June 4th: Paris raided – over 200 killed and 900 casualties altogether. Another brilliantly sunny day. Simply glorious. To the PT class, then to tennis with Edna Clarke. Played all night with Mr Harvey and the new manager of Stanton colliery. Freddie there, so brazenly asked him to take us home, and he did.

Thursday, June 6th: Another glorious day – a real scorcher. Clad myself in my flowered voile and yanked off to Burton to meet

Hilda T. She surprisingly remembered that tomorrow is my birthday and bought me *Rebecca*. I bought some sandals and a cream straw hat (which I now dislike) and by that time, to my relief, it was too late to go to the flicks so we had a sundae in the Ritz café, then I caught the bus to Geary. Freddie was there and he yelled that he had brought my bag etc for me, and didn't I think it was good of him, so responded fittingly, Oh yes. Played with Freddie v Cyril Poole and Delia, and beat them 6-0. Had a lift home in the dear Fred's car.

Friday, June 7th: My birthday! I'm 26. Had cards from various folk, including a most egotistical one from the ex-Bishop of Brimington. Dougie wrote and wants a snap of me. He says he's waited seven years for one, so thinks he deserves it . . . Glorious hot weather still.

Something always happens on my birthday, and this one opened at 2 a.m. with an air-raid alarm. The awful wail of the sirens broke out, so said 'oh lor'!' and clambered out of bed, downstairs, grabbed the gas mask, and we all migrated to Grandma's to the fringe of the cellar. Took us hours to get safely parked, as we were all pottering about in the dark, distrusting the efficacy of Grandma's blackout. My father got rapidly more and more annoyed and impatiently put the light on, while Mother decisively switched it off again. Mr Skerritt was darting about giving comfort and help to all, while my father groped in the shed for the sacks for the cellar floor and the sandbag for the grating. At a crucial moment the latter burst and emptied a torrent of sand in the bottoms of my father's trousers. Finally we moved into the cellar, Grandma leading. It took an age to pilot her down, and when she got there she decided she wanted to visit the lavatory and turned to come back but was firmly checked. Then there was the business of getting chairs down and a candle lighted, and whisky for Grandma's heart. The glass was passed round for us all to take a sip, but I couldn't swallow the awful stuff. Just as we were finally settled, the All Clear sounded, so we had to march aloft again. Drank tea and ate biscuits with relief before retiring to bed about 4 a.m. The birds were just beginning to chirp.

Monday, June 10th: Italy has declared war on us now. Hope they get well and truly squashed!

Letter from Swanee – Bill is safe in Aberystwyth, after having an awful time being evacuated from Dunkirk under shell-fire, machine-gunning and bombs.

Tuesday, June 11th: Fred (stiff and curt use of name – reason hereafter) took me to Geary. On the way home, he referred to a letter he had had from A Girl Friend in Hull!!! Was aghast. I thought I was the only light of his life, but apparently there are other flames flickering. I am most indignant. He has no right to transfer his affections – I have, but he hasn't! Even if I don't want him, he shouldn't swerve in his allegiance!

Wednesday, June 12th: Mr Skerritt had to face the tribunal, but steered a safe course and his name is to be kept on the register of conscientious objectors on condition that he remains in his present employment.

Friday, June 14th: Friday – thanks be! And the Germans have marched into Paris, which hasn't been defended, so that its buildings shall be preserved. Delia and I biked to Geary and returned about 10.15. Bill Swan is over after his ordeal.

Saturday, June 15th: Jack Whetton registered today with the 28s and so did George.

Delia and I went to Geary. I wore my new blue shantung frock

with the clover ribbons that Mrs W finished this week. Freddie –
I mean Fred – was there, with friend named Edgar. Had a singles
with Fred before tea and nearly beat him but he won by one
game. Simply boiling when we finished.

Discovered new and unpleasant depths to Fred's character
too – he is a Wolf in Sheep's Clothing. When we retired for a
drink after the set, he had no less than three (III, 3, iii) glasses of
beer straight after each other, and from friend Edgar's remarks I
judged this to be no rare occurrence. Had one more set with him
after this, and he kept serving doubles, which I am sure was the
effect of the beer.

A Very Revealing Day. Fred has revealed undreamed-of
depths – I don't think he's even Quite Decent now, but definitely
a Satyr.

Sunday, June 16th: No church bells this morn – nor henceforth.
They are to be rung only to warn us of invasion. Oh dear! How
grim! So tired this morn, and I have a mouldy cold in the head,
so missed Communion and slept on till 9 a.m. Went to Sunday
School and church twice. Doleful hymns, e.g. 'I know not what
may befall me.'

Wednesday, June 17th: They've got a mania on the wireless for
Talking Down Their Nose, says my father disgustedly.

The Reynaud Govt in France has resigned and is succeeded by
a new one under M Petain. Miss Smith affirms that the war will
have to be fought out in this country eventually and says that her
cousin believes it will start at the end of this week. How nice! J. B.
Priestley suggested on the wireless last night that all children
should be evacuated to the dominions and our country turned
into a fortress. I can see myself spinning out the rest of my days
under Canadian skies or the Australian sun.

Another dreadful and catastrophic bombshell announced at

the beginning of the 1 o'clock news – France has given in and is seeking 'honourable terms' with Germany, but the Premier in a very short speech at 9 p.m. said that we would fight on. Oh dear! None of us felt much like work but congregated with serious demeanour and asked each other solemnly What We Thought. I daren't even conjecture these days what is going to happen. So in view of all this, Delia and I thought we'd better go to Geary in case it's our last visit. We biked and saw Freddie's car parked there. Greeted him with marked coolness (I hope) and he babbled that it was late when he came and so he hadn't called. Made no reply. He asked if I'd play with him in the tournament for the Red Cross on Saturday, so in view of the worthy object I said I would, but in what were meant to be Tones of Indifference. Saw him trekking towards the bar again a few times and felt disgusted.

Wednesday, June 19th: Air raid over the Eastern counties last night – over 100 enemy bombers and 11 people killed and about 14 injured. We brought down one of their planes.

George rang up to see if I'd go to Geary to play off the first round of the tournament. Freddie and I surprised ourselves by winning. All congregated in the pavilion afterwards, drinking orangeade and listening to the news.

Friday, June 21st: Letter from Dougie adjuring me to take care of myself and repeating request for a photo. He discreetly mentions Tuesday's raid, but beyond telling me that he was out all night driving the ambulance, tells me little.

George says he thinks there'll be no tournament tomorrow – the glass is going down with a bump.

Mrs Tweed had just gone when I arrived home, after relating an alarming experience of the other night. In the middle of the night Amy leapt out of bed with the cry, 'Mother, they're here, they're here!' and in a second was frantically struggling out of her pyjamas while Mrs Tweed sat on the edge of the bed on the verge of hysterics. They couldn't hear the sirens but thought they must have stopped. Then the clock below began to strike, whereat Mrs Tweed screamed, 'The parachutists! We're invaded! There's the church bell!' Oh dear, I'd love to have seen them.

Saturday, June 22nd: Awoke to the sound of torrents of rain, so turned over and went to sleep again until 9 a.m. Hopes of the tournament dwindled, but nevertheless biked through the downpour to Mrs W's to fetch my new tennis dress. It looks quite nice. I would love the blue and white shoes I saw in Plant's to go with it, but it would be sheer extravagance. Besides, I have no money and had to borrow 5/- now until next pay-day – Friday, thanks be. Biked back about 12.30 to find that the tournament had been cancelled, so proceeded to ring up my partner and tell him. He didn't sound very distressed.

Sunday, June 23rd: Another wet day – very dull, gloomy and depressing. France has signed the Armistice and has now agreed to use her air force, fleet etc against us.

Reading *Tess of the D'Urbervilles.* Haven't done much reading at all lately – just can't settle down with a book. Have to be doing something. And on the move – whanging balls about or racing across the tennis court. Everything is so uncertain and so unsettled – one can't even look or plan a week ahead. It's just a case of living hopefully from one day to the next.

Spent part of this morn packing my little black bag – relic of college days – in readiness for potential air raids. Put in it the sal volatile, and spoon, beaker, bottle-opener, tin for biscuits, 3 handkerchiefs, a book, and the draughts, my efforts not being taken seriously, however, but more an occasion for mirth. Never mind! They'll be glad to munch my biscuits, sniff my sal volatile, read my book or play with my draughts when we're parked in that cold, damp, dreary cellar for hours on end.

Tuesday, June 25th: Oh what a long and weary day! Hardly had we retired to our slumbers sweet, than the unnerving wail of the sirens broke the silence of the night. Leapt up in bed with alarm, to find that it was only 12.40, so had only been asleep for about an hour. Fumbled in the dark for my dressing gown and little case – so thoughtfully packed, stumbled downstairs, grabbed the gas masks, and trekked up to Grandma's. Halfway there my case flew open, and I had to grovel on the ground redeeming the contents. Found later that I had also collected an empty cigarette packet. All the time the wail of the sirens continued, and I expected to hear the throb of the enemy planes overhead. Fell into Grandma's and Mother, Dad and Miss S followed. We were let in by Mr Skerritt, who in groping for his torch had put his fingers in the mousetrap. Then we proceeded as before, but with cushions, to the cellar, and had to wait there over two hours. We heard the muffled explosion of three bombs, and the enemy planes overhead, and shook like jellies. Then all was silent, so we decided to go upstairs. After a total wait of three hours, the All Clear sounded, and unnerved us all again. We thought it was the alarm sounding once more. Drank tea and then retired to bed about 4 a.m.

After all this, felt like a worn-out wreck for the rest of the day, and could have snoozed standing up. 14 of my class stayed away in the morn, but the majority turned up in the afternoon. We all had much to say to each other about the night's vigil. We'll all be going about soon enquiring about each other's morale instead of their health. Miss Harvey and her husband heard the whistles and thinking that it indicated gas, sat in their gas masks for three-quarters of an hour until their faces were bathed in perspiration.

In spite of all this, went to Geary after tea, and Delia followed later.

Wednesday, June 26th: Had hardly fallen asleep in the early hours, before the sirens tuned up and broke up our night's rest once more. Looked at my watch and saw that it was only midnight, so we wearily yanked ourselves out into the street and to the refuge of the cellar again. Fully expected a night's vigil, but to our surprise the All Clear sounded at 1 a.m. and we resumed our beds. And my stars – had only been in bed an hour before the sirens started again, and once more we migrated cellarwards. This time the alarm lasted about half an hour, but after the All Clear we decided not to be duped again, fearing another alarm, so we waited at Grandma's till 3 a.m. Thence back to bed.

Another day of profound weariness after this. Could hardly drag myself out of bed at 8 o'clock, so after school I went to bed from about 5.30 until 6.30, then biked to Geary. It turned cold and only a few there, so Mabel D and I decided to trot off home and get to bed early. Mabel had the ambulance so she put my bike inside and offered me a lift – spent the next half hour pushing it backwards and forwards because it wouldn't start. Finally it had to be towed.

Thursday, June 27th: Actually had an undisturbed night, thanks be! – though there were raids, and we had the red warning, but it was cancelled before the sirens sounded.

Tales in circulation to the effect that Crewe station has been bombed to bits, also Bristol station, the whole of Southend and so forth.

Went to tennis on my bike, accompanied by Delia, and the Faithless Freddie was there, giving lifts to Ivan B and his wife, Doreen R and Joan T afterwards. Brooded deeply.

Friday, June 28th: Enemy planes over again last night, but we're not going to have the sirens now until the situation is really very dangerous and we're actually being bombed. Mad, I call it! Shan't fancy zig-zagging my way up the road to the cellar between bombs and the flying shrapnel.

Went to school with a rebellious spirit today, caused by the fact that many schools – Miss S and Delia included – have today and Monday holiday, so both Miss S and Delia have packed their bags and tripped light-heartedly homewards. Still, it was pay-day, which helped to lighten the heavy burden of the day's labours somewhat, though once more I have had to disburse a large part of it immediately on receipt.

Awakened in the middle of the night by most agonising cries and moans, which proved to be Mother in the grip of a nightmare. She later explained that she dreamt someone was pulling her nose. Our slumbers do get disturbed lately.

Saturday, June 29th: Went to Miss B's to have my ends permed at 9.30 a.m., and emerged looking as though I'd had a prison crop. Tried to remedy this by combing out the curls with ferocious determination mixed with despair, but the result not very satisfactory, as it is impossible to lengthen hair that has been summarily cut off.

To Geary in the afternoon for the Open Tennis Tournament. Enjoyed it and had some good games. Ivy related tale of woman who heard only the All Clear last Monday night, so, thinking it was the warning, she got up hastily and stayed up till 7 the next morning waiting for the All Clear.

Sunday, June 30th: Awakened by enemy planes overhead at 1.30 this morn, but said nothing as the rest of the household was peacefully asleep. However, when they had nearly gone, and were just a hum in the distance, Mother and Dad woke up. News later reported bombing raids, over SE, SW and E England and the Midlands and said that a town in the Midlands had its infirmary bombed.

All slept at Grandma's in case we had to get up in the middle of the night. However, we all had a peaceful night.

Monday, July 1st: Heard via May Staley that parachutists were dropped last night round Rugby and Leicester. She was on the train from London about 9 p.m. when the guard dashed round ordering all lights to be extinguished and all blinds drawn, as parachutists were about. And Mrs G has brought the tale that some refugee Jews who have taken a house in Southwell near Nottingham are Germans, and have been signalling during the raids. They've been rounded up. Mrs L says that there is some-one in Derby who signals too, during the raids – her brother has seen the flashes, and lots of people have been reporting them to the police. Our coalman has been visited and warned by the police against spreading false rumours.

Got ready for tennis and set out about 6.30. Was just trailing up when I heard an unmistakeable chuff-chuff behind and turned to see my father in hot pursuit on his little motorbike. Dismounted and waited and he drew up, saying solemnly, 'If I were you I shouldn't go tonight!' All sorts of possibilities flashed through my mind but asked 'Why?' 'They've had the Yellow Warning,' said my father seriously. If he'd said the Yellow Fever it couldn't have sounded more ominous. Hesitated, but finally accepted the way of caution and returned home. Hadn't been home more than ten minutes when the All Clear was given, whereby I gnashed my teeth in rage and frustration. Slept at Grandma's, because everyone was sure there was to be an air raid – but there wasn't. So in spite of having to sleep on a mattress on the floor I had a quiet and peaceful night.

Tuesday, July 2nd: Delia and I wandered forth to Geary again and I arrived to find I was notorious – the tale of my retreat last night having been spread abroad. Mrs Smithard asked me with a smirk if I was still standing by. The False Fred said he Laughed His Head Off when he heard. Played with him in the first set and he cracked his racquet (felt like Laughing My Head Off). Played a set with Mabel D, Esme, and Hildred M, and we left for home quite early in case of raids.

Wednesday, July 3rd: Tales about Miss Foster's Man-in-the-Red-Car – which have been effaced by War Rumours – are to the fore again. Mr Wheat saw him and Miss F sitting in his car about 6 p.m. last night, and they both ducked when he appeared. And it is said that he has been writing to her daily while he's been away and that his wife knows and is distressed. I think Miss F is the limit. She's leaving, and Mr Wheat thinks that this Underhand Work is the reason for her departure.

Letter from Dougie stating with ghoulish importance that he has already picked up one case that refused to take cover in a raid – he will see no more raids, says Dougie grimly. He also goes on to relate morbidly the deaths of (a) his aunt, (b) a fellow next door and (c) his old school pal, but adds viciously that We Shall Make Those Blighters Pay For It, and he'll kill everyone he sees if he has the chance, which he hopes he will. (He gets rather involved and ungrammatical at the end.) He ends by stating simply that this is not a very cheerful letter – which sentiment I heartily endorse – and the usual solicitous admonition to me to take care of myself.

Letter also from Maretta Madge – now having a marvellous time with her RAF husband in Ireland – making me green with envy.

Saturday, July 6th: After dinner Delia and I went to Geary. Were having a last set at 9.30 when an aeroplane sounded overhead and everyone stopped playing immediately and gasped 'German!' We promptly stopped our play and made for home. Slept at Grandma's again.

May with Ivy (front left), and George and a friend

Monday, July 8th: Went to tennis. Ivy and George there. We watched the LDV drilling – some of them were very 'raw' but there were two obvious old hands.

Wednesday, July 10th: Torrents of rain fell all day long. Rumbles of thunder also sounded – very ominously – this afternoon, whereat I received a frenzied note from Miss H, asking Was it Thunder or Bombs?' Replied in consolatory vein, and shortly afterwards lightning appeared, confirming my diagnosis.

Thursday, July 11th: Was in the act of washing this morning when an aeroplane went buzz-buzzing overhead. Sounded to me like a German, and I idly speculated that if the sirens went I was at least up, and it would mean being late for school. However not perturbed until Mother came rushing in exclaiming, 'A German plane!' and announcing that Others Had Heard it Too and had pronounced it a German. Mrs Fearn even declared that she had heard bombs dropping, but we all pooh-poohed the idea. However when I arrived at school, found that Miss Harvey had also heard the bombs, and so had many other people. When I arrived home for dinner, I learned that news had filtered through. The raid had been at Melbourne, where a silk factory had been hit, and a house where soldiers were stationed. 8 soldiers were killed and about 30 people injured, and as Melbourne disbanded its ARP organisation a fortnight ago, ambulances, doctors, fire engines etc from here had all rushed to the scene. No air-raid sirens sounded at all. Everybody is highly incensed. The raid much discussed and the principal topic of conversation throughout the day.

Saturday, July 13th: Had my hair set. Much better day – actually saw the sun after about a week's sulking behind the clouds. Amy, Joan G, Delia, Joyce and I set forth about 2 p.m. on a picnic on our bikes, through Ticknall and Melbourne. When we got to Melbourne we saw evidences of Thursday's raid – windows boarded up, roads closed, and shop windows shuttered but with 'Business As Usual' chalked on the outside. We saw a crowd of people in one street, and a special constable stopping people at the end to enquire where they were going. I asked a woman what it was all about, and she said the soldiers who were killed in Thursday's raid were being buried.

We all retired to Grandma's to sleep, but had scarcely crawled into bed before we heard a German plane – or so we thought – overhead, and then air activity with a vengeance – our own machines buzzing backwards and forwards unceasingly for the next hour, dropping flares, so we discovered. Every time a plane went over, either Grandma or Mother appealed to my father for his verdict – German or British? Mother was in and out of bed like a dog at a fair, hanging out of the window, scanning the sky. About midnight she spied Mrs Merchant speeding up the road and flying to the refuge of Grandma's cellar. Mr S let her in, and she was offered a share of my bed. Obligingly made room for her – and my hat! Never again! What a night I had! Didn't seem to have two consecutive hours' sleep all night. Kept having jolts from her, causing me rudely to awake. 'What's that – gunfire?' she exclaimed in the depths of the night. Just as I had fallen asleep again she'd leap up exclaiming, 'Was that a bomb?' Then she roused me three times to know the time, so I despaired of ever having any rest.

Sunday, July 14th: To Evening Service – we're having sermons about the small but valiant (like David) defeating the great and unscrupulous. To G's to supper, then home to listen to the news, and to a speech by Winston Churchill. Mother remarks grimly that, He Tells You Straight. A very good commentary on an air fight followed, then a talk by J. B. Priestley on a voyage to

Margate which was very good indeed, and very graphically told. He described the journey down, with Bren guns amongst the agricultural machinery, cows beneath the trees which might have been tanks, and soldiers materialising from nowhere to demand identity cards. Arrived at Margate, he found it deserted and desolate, with no sign of life. The bandstand was there, and the seats and flowers, but the beach, promenade and boarding houses were all deserted – how different from normal times. The sirens sounded as he was about to begin his lunch, but apparently he was undaunted and continued.

Mrs M called at Grandma's and I was in a frenzy in case she decided to stay the night. Mr Skerritt provokingly told her I'd be most disappointed if she didn't. Luckily she didn't stay – There would have been a murder if she had done.

Tuesday, July 16th: Oh boy, oh boy! Something rare, something precious – a holiday! Celebrated by lounging luxuriously abed until 9.15.

Very surprisingly, the Faithless Freddie rang, asking me if I'd go to the flicks with him. Apparently he was at a loose end! Said Ivy was here, so he said Ivy could come also, so I said we'd go. Told Ivy, who fetched George, so in the end there were four of us. We went to the Ritz to see Greta Garbo in *Ninotchka* – very funny. George a most generous soul – he brought the Faithless Freddie up to scratch. Instead of going in the shillings, we graced the balcony, and George bought Ivy and me a half-pound box of chocolates and an ice. Afterwards we had coffee, and so home.

Wednesday, July 17th: School once more, woe's me, woe's me! Miss F returned in a bad temper and snapped, then came to test my class's reading but marked very leniently.

Went to a meeting of billeting officers at 6.30. 1200 more B'ham children expected any day. The usual dilly-dallying and silly questions, so I left before it was all over, at 7.30, and biked to Geary. Hitler is to invade us next Friday, say the papers.

Thursday, July 18th: Wrote a very belated letter to friend Vera, thus clearing up all my arrears of correspondence ready for the invasion. Now I can be invaded with a clear conscience!

After a dull and doubtful day, the sun came bounding forth after tea, and it was a lovely evening, so I wended my way to Geary.

Friday, July 19th: Dull and showery. No tennis. Delia, Amy and Mrs T here to supper. Slept at Grandma's in case of raids.

Sunday, July 21st: To Church at 8 o'clock and 10.45, but not again. Instead we went to Auntie Nell's to tea and didn't come home till suppertime. Ate a massive supper, and retired to bed at Grandma's again. Fell fast asleep almost as soon as I was in the bed because I was so tired but had not been long asleep before I was rudely awakened by the sirens. We all awoke at once and tumbled down to the cellar, fully expecting a 'proper do' this time, with bombs exploding all around, and as it was not quite midnight, thought we were in for a long wait. But the All Clear sounded after half an hour, so we crawled back to bed.

Monday, July 22nd: Jack W had his medical today and passed Grade II on account of his bunions. He's most disappointed because that stops him entering the Air Force.

To bed at Grandma's again because Mother feverishly convinced that there would be a raid. And there was. The sirens sounded just after 12 and we tumbled out of bed and into the cellar once more. But we had scarcely time to get the cushions, stool and sacks down before the All Clear sounded after 10 minutes. And so to bed once more.

Wednesday, July 24th: Had decided to ignore the Bishop's birthday, but at the last moment, as a concession to my weaker nature and in view of the uncertainty of the times, sent him a letter card with 'Many happy returns – and a safe passage through stormy times' poetically inscribed thereon.

Thursday, July 25th: Staggered when dear Freddie condescended to ring me up and say he'd call and take me to tennis. Mother was busy in the midst of a Little Whist Drive for the Waifs & Strays, so glad to get out of it.

Budget this week has increased income tax by 1/- to 8/6 (taxable at the source) and increased the price of cosmetics, clothing, beer and tobacco etc.

Friday, July 26th: On the way home from tennis, who should we meet but Swanee! – over for a fortnight's holiday. After one critical look she asked me what I'd been doing, as I looked worn out, with Bags Under the Eyes, etc, etc, adding that she had never seen me look so washed out before. Immediately felt like a hag and on the verge of a complete collapse from exhaustion, so biked home feeling really ill. Decided that bed was indicated, so retired before 10 o'clock.

Saturday, July 27th: Lay in bed until 9.15, in view of Swanee's outspoken comment, hoping thereby to eliminate the Bags Under the Eyes, and had a really good night's sleep. Having had my hair set, launched myself upon another billeting campaign, with the utmost reluctance, to ensure billets for the additional 1200 B'ham children who are to come. All my potential clients exclaimed in horror when I told them where the children were coming from, having seen Direful Things from the entry of the first batch of Birmingham evacuees. One, Mrs B, told me that she found Five Bugs in her bed after her evacuee had returned. Trailed miserably round, but finished about 3.15, so sped joyfully homewards with the comfortable feeling of duty done, had a bath and felt considerably refreshed.

Joyce, Auntie Nell and Brenda to tea. Decided after trying Joyce's on, to indulge in a turban – now very fashionable, so Joyce went with me in quest of wool for one. Bought some green and blue. Seemed to have an orgy for spending again, because, after going into Boots for a 6d. cold cream, I emerged with talc and face powder also – before they go up. Slept at Grandma's as usual – as we have been doing for over a week. I occupied my little feather bed and had a very good night's sleep. Retired before 10 and didn't get up till 8.30. Felt much rested.

Sunday, July 28th: Scrutinised my face to see if the effect of two good nights' sleep had erased my careworn look – felt much less tired, but think I can still detect the Bags. A sad state to be in! Went for an hour's bike ride as far as Stanton with Delia at 3.30.

Thursday, August 1st: To Geary again, played with Freddie v. Edna Clark and Mr Gulliver (who had biked up with us – he talked about Ants all the way). Ivan B and Ruth there – they're all breaking up tomorrow! They're going to Ilfracombe with Freddie on Sat – he's taking them but isn't staying with them. I imagine he must be taking his Girl Friend From Hull. Bet she's a Flashy Piece of Goods.

Friday, August 2nd: Oh mouldy! Normally we'd be looking forward to holidays by the sea now, and a month off.

To Swanee's to tea, then to Belfitts to play tennis. Mrs Belfitt said I didn't look too well – which made me feel washed out and decrepit. Sank into bed after playing tennis, exhausted, but we were awakened at 12.25 by the sirens. Alarm lasted for an hour, then we crawled back to bed peacefully and undisturbed for the rest of the night.

Monday, August 5th: Bank holiday for nearly everyone but us. Oh mouldy having to go to school when everyone else was in festive holiday spirit. Still, we only had 30 children instead of 46, and we finished at a quarter to 4.

Thursday, August 8th: A blow awaited us at school – all windows to be covered with net – by us! Trissie offered to come after school, and Miss H, but I didn't intend to. When I leave school at 4, I leave for the day, when the bally Education Committee is mean enough to pinch our holidays. So we all made a start in school time, and the children stayed in the yard for an hour in the afternoon while we got on with the job. Glory! What a job! Began by conscientiously doing every pane myself, but after a while let the children help – and of course they were all too willing to have a finger in the pie. Derek D cut the net so vigorously that he raised huge blisters on his fingers.

Friday, August 9th: Lots of people heard bombs dropping last night. They were subsequently found to have been dropped at Erdington. Auntie Nell of course heard them and they all got up and went downstairs. Glad we heard nothing of them – I for one had an extremely peaceful night and didn't wake up once. Grandma vows however that she heard an aeroplane go buzzing overhead.

Another day spent daubing net over every inch of glass we could find in the building. Got thoroughly weary, sticky and fed up, so biked home with relief at 4 p.m.

Sunday, August 11th: We all went to Mrs Tweed's for tea and supper. Home to bed by 10 p.m., but had to rise again about 10 to 12 because the sirens went. Luckily we were only up for about 20 mins and we didn't hear or see anything. The enemy was reported later to have been in the Lichfield region.

Tuesday, August 13th: Biked to Geary. Very few there. To bed quite early, and was in a deep sleep dreaming that I was ordering milk shakes in a café, when the sirens went at 3 a.m. Came down, but after 5 minutes the All Clear went, so we returned to bed and I quickly resumed my nice sleep.

Wednesday, August 14th: Oh dear! We did miss something last night. Everyone seems to have been up all night. The raiders came over in waves – 7 or 8 waves from 10.30 onwards, dropping bombs all round us. Everyone was in the street watching the flashes and hearing the thuds. It was like Bonfire Night, I'm told. Glad I slept through it, but Mother rather peeved because she says she doesn't want to be bombed in bed. She has therefore arranged to be knocked up if anything like that should occur again.

Thursday, August 15th: Only two more days now until we break up, thanks be! *If* we get our holiday, that is. I've had my doubts all along. Oh dear! I shall die if it is wrenched from us at this last moment.

Friday, August 16th: Had to get up twice last night. The sirens sounded about 1 a.m., and down we trooped in instalments – Mother first bolting towards the cellar like a rabbit to its burrow, then me, then Mr Skerritt, who proceeded to lay the sacks on the floor of the cellar, and the cushions on the plank, then Dad, Grandma and Auntie – the latter three all decently dressed. My father marched boldly outside on his patrol duty, but returned a minute later telling us to descend to the cellar as he could hear enemy planes overhead.

We all troop solemnly down, and sit in a row on the plank. We are able to go up about half an hour later, then the All Clear sounds and we file off obediently to bed again. Oh glory! We're not in bed long before the all-too-familiar wail starts off again, though fainter, and once more we troop downstairs, my father remarking that the siren has blown itself out, it sounds so faint. Or else it has a cold, he suggests. We all chuckle appreciatively, then Grandma is heard wailing on the stairs that she can't get the blessed thing on (she's trying to get dressed). She stumbles down with the heel of her stocking round her ankle and looking very dishevelled. We discover later that this warning was a mistake – it was the Newhall sirens that sounded, after a mysterious telephone call. Huh!

Overwhelmed with weariness all day after this, but struggled manfully through, buoyed up with the pleasant feeling that today is the Day of Days – breaking up day! Hallelujah! Children all wild and uncontrollable, but managed to cope with my brood, and breathed a fervent sigh of relief when 4 o'clock came. We all filed along to Miss Foster's room to say goodbye to her. Oh dear! I wish she were not going really. She has some funny ways but she's most decent to work for. I bet we'll get a Tartar! Oh woe is me! If we get Miss Perkins, Trissie has vowed to leave, and if we get Miss Howard, I'll die.

Saturday, August 17th: Renie bolts in during the morning, breathing hard and gasping that They've Had the Purple Warning, and that a warden has told her they'll be blowing the sirens before she gets home. However, they don't. We spend the day in peace, undisturbed, and the even voice of the BBC announcer declares later that there have been no raids on this country today. Mabel D says ominously No, they're saving them all up for Tonight.

A glorious change in the weather again – hot and sunny

instead of cool and dull. Retire to bed early and have a peaceful night apart from two nightmares, during which I am first marching in front of German tanks along West Street, then fleeing on foot from a bombarded Nottingham. Awake with a gasp of relief.

Sunday, August 18th: Lie in bed like a Lotus-eater until 9.15, instead of making a Spartan effort and presenting myself at church for early Communion. Eat my way solidly through massive sausages, tomatoes, and hunks of bread and butter and marmalade, and then think with remorse upon the potential future state of my waistline. Spend the morning service feeling like an Advent Turkey.

Several people with either insomnia or very acute senses declare that they heard bombs drop last night. Winnie vows that she counted five. In the throes of my nightmare I heard nothing.

To Grandma's for supper. Bask in the comforting thought that tomorrow is a holiday – whoopee, whoopee! Read *The Diary of a Nobody* for about the third time. Grandma etc talk about Property, Coppers, Nellie's Dismal House and Houses in General. Discuss the 9 o'clock news as soon as it comes through – two attempts on London since dinner, and an air battle going on over the Hampshire Basin, but we have brought down 86 planes with a loss of only 15 of our fighters. Good for our RAF!

Monday, August 19th: Have not been in bed long last night before the now well-known wail screeches through the air. Immediately all is astir in the house – we scramble out of bed, nip downstairs, and sit in our usual row on the plank in the cellar for about 20 minutes, but we beguile the time away and minister to our sleepy senses by drinking large hot cups of tea. After half an hour the All Clear goes, and we stagger off to bed again, declaring ominously and in turn that They'll be Back Again before the night is out. This however doesn't keep me awake and the rest of the night is surprisingly peaceful.

Celebrate this first day of the holiday by lounging luxuriously abed until 9.45, thinking compassionately of those who are starting back at school today. Compare their state mentally with mine and beam with satisfaction.

To bed with the usual query on our lips. I begin to dream in horrible fashion that I am scrambling through barbed wire round Bretby to get out of the way of machine gunning by German planes. Awake abruptly from this to hear Auntie F telling the sleeping house to 'Hark! – What was that?' She has, she observes, already heard three bombs drop! Lie and listen, and to my horror, hear thuds and so do we all, except my father, who positively and stubbornly refuses to get up. We begin the usual migration downwards. On the way we hear a thud that shakes the house and I shake in sympathy. The cellar receives us into its sanctuary again, and we stay there until things around seem more peaceful. After this we sit about in the kitchen, with the usual comforting cup of tea, until about 1 a.m. Then we decide to retire to rest again.

Have not been long asleep before the sirens begin to trill, so for the second time the house is astir. This time there is a perfect avalanche of thuds and we sit in our row on the plank in the cellar and shudder at them. Mother sits with her fingers plugging her ears, and as we hear an extra loud bang Auntie Frances clasps her head. Grandma meanwhile sits stolidly through it all until she begins to feel chilly, so I lend her my chiffon scarf. She opens it out and places it over her head like a veil. After two hours of enemy planes overhead, anti-aircraft fire, and bombs, the All Clear finally sounds at 4 a.m. and allows us to begin our night's slumbers. Fall soon asleep.

Tuesday, August 20th: Make a belated appearance downstairs at 11 a.m. this morn to find the one topic everywhere is that of last night's activities. One says that 69 bombs were dropped, another

16, another that Derby station was hit, another that it wasn't, someone else that the raider was brought down at Repton and someone else that two bombs fell in Bretby Park. Anyhow, everyone has an inexhaustible topic of conversation, even though the reports are too conflicting to tell much.

Wednesday, August 21st: Up a little earlier in view of projected outing to Leicester. Am just donning my coat ready to set out, when the most astonishing and utterly unexpected noise is heard. 'The sirens!' we gasp, and look at each other stunned, as it is only 10.15. Then we collect ourselves and make hurriedly for the cellar – Renie, who is here, moaning frantically about What Will Her Mother Do? When we get to the cellar, someone raises the sacking which blacks out the grating, whereupon Mother in a frenzy orders him to put it down again – it will show the light! Then she remembers that it is broad daylight outside and we all giggle. At this, after 7 or 8 minutes, the All Clear goes and we emerge with relief.

Mother says, 'Surely you're not going to Leicester now!' but reply, 'Why not? Leicester's safe enough!' and set off. Meet Ivy and Mabel on the bus, and when we get to Leicester, we find we are at the very place that has been bombed this morning! Make straightway for our lunch, which we eat in style in the Grill Room of the Grand. Have grilled halibut which is lovely, and ices. After a massive meal we stagger forth replenished, and totter around Lewis's, the market, and other shops. Buy a pair of green string gloves. Make a frantic dash for the 4.35 train back, and just catch it, as well as the 5.30 bus at Ashby.

All meet at Geary later in the evening, but a gale is blowing. A peaceful night, except that I am in much perturbation and stress of spirit about my promised visit to Swanee's. Don't want to go at all, but don't see how I can get out of it.

Thursday, August 22nd: Oh dear! Decide I ought to go to Swanee's but proceed to moan about it all day. Tale now in circulation that five dead Germans have been found in Bretby Wood in the remnants of their plane and are to be buried at Hartshorne tomorrow. My father scoffs at the thought and says What Next.

When we retire to Grandma's for the night Mrs Gee storms in and declares that Bob was blown out of bed during Monday's raid, and that they had bombs all round Nottingham. Recrudescence of feeling against my going to Wilmslow comes up here, and I retire to bed not knowing what to do.

Friday, August 23rd: Decide to send telegram to Swanee saying I can't go, so lie in bed and feel mean, but Mother dashes up with a card at 8 a.m. from Swanee saying that she will meet the train, so realise that I can't possibly not go now. Just manage to catch the 8.15 train at Burton. Discover later that I have come without additional dress, comb, powder etc. Arrive in Wilmslow at 12.40, to be met by Swanee. Geoff is as pompous as ever. Spend the afternoon buying necessities that I've come without, and after tea Geoff conducts us on a Tour over The Bog. To my relief we go to the flicks after this, to see Charles Laughton in *The Hunchback of Notre Dame.* Very good.

Saturday, August 24th: Swanee and I took a trip into Manchester this morn, shop-gazing. After lunch at Lewis's we caught the train to Stockport and met Geoff. The afternoon we spent trailing around a huge market. After tea we again visited the flicks. After we had returned, my heart missed a beat when I heard a faint sound – the sirens. Swanee and Geoff however took it most calmly and we just sat about and talked until the All Clear went about an hour later.

Sunday, August 25th: Geoff kindly offered to take me for a walk round Wilmslow while Swanee prepared the dinner, so I was trailed for miles and miles, Geoff pointing out houses all the way and telling me what their rates were (he works in the Rating Office).

Monday, August 26th: Swanee and I go to Manchester again in search of a coat for me, but find nothing I like. We go once more to the flicks at night.

Tuesday, August 27th: Rise with the lark but with reluctance also and catch 8.35 home. Arrive in time for dinner, bath and ride up to Auntie Nell's.

Wednesday, August 28th: Another raid – and glory, what a night! Awakened by bombs about 10.30, so troop downstairs. Spend my time crawling up to bed during moments of peace, down again at the sound of bombs, into the cellar when the aeroplanes are overhead and up when they have passed over. Finally crawl back to bed when the All Clear goes about 4. Learn that bombs have fallen at Hartshorne.

Thursday, August 29th: Time bombs have fallen at Hartshorne, so 31 families have had to be evacuated. Accordingly, when Joyce and I set forth on the way to Nottingham for a few days, the bus takes a different way, avoiding Hartshorne, and the driver gets lost and has to go back part of the way.

Glorious day and a lovely journey, but see houses with their windows smashed in Long Eaton and hear that there have been casualties. Two houses have been demolished there. View Chilwell Ordnance Factory as we go through, and am pleased I don't live there. Would seem like living on the edge of a volcano, I should think.

Meet Barbara in Nottingham, and after lunch we go to the Ritz to see *The Invisible Man Returns*. After this we have tea at the Mikado, then to Mapperley, where we have supper. After this we get everything ready for the raid, and place warm dressing gowns etc over the banisters where they will be easily accessible. In the midst of these preparations, loud bangings are heard downstairs, then the voice of an air-raid warden tells Barbara ferociously that the house is Ablaze with Light. At this we extinguish every light in the building and stumble into bed in complete darkness. See flashes in the sky as we do so, and hear enemy planes, but no sirens sound so we fall asleep. Much to our amazement we sleep all night undisturbed.

Friday, August 30th: Spend the day in Nottingham prowling round the shops, and I buy a few oddments such as belts and bath cubes. After tea we go to the Empire to see a Variety Show. Not bad. Catch a bus back to Mapperly. We are just alighting about 9 p.m. when we are galvanised into action by the early sound of the sirens. A couple in front of us promptly take to their heels and disappear down the road like fleeing stags and we follow suit. Hear Joyce panting in the rear. Arrived at Mrs Watts, Barbara's neighbour, we go straight to the cellar, where we find Mr and Mrs Adams and their twelve-year-old daughter, June, already assembled in deck-chairs and looking very comfortable. Another man and his wife are upstairs too, and every time they come into the cellar with their dog, Mr Adams looks peeved and remarks when they are gone that That Dog Smells and asks sulk-ily and unreasonably Why They Can't Go Home. Hear all sorts of activity in the air, bombs and gunfire, and a most awful screech as a screaming bomb drops. Then Mr Watts comes dash-ing into the cellar telling us to come up and look – it's worth seeing. We go, and see that we are ringed by fires that make the night as bright as day. A hundred incendiary bombs have been dropped in a field across the road, but the fires are all under control within half an hour. We hear the fire engines hard at work. The woman with the dog says gloomily that He Can See His Target Now – we shall all be Wiped Out.

The minutes drag on – we get colder and colder and shift about in our seats to try to find a comfortable position. We talk, then listen, then giggle, then talk again, and Mr Adams glues his nose to a book for about two hours. At 2 a.m. we have a cheering interlude in the shape of tea and biscuits, and begin to tell each other that it Won't Be Long Now. Finally as we are exhausted and frozen, the All Clear sounds at 4.10 a.m. We are jubilant, but wearily so. We finally crawl into bed about 5 a.m.

Saturday, August 31st: Oh so weary today. And such a hot day! Get up at 9, have lunch in Nottingham, and Joyce and I catch the 1.05 p.m. bus home. Every little place from Nottingham to Castle Donington shows signs of the night's raid – windows out, roads blocked, buildings down, tiles off etc. Buildings were shattered not 100 yards from Chilwell Ordnance Factory – someone's aim was nearly a bull! Glory, what a bang there would have been!

Bath and wash my hair and have it set when I arrive home. Go to bed just after 7, to get some sleep, before the sirens sound at 12.30. Sit up till 2.30, then go back to bed. The All Clear goes about three-quarters of an hour later. Hear planes but no bangs, thank goodness!

Monday, September 2nd: The time bomb at Hartshorne is now 24 ft in the ground and still hasn't gone off!

This sad and dreadful day has come to pass at last – school once more, after the most mingy little holiday. Feel ready for another already. Have a new class – 47 children – so spend the day settling in. Our new head has been appointed – Miss

Howard – who, I fear, will prove a Tartar. She looks very august, stately and unbending, so the future looks very uninviting. At the moment, Trissie is fluttering importantly about in charge, until she comes.

Two lots of sirens tonight – one from 10 till about 1.30, and the next from about 2.15 for about an hour. My father's friend Mr Shaw is staying with us this week, so that he can get some sleep. They're getting none in Birmingham. However he spends the night prowling round and saying that he is enjoying it, and he refuses to go to bed.

Tuesday, September 3rd: The first anniversary of the war. It seems to have been going on for ages. I wonder how many more anniversaries there will be.

Glorious hot, sunny day. Much too nice to go to school, but potter off to the usual grind. Joyce and Ivy call for me to go to the flicks, but far too fine and sunny, so bike to tennis instead. Hear a German plane go over as we are playing. Dither and suggest we finish, but the others insist on continuing. Retire to bed expecting the sirens, but we have the first peaceful night for over a fortnight.

Saturday, September 7th: To Derby by bus with Mother, Auntie N, Ivy and Joyce. A glorious day and a lovely ride, through Hartshorne, so we conclude that their bomb must either have exploded or been put out of action. Most of the balloons around the town are only a few feet up, and look colossal as we ride by. Wander around in search of material for a coat – can't afford to buy one this year. Can't get my cherished blue at all, so feel very peeved. Leave the others still shopping so that I can go to tennis.

Another raid alarm, from 12.30, but only stay up for an hour. Not much doing here, thanks be! Ethel B says that Swanee is getting it in Wilmslow now. They had an awful raid the day I left and have had them ever since. They have had about 18 bombs in the village – and lots of delayed-action ones among them.

Sunday, September 8th: A day of national prayer – and we need it too! A dreadful raid on London yesterday, from 6.30 intermittently until 8 and then from 8.30 till after 5 this morning. 400 are killed and over 1300 seriously injured – and those are only approximate figures. Oh dear! How dreadful. Church packed – lots of people appear for the first time in years, I should think.

Letter from Dougie – he has to go for his medical next week, and is fattening up a young cockerel for me for Christmas.

Auntie Nell imparts scandalous and shocking news about Miss Foster, to the effect that it isn't a school she has gone to but a maternity home!!! Oh dear! Can I really believe that it can be true?

Monday, September 9th: Another dreadful air bombardment of London, for 9 or 10 hours. From 200 to 300 killed and about 1000 or more seriously injured. Oh how dreadful! Really autumnal today. Brown leaves fluttering about, and a bright morning with a nip in the air. Quite frosty at night too, with a bright yellow moon – of ill-omen these days, when it heralds fresh air onslaughts.

Three air-raid warnings before midnight tonight, but all very short, and none after 12, so a comparatively peaceful night – for us!

Tuesday, September 10th: Oh dear! Another raid from 8 p.m. till 5.30 a.m. in London last night. They're bombing indiscriminately now. It seems terrible.

Wednesday, September 11th: Go to an NUT meeting – the first in many moons, but there is a free tea provided, so make an effort to go. Quite a sumptuous meal of fruit and cream, scones and cakes etc. All listen in to the Prime Minister's speech at 6 – a warning that invasion may be imminent, and a call to every man and woman to stand firm . . . How ominous!

Rest of the meeting very boring – just to welcome the Southend teachers who have been evacuated here. Left to go to tennis, then changed my mind as it didn't seem worth it to go at 7. It begins to get dark at 7.30 now. Night raids on London still continuing in their intensity.

Have to get up at 11.45 but nothing doing so return to bed and the All Clear goes about an hour later.

Thursday, September 12th: Oh dear! Have a mouldy sore throat and my dear little tonsils have come up like footballs. Delay going to Grandma's. Grandma is cultivating a habit of Great Meanness, which is both annoying and amusing. She makes us sit until it is too dark even to see each other, before she'll put on the light, and she won't have a fire for our comfort during the raids.

Mrs Merchant is at Grandma's – declaiming viciously and at length about the Germans. They make her feel That Evil, she says – she'd like to have a Pitchfork to run into them. Had an air-raid warning from 11.30 to 3, but I slept through it quite peacefully. Nothing disturbing occurred.

Saturday, September 14th: Jack W has had his papers and has to go on Monday to Sheffield on the anti-aircraft. He came down with Ivy to see us tonight.*

Monday, September 16th: Go with Joyce and Ivy to Salts and buy a pair of black suede boots with lambswool lining in readiness for the winter. To Grandma's quite early – about 8 o'clock, and

*Ivy is the wife of (cousin) Jack, not to be confused with the girlfriend of George.

the sirens go about 8.15. The All Clear goes about 10, so we retire peacefully.

Tuesday, September 17th: Very windy – a lashing gale tears around the countryside, but comfort ourselves with the assurance that perhaps it will keep Him away. 'He' is unspecified but nevertheless understood. Spend the evening at the flicks with Delia. We see Leslie Banks trying to be funny with a large assortment of hats as the Police Detective Inspector in *The Arsenal Stadium Mystery* – wherein the real Arsenal team features and is therefore considered a great attraction. It is all very involved and I don't know quite who did it or how, or why. The second picture is really straightforward – a proper roaring rampaging cowboy film, featuring Hopalong Cassidy with his white hair, and black suit and white horse. As usual he routs all the desperadoes.

No raids or sirens tonight, but learn later that attacks have been more intense than ever over London. Bourne & Hollingsworth, D. H. Evans, and John Lewis have all been hit and many dwelling houses in the SE.

Wednesday, September 18th: Find that I have a lump on my neck – hope it's from my sore throat and nothing more! Have visions of Infirmaries and Operations. Mrs M pops into Grandma's during the course of the evening and declares that an airman called Jim in Spondon has prophesied that the war will be over by Christmas! From this she switches quite irrelevantly to remember that on the day she became engaged she had Pork Chops for Dinner.

Have to submit to my lump's being doctored with most vile and noxious-smelling goose grease. Have it swathed around in warm layers, then ooze miserably to bed reeking of grease. The sirens perform their nightly solo round about one, whereat I trot downstairs, gulp down a cup of tea, then decide to retire again, but the All Clear goes within an hour and we hear nothing awful.

Thursday, September 19th: A bomb has been dropped at a hall near Netherseal, says report, but it has only made a crater in the lawn, and it serves the owner right, because she would persist in showing lights. Just retribution!

Have my striped frock fitted, and learn on my return that the spasmodic Freddie has rung up to say that he will take me to tennis. He does – before I have washed, so he has to kick his heels in impatience, while I perform my toilet. He asserts that I am not sufficiently grateful for his bringing me to tennis. I remind him with sarcasm that he only brought me in case no one else had arrived! At this he chuckles.

Home by about 8.30, and the sirens go just before 9. Strange reaction to the alarm – we all look at each other and giggle. The All Clear sounds before 10. Bombardment on London still continues.

Friday, September 20th: The photographer – a funny little man with a smirk – invades the school and tells us all in turn to smile. We all try desperately hard to look as beautiful as possible.

Saturday, September 21st: Decide to have the blue coat I saw in the Jaeger shop in Nottingham, so phone Barbara to inquire the price. She does – 11 guineas! Too cheap! Wouldn't dream of wearing such a Common Garment.

Go with Joyce and Ivy at 1 o'clock to the Ritz to see Rex Harrison in *Night Train to Munich* – very good and thrilling Secret Service stuff, in which dear little Rex outwits the German SS, Storm Troopers and Gestapo in toto. Naughton and Wayne – as the two old school Englishmen who discuss cricket when the nation's fate hangs in the balance – are very good. Struggle through a crowded Boots café then and just manage to find a table.

Find there's a seething mass of people waiting in queues for the buses. We tack ourselves on to the extreme end of one and gaze despairingly along the length of it. However, we move forwards by degrees, and finally leave the park after three-quarters of an hour's wait. The one topic of conversation on the bus seems to be whether we'll get home before the sirens go. We do. They don't go till about 12, and only for a very short time – not enough to disturb our rest very much.

Wednesday, September 23rd: An evacuee ship has been torpedoed and over 80 children drowned. Oh dear! How ghastly! The horrible creatures! I hope the commander of that submarine has it on his conscience for the rest of his days.

Listen to the King's speech at 6. He speaks quite well. Hear the All Clear faintly through the wireless as he speaks.

Tuesday, September 24th: The dear Freddie phones to say Am I Doing Anything and would I like to go to the flicks? Ask him tartly if he's sure *he* isn't doing anything, whereat he says he hopes I haven't any more sarcasm to offer him and as a matter of fact he particularly wants to take me . . . Hmm! We go to see *Mr Smith Goes to Washington* – quite good. My sarcasm has evidently done the dear fellow good – he lavishes a box of chocolates (small) upon me and also asks if I'd like an ice. Nearly swoon from shock. Seem to spend the evening munching. He becomes skittish and tells me that I'll put on weight, ha ha! Produce an answering but sardonic ha! but continue munching.

Cold when we emerge, so he lavishes his scarf upon me – once more wilt beneath this attention and stifle a gasp of amazement. He then tells me under ban of secrecy and after much persuasion what a London detective has said – that the Londoners are ready to pack up, and that the women are terrified when night comes. Oh dear! But no wonder!

Start off homewards and discover that all the traffic lights are out, and can see no cars with their headlights on. Begin to dither and think that the sirens have gone, but we arrive home safely to find that they haven't, much to my relief.

Wednesday, September 25th: Butter rations are to be reduced again – to 2 ounces a week. Oh glory! I'd rather cut down on anything before butter. After many moons of silence the neglectful Swan deigns to write. Since I left they have had only two peaceful days – they have had air-raid warnings day and night alike and had 28 bombs dropped on Wilmslow three days after my departure. The night I left they had a dreadful raid. But she seems quite cheerful about it all – and is spending lavishly on her winter outfit.

Bill is now in Egypt, after a luxurious passage on a converted liner complete with swimming pool.

Short warning from about 9 till 9.30, but nothing untoward occurs, and we have yet another night of peace.

Thursday, September 26th: The first WEA English lecture tonight. We seem inundated by Southenders, who make me silently annoyed by trying to run the meeting and dictate the syllabus. They are all plain to look at. One large female next to me with a heavy jowl, spectacles, and straight wisps of untended hair, staggers me by a reference to her husband. Would never have credited her with such an acquisition. We decide – to my silent disgust – against the proposed Art of Expression, and choose a course similar to last year's.

Enjoy a supper of potatoes roasted in their skins, with lots of butter. Mother reads from the *Mirror* the lurid tale of a German who deserted his young wife and baby – to come back apparently to rain bombs on both. A pack of lies, I consider. Our *Telegraph* has been unobtainable for the last few days.

Letter from Dougiedear. More news of bombs dropped in and around Ely – two dropped 200 yards from dear Dougie himself. Both he and Gags have passed their medical A1. He ends by remarking, 'Well, I'll just go and get ready for the next siren which is due, and don't forget to write soon, yours very sincerely, Doug.'

A quiet night again, though planes were heard cruising around during the night.

Friday, September 27th: Friday and a pay-day too! These two pleasing facts combine to produce in me a pleasant state of exhilaration.

Out to tea with Amy – so call to see Mrs Swan en route. She says that Geoff has been called up and goes tomorrow, to Foremark Hall, so Swanee is packing up and coming home. Another home disrupted.

Saturday, September 28th: Betake myself to a rendezvous with Miss Tooth in Burton. Over tea she shows me photographs of Bert, herself and Bert (studio), and Bert's sister's wedding, and tells me all about Bert in the Marines. References to Bert are plentifully sprinkled throughout the conversation, and she announces that she is going to do her duty Like a Soldier, and visit Bert's parents next weekend. Not that she wants to, she adds. She says she is a Stoic.

The usual long wait in the bus park, but I reach home at 8, an hour before the sirens sound. Only a quarter of an hour's warning, and another little one round about 3. Don't get up. Huddle further into bed when the planes go over. Start violently when the All Clear sounds, then relax, and sink into sleep once more.

Monday, September 30th: Awake from undisturbed slumbers and am soon plunged into school and the common task again – to the accompaniment of many groans.

Bike to Mrs W's after school to have my greeny-blue dress tried on. Am having a high, straight neckline and pink corded ribbon round the belt and the hem. Mrs W groans when she sees the ribbon and says Why Do I Always have All My Dresses Made Alike? Realise the futility of replying.

Amy comes down in exuberant spirits, seemingly, to say Goodbye. She goes to Goldsmiths tomorrow, now evacuated to Nottingham. Only hope she has as good a time as I did. Mrs Tweed also comes down, in great tribulation because Amy goes tomorrow, and Bob into the Army, near Bath, on Thursday. Poor Mrs Tweed – she is very upset, and weeps in spasms.

Tuesday, October 1st: A telephone call for me during tea from the False Fred who seems, I fear, to be waxing affable again. As soon as he inclines towards a rapprochement, I instinctively sheer off. I wonder why it is. If only he were cool, and referred continually to Girl Friends in Hull and the like, he'd find me far more friendly than when he warms towards me. I'm made strangely that way. Anyhow, he rings up to invite me to the flicks, so as I am eager to see *Rebecca*, I say I'll go. When we get inside and are seated, I have a fit and palpitations, because he says he's got Cold Hands tonight, and I think for one ghastly moment that he's said he's come to Hold Hands tonight. Would rather die than flirt with dear old Freddie. Watch the film with absorption, while dear Freddie makes flippant remarks which I choose to ignore. Chocolates fail to materialise. To my amazement, Freddie takes my arm as we go to the car, but suffer this in silence and hold it rigid and unyielding. He offers to let me (a) hunt mushrooms in their fields (b) go to Manchester with him to see Swanee the next time he visits his relatives there and (c) go with him to Blackpool for our week's holiday at the end of this month. Recoil in inward horror from the latter suggestion and treat it as a joke, and add for his enlightenment that Mother wouldn't dream of letting me go, to which he replies that she would if he talked to her. Ridicule this idea with all the scorn at my disposal, so he says Ah well, perhaps he'll go on odd outings, instead of to Blackpool. Leave him with relief.

Wednesday, October 2nd: Mrs W sends my new greeny-blue dress, and I garb myself in same ready for the Church Sale of Work. Feel very fetching in it. Keep my coat over it in school so that I shan't excite comment, and to keep it clean. The Sale of Work is dull as dishwater.

Meet Betty Dinnis at 5.30, and set off for Geary for the Presentation. Toil on foot, pushing our bikes up Springfield Road and have just reached the top when we stop dead, listen, and exclaim together, first in horror, then in disgust, then in unwilling mirth, 'The Sirens!'. We turn ourselves about and journey homewards. Am just rounding the doorway when the All Clear goes. Comment is needless.

Night of peace. Loud and fervent thanksgiving.

Thursday, October 3rd: Trail along to Swanee's to tea, and stay till about 9 o'clock. She seems quite cheerful at the thought of being without Geoff – no cooling of the air with sighs for her! Instead she is very brisk and hearty, and tells me that she suffered from acute indigestion for three days and could eat nothing, but when Geoff's papers came for joining up, she was better immediately. Perhaps the shock, she suggests! Though an unkind observer might suggest other reasons. After all, she says, she's only lived with him for a year, so it won't be a hardship to be without him! She's hardly ecstatic about him, to say the least – she might even be called Sublimely Indifferent. Have to walk home in inky darkness. Glory! What a night – and wet too. Learn that Delia has got the job she went after yesterday on the Wirral, so she'll be nearer home.

Saturday, October 5th: I am penniless – the result of a shopping expedition to Derby. Set off with Auntie Nell on the twenty to ten bus in bright morning sunshine. The countryside looks very peaceful – no signs of war except a few broken windows, a house with one side missing just outside Derby, and quite a fair sprinkling of khaki everywhere. Wander along to Bracegirdles, where I feel very insignificant, as usual, though I tell myself before we go to Feel Superior to the assistants. Those exotic, black-robed creatures make me feel Shabby, whatever I'm wearing, and so do the long mirrors that loom in every corner of the place. We are shown a mouldy selection of coats for 5½ guineas – decline to try any on because I know I hate them all. Find a hat shop and manage to get a very chic-looking black hat. Return to Bracegirdles and decide to plunge on a lemon-fawn camel hair coat with suede buttons and belt and slit pockets, though it is 9½ guineas! Still, quiet my conscience by telling myself that it will wear and wear – I'm afraid it will have to! Have the coat fitted for alterations, and they promise to send it. Have lunch at Boots, dive round the Midland Drapery and catch the bus at 2.

Parade in my new headgear when I arrive home – it is greeted with jeers. My father says we only want half-a-dozen rubber balls and we've got a grand Aunt Sally.

No sirens.

Monday, October 7th: Trissie, looking very worried, informs us that she has heard of someone visiting Miss Foster. The unknown reports her to be living in two rooms and expecting the Happy Event at the end of next month.

George P who used to work for my father, looking very smart in Air Force uniform, descends upon us at dinnertime, while he is home on leave. He states that there have been four attempts at invasion – one from Scotland, one from Merseyside, and two from the south. He says that at the latter the Germans lost 60,000 men, and that was a fortnight ago, because they were all called out for 56 hours and saw the naval guns pounding away. He also spoke to a young German pilot, who gave in without a blow, bringing with him an attaché case containing hair oil etc.

Visit from Ivy at teatime, resplendent in her new winter coat made by Mrs W and a beautiful fit. Immediately feel dissatisfied with my own that I paid so much for. Wish I'd waited and had one made – it would have been much cheaper and would have looked equally as well.

Wednesday, October 9th: Tearing gale all day. Carry home with me the results of the photographer's visit, 4 photographs of me – one good, 2 indifferent and one bad – I am screwing up my nose and baring my teeth in a large grin, so I am forced to the conclusion that I must look like that on occasion, however much I prefer to believe otherwise.

Saturday, October 12th: Oh dear! I'll be glad when pay-day comes. I have 2/6 to live on until then.

Mr Skerritt warns me not to leave my diary about, so I gather he has caught someone prying. Some dishonest creature with no idea of *meum* and *tuum* apparently!

A quiet day. Am reading *The Code of the Woosters* – very funny. A letter arrives from Dougie this morn, couched in the usual vein, and composed entirely of references to bombs and bombing and with the usual kindly adjuration at the end to take no risks. Am as much concerned about the health of my cockerel as anything, but Dougie omits to tell me how it is faring. Think I'll advise him to keep it in a bomb-proof shelter. Wouldn't want my Christmas dinner to get bombed. He says that the 'blinkin' post' gets worse and worse, my letter having taken 5 days to arrive, 'but we can't expect any other in wartime'. I shall omit to tell him that the letter reposed on our mantelpiece for about 5 days after it was written. His cousin Bert has had a narrow escape. He was sleeping in barracks in London when a 2000 lb bomb 8 ft long came crashing through the roof and buried itself 36 ft in the earth – without exploding. Gosh!

Sunday, October 13th: The Germans have marched into Romania – wish they'd march into the sea and forget to march out.

Wednesday, October 16th: Very bad raid on London again last night and on one town in the Midlands, presumably Coventry. To the flicks with Joyce to see Ralph Richardson and Diana Wynyard in *On the Night of the Fire* – very good, though very pathetic. Very mild and stormy night – torrents of rain, though this does not deter Adolf's brood, who buzz over the country on their flights of destruction.

Thursday, October 17th: Wend my way to the English lecture upon the works of Arnold Bennett. Still haven't perused the noble work. Sit by the massive married woman with the lank hair and the baby – she has too much flesh and heaves slightly as she breathes. She says Do I think she could bring Baby in the pram if her husband gets moved? He's a Good Baby, she adds. Am rather nonplussed and say discreetly I Should Think So.

A peaceful night.

Friday, October 18th: Delia blows in from an expedition to Burton about 9.30, explaining that there is something 'fishy' about tonight – all the traffic lights are out, police wherever she turned, stopping all cars. She suspects parachutists. Letter from Eric. He says that stacks of rumours fly about their camp – even in the officers' quarters – and refers to one very hair-raising one that he wouldn't like to believe, but doesn't specify precisely – or even vaguely – what it is. Imagination therefore plays wildly upon all sorts of possibilities.

Saturday, October 19th: There are to be no more silk stockings after Dec 1st. And I've only one pair to my name and no money to buy any more. I am now £2.14.3 in debt, and 4*d.* in hand.

Take my last few shekels and rake off – as my father would say – to Burton, for my rendezvous with Hilda T. We see *Pinocchio* – oh, lovely! Really very very clever – marvellous, in fact. I do admire Walt Disney – he must have a wonderful imagination to create such dear little things as Pinocchio, Figaro the Kitten and the coy lady-goldfish, and Jiminy Cricket, whom I admire most of all. The colours are beautiful.

Sunday, October 20th: Am in such desperate straits financially that I am in that dire position when I cast a speculative eye around, wondering what I may pawn. If I am seen wandering hatless to church, it will be understood that I have made the Great Sacrifice and pawned The Plate – not the family plate, but the milliner's one.

Read in the Sunday paper that the best way to keep fit and the complexion clear is to Drink Water, lots and lots of water, at all hours of the day. So in future I intend to do this.

The Purchase Tax – 1/3 more added to the wholesale price of goods – goes on tomorrow. I want stacks of things that I can't afford until we're paid – by which time they will all have risen to colossal prices.

Managed to gulp down 2 extra glasses of water today. Have the sirens from 9–12.30, but go to bed at 11, despite the hosts of planes buzzing overhead.

Monday, October 21st: Rise to find that I have 3 pimples in a row across my forehead. Huh! Mentally compose a narky letter to the mendacious Health Expert in the *Sunday Graphic*. Still, decide to give it a longer trial, so get a glass of water at playtime and painfully lower it into my innards.

Wild tales in circulation today say that the parachutists have been seen bobbling from the clouds, and bombs have been heard not far off – about noon. Lord Haw Haw is also reported to have warned Derby to expect a Pasting this week.

Tuesday, October 22nd: This morning we are performing our daily tasks in the usual dutiful, and conscientious, not to say inspired manner, and then the Sword of Damocles falls. In the middle of the morning, about 11.20, the sirens begin to wail. Start up in horror and consternation on this first occasion in schooltime. The children yelp, 'Sirens!' and begin to perform their capers. I vainly bellow 'Sh! Quiet! Silence!' and other intimations for them to 'Pipe down'. Meanwhile, with frenzied fingers, I unlock the back door. We all scramble up the bank towards the shelters – a feat as difficult as climbing the greasy pole, after the recent rains. Big Miss Smith succumbs to the mud and gracefully falls headlong, taking a mud bath in the process. After much bellowing and poking, we find ourselves seated on our benches in the shelter, while I unearth the torches and distribute them over the length of the shelter. Once more in frenzied tones I call for silence and at length compose my flock. They are not in the least frightened, but merely very excited, very turbulent, and very happy at this departure from the normal routine. I read a story to them by the light of my bicycle lamp – but all I can see of them are shadowy forms and the indistinguishable pale ovals that are their faces. After this we sing two songs, then the gathering begins to get uproarious, so I hastily begin another story, then we have a sweet each to suck. Having quietened the mob in this Machiavellian manner, I rise to my feet and tell the children that we have been in the shelters three-quarters of an hour, and at this precise moment a head is poked round the door, and a voice announces that the All Clear has gone. So we troop down, and out, and home, much to my relief.

Hear during the course of the afternoon that we are to receive 800 London homeless mothers and children tomorrow, so the schools are to be closed while we yank them round to their billets (if any!), and a meeting of billeting officers is called for 5.15 p.m. Present myself at the Town Hall with Miss S and Delia, and see the rest of the local teaching profession assembled there. The meeting lasts until 6.30.

Wednesday, October 23rd: No school today. Consequently rise in a leisurely fashion about 9 a.m. A murky morning – cold, with a drizzle of rain in the wind – so stay indoors by the fire.

Canter along to the Town Hall after dinner, and sit about in groups in that depressing edifice, awaiting the coming of the homeless. The minutes drag by; the groups continually fluctuate and change, grow restless, then settle down to gossip again. Every time the door opens all heads turn that way, expecting the homeless. They arrive about 4 – all mothers with families of anything up to 5 young children each. Trissie achieves a master-stroke by billeting what looked like an impossibility – a mother and her tribe of 5. She tucks them into a remote spot in the wilds of Cadley Hill. Wander about, but can find no unaccompanied children to billet, so after helping with luggage, drift home for a late tea about 5.30.

Delia saunters in with her knitting and we discuss the day's events. Fierce argument between my father and Miss Sanders upon the general situation.

Thursday, October 24th: To school as usual this morn, but only to be turned back when we get there, because there are, report says, stacks of women still unbilleted at Gresley and some also at Hill Street. We groan in spirit and wend our way to Hill Street, where the most impossible situation exists – a group of about 10 or 12, refusing to be separated but demanding a house, and two sisters with their families who weep at the thought of separation. Also a deaf woman, and one who speaks nothing but Belgian. Manage after a long and tedious struggle to separate the two sisters, and billet one in my area. As soon as we get her there and her hostess opens the door, the small boy Ronnie starts to howl and yelp and scream that he wants to Go 'ome, and the baby, hitherto quiet, starts to howl in sympathy. The boy runs off, with the hostess in pursuit, and I leave them with no little relief. Then home for dinner. After this we get them all billeted, so off to Gresley to help there. A most dejected scene – lots of unbilleted women and children looking weary, untidy, and fed up but some of them grimly refusing to be separated, while others are ready to go anywhere. Miss Peat and I bike to the top of Springfield Rd after a possible billet, then back, and after this trail wearily home. Collapse exhausted, with a face sore from the cold wind.

Friday, October 25th: To be or not to be is the question that trembles fearfully on the lips of the Springfield Road staff on this, their morn of breaking up. In other words – shall we be Paid? The cheque comes, we draw our meagre due, our faces are wreathed in smiles as we sign on the dotted line. Then we break up for our week's holiday. Unfortunately have to hand over some £3 in debts on my arrival home.

Bella tells us that all the evacuees aren't billeted yet and have had to spend another night in that smelly chapel schoolroom, so this is their second day without a wash. But the council has commandeered certain empty houses for them to use, and is now having to face storms from irate householders. Still, they must be put somewhere. But some of them are not at all grateful. When Miss T offered to house a woman and her three children and to allow them three rooms for themselves, the woman expected hot and cold water laid on in the bedrooms, and left when she found it wasn't.

Another letter from Dougie – just a replica of many that have gone before. The latest bombs there have hit a celery patch. Dougie has seen one of the pilots try to bail out only to find that his parachute wouldn't open. He adds grimly that I can imagine his fate. Prefer not to. He ends this by exhorting me to take care of myself, and to 'keep clear of the bombs'. I don't need telling!

Take my camel hair to Mrs W's to have an inch off the hem, then go to the Majestic with Swanee to see Arthur Askey in *Charley's Aunt*.

Sunday, October 27th: It is now One Week since I read about the wonderfully restorative qualities of water. Since then I have drenched my tonsils with water. My diaphragm has become worn by the daily passage of this estimable liquid. With what result – three Pimples and a Foul Cold. Huh!

Monday, October 28th: Oh glory! What a long and enervating day. Awake, feeling muzzy and thick-headed from my cold, and get up late, which makes me feel worse. Sit huddled over the fire, pitying myself with the utmost compassion. Manage to tear myself away while I chew a moody mouthful of dinner, and take advantage of the wrench not to return until I have fulfilled a promise to get four blankets for the evacuees I billeted. Once out in the open air I feel a little better.

We are reduced to sardines and margarine for tea – dreadful plight.

Go to Grandma's early. We are just about to sit down when the sirens go, but after the first start of surprise we carry on as though nothing has happened. Italy has declared war on Greece today. Soon the whole world will be at war. And this is 1940, and we are civilised human beings – or so we say! What a world! Still, I suppose it isn't the world that is to blame, but the people in it.

Tuesday, October 29th: Go to Burton and buy some blue ribbon and a pair of thick crepe-soled shoes for the winter. Display these with defensive pride when I arrive home, anticipating the reception they will invoke. It comes. My mother remarks that she doesn't know what I've bought Those Things for; she doesn't like them At All; she likes Dainty Shoes; I can't wear those on Sunday; I'd better ask Mrs Davies to knit me a Pair of Woollen Stockings to go with them (this with deadly sarcasm). My father approves, however, and says they are Sensible (the highest praise he could offer).

Thursday, October 31st: My father and I go to the Majestic to see *Raffles*. Arrive to find the box office, surrounded by a little knot of people, not open. So we prowl disconsolately round, and I spot a small notice on Mr McCann's door, to say that *Raffles* has not yet arrived. My father, never very enthusiastic from the start, thereupon announces his intention of returning home. However, Mr McCann strides in with important step that minute, exclaiming to my father that he has *Raffles* with him – he's had to fetch it from Walsall – two air raids on the way – machine gunning in the streets – and with this he disappears into his sanctum, so we go into the pictures, where Mother joins us some minutes later. *Raffles* is awfully good.

Friday, November 1st: Mrs H comes through the rain to our back door to return her billeting form, her three evacuees having departed for London again today. She remarks grimly that she has never before had such a week. 'Idle?' I suggest, to which she retorts, 'Idle! Huh! *And* dirty!' etc, etc, 'And the *lad*! A *dreadful* child.'

We make our nightly migration through the wet blackness to Grandma's, where Auntie sits knitting the back of my jumper and Grandma sits poring over some absorbing and heart-throbbing drama in *Flame* or some such scorching periodical. Mr Skerritt has turned into a recluse, and is closeted in solitary confinement in his bedroom. I take up the front half of my new jumper and begin to plough grimly on. We hear an aeroplane of sorts, but nothing happens, thanks be.

Monday, November 4th: School again – a return to the prison house, and under what conditions! Rain, relentless and remorseless. It gushes down all day, and I have to rise in darkness, bike through the driving wetness, and apply myself to the daily grind once more – with groans. And still it rains, so the morning never seems to get light. Just before playtime Miss Smith comes tearing along the corridor, banging frantically at the windows as she comes, and she skids into the room panting, 'Whistle! Whistle!' palpitating visibly. Eye her warily, suspecting a sudden seizure or a brainstorm. She gasps, 'Sirens! The sirens are going.' This galvanises us all into action. We fling open the door, clamber up the greasy bank, slide over the grass through the driving rain and to the shelter. Shelter? Huh! I beg its pardon. More like an indoor swimming pool. A calm, placid expanse of water greets our eyes as we open the door – a pond, some 4 or 5 inches deep. Fall back in horror, hesitate, and we all get soaked but see the other classes being remorselessly herded into their refuge, so drive my class into ours. Splash, splash! We wade in, and sit with the water up to our ankles. A mad idea! The noise is deafening so bellow like a bull until I am hoarse, order the children to tuck their toes under the forms, and the noise subsides a little. After ten minutes of this agony, we return, and have to endure three-quarters of an hour of composition before going home. I feel as though I am just returning from 6 months' hard labour at Pentonville, instead of one day at school. And it is still raining viciously.

Home to find Mrs Tweed by the fireside. She reads us the latest editions of war and college news, in the shape of letters from Bob and Amy both doing well in their different spheres. The conversation then drifts back to the war. Mrs Tweed states that after a raid in Birmingham you could pick up arms and legs in the streets – then, as if that were not enough, she adds with gruesome emphasis that They Carried Fifty-Seven Dead Bodies out of a Cinema there. We try to guide her talk into less depressing channels. She departs about 7.30, and we trail up to Grandma's with our basket of supper, books and knitting.

Tuesday, November 5th: Bonfire Day, but the bangs, flashes, flames and whatnot are prohibited this year as the Germans are supplying them free, with their compliments.

A circular arrives from Derby decreeing that from the end of November until the lighter mornings, we start school at 9.30. My goodness! I bet it caused them spasms of acute agony to put their hand to such a document. They hate us to have any extra free time, and are perfectly in their element when they wrest our holidays from us, and pile on us extra work.

Wednesday, November 6th: Decide to sacrifice my evening on the altar of the mauve cardigan, so settle myself comfortably by the fire, feet in the fender, and knitting in hand. Ply the pins assiduously for some two or three rows, when they are arrested by the sound of an abrupt knock on the door. It is opened, and there stands the Faithless Fred, reappearing after some weeks' absence with a fatuous smile. He remarks by way of explanation, that he is on the way to Burton, and wondered if I would like to go with him. Ask redundantly if he is going to the pictures, knowing full well that he is. I throw on a hat and coat and we depart. We see an English detective story – improbable but not too bad. Find myself wondering anxiously, with an eye on the clock after 8 p.m., whether the sirens will tootle, and if so what we'll do. But they don't, and we arrive home in safety. Manage to get in 4 rows of the neglected Mauve Cardigan before bed.

Thursday, November 7th: The usual type of letter from Dougie, beginning with bombs and ending with the wonted adjuration to take care of myself. This, and a chunk in the middle about dances in the locality that end with brawls between the Army and the RAF, compose the regulation two pages. Grandma sighs when she sees me reading it and exclaims ambiguously that it Does Seem a Pity. Wisely refrain from asking her to explain herself.

Victory is ours – the Mauve Cardigan now glitters forth in its entirety. Thread a feverish needle and begin to stitch in the sleeves with a wary eye on the first as I remember previous efforts in which I have finished with the sleeve on inside-out. And blow me! Manage to get the first in correctly, but find myself falling into the pit with the second, so have to take it out and put it in afresh. Gnash my teeth.

Mr Addison dilates upon the life and works of H. G. Wells in English. A Southend teacher exclaims dramatically that Bennett is a Pedestrian, then she pauses expectantly. Have visions of the man plodding a weary way through life without mechanical aid, but she explains after due pause that she is referring to the pace of his novels.

I quite forgot – the most important part of Dougie's letter! The cockerel is doing fine and is Quite a Big Boy now, he says. Am very relieved.

Friday, November 8th: Read an exultant article in *Time & Tide* about Mr Roosevelt's election last Tuesday to a third term of office – Mr Willkie having been defeated. It predicts almost unlimited help for Britain, and that long hoped-for eventuality – the break-up of the Nazi regime. Very optimistic. Mr R is then painted in glowing terms as 'an embodiment of generosity and humanity, of statesmanlike vision and just dealing'. My, my! I wonder if he recognises himself beneath this aura of glorification?

Pay 5/3 for a pair of new stockings from Salts', and the transaction almost breaks my heart.

The sirens sound very unexpectedly just after 7 o'clock, and catch Auntie Nell, Joyce, Renie, Brenda and Ken at our house. They dally uncertainly, envisaging bombs falling round them if they go, and a period of calm if they stay. Finally they stiffen the sinews, and summon up the blood and taking the risk, plunge out on their way to Midway. A few minutes later the All Clear sounds. Mother says Thank Goodness.

Saturday, November 9th: A journey to Derby these days is like a voyage to the unknown. Never embark upon it without fearing an impending air raid in which I am one of the severest casualties. Yet I find myself travelling serenely homewards and without mishap, each time reproaching myself for such foolish fears. Woman at the back of the bus carries on a spirited conversation with the driver, before we start, on the subject of food in wartime. She thinks that it is Wonderful what we get – lovely Bread! The driver echoes reverently, Yes, bread, lovely White Bread! This inspires the woman to a fierce indictment of those who Grouse. She would like to Hit them On the Head. Once again the driver echoes her sentiments, and they part on a basis of mutual sympathy.

Delia and I both buy a pair of shoes, then we wander round the Central Educational, where I buy *Tono Bungay* by H. G. Wells. Buy trimming for my blue dress, and Xmas cards, then we catch the 1 o'clock bus home. I love prowling round the shops. Tell myself, 'You see, nothing to fear', on the way home.

Have to set out on my travels again almost as soon as I return – this time to Burton to fetch my hat back. Have no qualms whatsoever about journeying here – then lo! We are just on the outskirts of Burton when the bus stops and an all-too-familiar wail is heard screeching through the murky afternoon air, and the word passes round the bus 'Sirens!'. Think, 'Well, my hat' but to my surprise feel no qualms or tremors, so decide not to be turned back but to proceed with my shopping. Feel very brave, and pleased with my courage as I do so. Everyone else seems to be instilled with the same idea and the streets are full of people. Buy buttons for the cardigan, wool for gloves, and fetch my hat. On my way back to the bus the All Clear goes. Feel relieved, despite my bravery.

Large headlines in tonight's local *Mail* – 'Serious Charges Against Newhall Vicar'. Large piece goes on to relate how he was drunk during the service on the day of National Prayer etc. Still, I don't think it ought to have been splashed all over the *Mail* like that. These bally news-hounds! Feelings don't matter to them so long as they get some spicy news.

Sunday, November 10th: A service of National Prayer at church today. BBC announcer regrets to report the death of Mr Neville Chamberlain, at his home last night. Poor man! Feel sorry for him now. The last two years must have been dreadful for him.

Amy is over for the weekend, running Goldsmiths College

May and Amy Tweed

still, and having a simply *marvellous* time. In her first 6 weeks she has had supper with the warden and his wife, is Group Rep and in the hockey XI. My stars! A quick mover. She'd be an asset to any firmament – only I'm afraid the other stars would be jealous. (Sounds very much as though I might be accused of the same thing, after all these remarks.) Amy departs as exuberantly as she came.

Monday, November 11th: A mouldy, murky Monday, with the usual daily downpour. As a concession to Remembrance Day, we have an extra hymn in Prayers – 'For Those in Peril on the Sea', and we end with the National Anthem. Mrs G expresses the fervent hope that Hitler doesn't find out the date of Mr Chamberlain's funeral, or he'll be sure to drop a bomb on him and blow him out of his coffin.

Freddie rings up to say What About Going to the Flicks, but tell him sorry, I've promised Delia. He says Oh and is silent. He then mumbles something about the dance on Wed. Say I don't mind, so he says All right, but if anything happens, he'll let me know. Vague.

Delia and I go to the Majestic to see wise-cracking American reporters doing their stuff in *His Girl Friday*. Not bad – but as a type of picture I dislike it. Delia and I sit and chew boiled sweets throughout, in the lowly tenpennies. Thence to Grandma's, where Mr Skerritt relates awful tales about air raids – with bombs falling on mortuaries and scattering the dead bodies on people's houses. Oh horrible!

Wednesday, November 13th: Fulfil the promise to go to the dance with Our Fred. Delia comes with us. My expectations are not belied. Spend the evening regretting going. The room is crowded to capacity, and it is no pleasure to dance, but think complacently that my dress is as nice as any in the room. I am accosted by a young man who asks for the pleasure, etc. Grant him a dance, feeling that I have made a conquest. And so we sail away. Suddenly he asks if I am still at Springfield Road School, and tells me that he earns £4 10s. at the Brewery. Think him a little premature in outlining his prospects at this early stage, but decide

to sound interested. Then he says that lots of the Old Boys are at
the brewery with him – and goes on to mention them by name.
Realise with horror that he is an erstwhile pupil, whom I once
taught at the Church School – and possibly smacked. Feel as old
as Methuselah. Oh dear! I shall have to give up dancing.

Grandma says Thank Goodness I'm Back when I return, but
fails to enlighten me further.

Thursday, November 14th: Rivalry between Miss Harvey's class
and mine has reached a pitch of great ferocity. It is hospital week,
and our two classes are racing neck and neck with our collec-
tions. To date, we are a dead draw, with a grand total of 9/- each.

My order of books arrives from The Phoenix – *The Fountain*
(Chas Morgan), *Testament of Friendship* (Vera Brittain) and the
Pick of Punch for 1940 – so gaze gloatingly upon them and put
them aside for future reading. George rings up to say that Ivy
would like to come over tomorrow, so say cordially 'Oh good!'.
Thence to the flicks to see a George Formby flick – *Let George Do
It*. We are no sooner out of the Majestic than the sirens go.
Mother immediately falls over herself to get up to Grandma's and
scrambles up the road like a hunted hare. We eat a peaceful
supper, and as nothing is happening except a few planes buzzing
about, we retire to roost. No sooner settled down than bombs
begin to thud, so I precipitate myself hastily downstairs. Calm
reigns again, so yank myself aloft and curl myself comfortably
between the sheets again. Just beginning to snooze when bump,
bump! More bombs! Dive headlong to the safety of the ground
floor again, but only to return a few minutes later. Stay up this
time, braving the sound of questionable bumps, and continuous
buzzing of the planes, and sleep well but spasmodically. Drowsily
hear Mr Skerritt's alarm clock about 7 and think half-consciously,
'Oh blow! another raid!'. The All Clear actually went at 6 a.m.

Friday, November 15th: All confusion this morn, before I set off to school, the chimney being on fire, and grim prognostications of heavy fines being made. Seen from without, the house looks like a munitions factory working full blast. News about last night's raids already filtering through – Coventry bombed by 240 planes – 1000 casualties – considerable damage. Dreadful. Also tales of more unexploded bombs at Hartshorne but these are later disclaimed. Mr Wheat tells dramatically of shrapnel from the naval guns that whizzed by his nose. He shouldn't have been out. And a man who has been on his lorry to Coventry says the pictures of Belgian refugees on the roads are nothing compared with the poor people leaving Coventry, with their pitiful little bundles and nowhere to go. Oh dear! It is simply terrible. War is so wicked and its whole machinery so relentless and deliberate once it is set in motion.

Mrs Tweed comes to tea, on her way back from Derby. She tells us how the naval guns were in action all last night, sending them scuttling into the cellar each time they opened up. But she is quite confident the enemy will never damage Derby, because the smoke screen is so effective. Glory! Wish I could think so too, but if they have penetrated London's defences, I don't think those of Derby will keep them out.

Saturday, November 16th: Dreadful tales about Thursday night's raid on Coventry are coming into circulation – 10 ambulances went out to rescue, but only two arrived, a shelter containing 500 people hit, no water, inadequate supply of ammunition, all the telegraph wires down and the post office bombed, and so on. The King has been there today.

Tuesday, November 19th: Ooze out in the early morning hours into a wall of fog, which lingers about for the rest of the day.

Sirens sound about 7.20 p.m. and we hear bumps and bangs

all around us – chiefly anti-aircraft fire from Derby, but we go to bed about 11.30. Don't sleep much – have a cold impending, which gives me a stuffy head. All Clear goes at 1.30, but we have another warning lasting till about 5.

Wednesday, November 20th: Leicester, Derby, Nottingham and Birmingham reported to have been visited by our aerial friends last night.

Delia comes down about 6.30, and the sirens sound again at 7.30. However, we take no notice, preferring to continue with our peaceful pursuits of knitting, reading and chatting. We recall with hilarity how the first note of the siren sent us scooting into the cellar like hares to their lairs at one time. We contrast this proudly with our present courageous attitude of Taking No Notice. The thought of our one-time foolish timidity moves us to no little mirth. The evening wears on – planes buzz over but we hear neither bombs nor gunfire, so about 10.30 we retire bravely to bed. Doze, wake to hear bumps and gunfire, but turn over and try to doze again. More planes, sounding very near, then there is a flash that lights up the room and, bang! A most terrific and violent explosion, accompanied by the sound of shattering glass and rattling doors. This is followed almost immediately by another deafening crash – as though a bomb had fallen in the back yard. Stop for no more bravery, but hurtle out of bed, claw on the top of the bed for my dressing gown, and dive headlong downstairs. Find that I have brought the eiderdown instead of my dressing gown, but drape it round me like an Indian squaw. Feverish activity in the house – everyone is stumbling in the dark, down the stairs, and into the cellar, shouting all at once. Grandma is heard groaning above all the confusion, and Mother blaspheming about Hitler. None of us has been inspired to lie bravely in bed, nor even to call and ask the rest what to do. Like bullets out of a gun, down into the cellar we shoot.

There on the floor lies, mildewed in patches, but recognisable in its former glory, my Lost Purple Cardigan, last seen in July. Gasp and fall upon it with a glad welcome, but everyone else is too concerned with the air raid to share in my joy. Things begin to subside, so up to the kitchen we trek once more. Wander outside, to find the street alive with men, who have popped out of their holes like worms after a shower, to investigate the extent of the damage. We find that Grandma's shop window is half out, and littered over the pavement, then see the fire engines go clanking by at great speed. Learn that most of the shop windows along High Street are out, and that the bomb has fallen just opposite Hastings Road, in Baker Street, demolishing four cottages. We immediately think of the effect it will have on all our friends and relatives. Delia would get the full force of the impact. Much activity from the region of the fire station for the rest of the night. Engines, lorries and motor bikes go hurtling by at intervals. Meanwhile we light a fire, boil the kettle, make tea, and sit round drinking it as we discuss the nocturnal activity. Each time a plane looms over, we grab the cushions and down we tumble into the cellar again. No more complacency and optimism, but rather a state of caution and preparedness. Towards 4.30 a.m. we hear another bang – about 2 or 3 miles away this time, but too close for comfort, so helter-skelter we go again. By this time Mr S and Miss S have crawled wearily back to bed, and I am feeling like something washed up on the beach by the tide. Can hardly keep my eyes open, so stumble dazedly to bed about 5 a.m., and 8 o'clock comes all too soon.

Thursday, November 21st: Awaken to hear my father telling Mr S that Wraggs' works have been hit. Think this to be an instance of my father's leg-pulling, but find it to be correct. Wraggs' works indeed hit – with a land mine that has caused a 30 foot crater and flung a truck weighing 10 tons over a nearby wall, and hurled iron girders the length of the street. Swadlincote agog this morning. Never was there so much excitement. Poor, harmless, humble little Swadlincote! Mother exclaims that she thinks the People of Swadlincote are Wonderful, in humorous imitation of the newsreels about London.

Knots of people stand in the streets, while shop assistants the length of High Street and West Street are engaged in sweeping up the shattered glass and boarding up their mutilated windows – Belfields, the Co-op, Fosters, Salts', the Food Office, the Vicarage, etc, etc.

After all this, make my way to school to turn over the matter there, and we all excitedly air what we know. Trissie affirms that they have brought the plane down. We open school, with only a quarter of the children, but learn later that the Church School and Hastings Road have not opened, because the schools were damaged. Work goes down very badly. Miss Harvey and I send notes to each other all morning to pass away the time. Give the children tables to write, yards and yards of them – poor little brats! – while I sit and snooze at my desk. Think of enacting *The Babes in the Wood*, with me in the part of the Babes, while the children shower paper on me for leaves. It would at least give me an excuse for lying down. Think we ought to have closed early, but Oh no! Hail 4 o'clock with open relief. A wet evening – downpours of rain, but they evidently preserve us from further bombing because although the siren goes at 7.15 and we hear planes and a loud bang, the All Clear sounds about 10, so we are able to go to bed and have a good night's sleep.

Friday, November 22nd: Thank goodness for Friday. Letter from Dougie yesterday, full of the latest bombs that have fallen around Ely (not literally!), but he forgets to tell me to take care of myself. Oh dear! He also omits any mention of the cockerel.

Children all trot to school clutching pieces of shrapnel, and some have parts of the parachute cord that brought the diabolic magnetic mine down. They display these with the greatest of pride. Grow a trifle weary of viewing these grim trophies by the end of the day.

Delia comes down at night, prepared to stay and suffer with us, if the sirens go, but they don't, so we all sleep peacefully and thankfully in our respective beds.

Sunday, November 24th: Panic – evacuation in progress from Birmingham, so have to go to a meeting of Billeting Officers in the Town Hall. The usual scene – dingy hall with bare patches on the wall where the plaster has flaked off, a disgrace to the town, yellow gaslight even though it is only 11 a.m., and the usual familiar faces, plus those of the councillors, who take it upon themselves to bounce to their feet, give long speeches, and then refer modestly to their Brief Words. Miss B, clad in green with a fur, sits behind us muttering that she Hasn't Come to listen to Socialist speeches, that it Bores Her to listen to such English (this with indignation) and that they keep Chewing over the same thing. She wishes that they would finish This Gobble and get down to Brass Tacks. The meeting drones on, half the speeches are inaudible, but at last we are told something definite – that no one knows whether the evacuees will arrive today or not, but if so we shall be notified and must therefore turn up.

Leave the meeting with relief, and we trek up to Auntie Nell's to tea. We go via Wraggs, to view the damage done by the land mine, but when we get there, we find that the crater is already almost completely filled up, and men are at work mending roofs and windows.

Monday, November 25th: Miss Harvey says she hasn't had a minute's sleep all week. She thinks she may have to give up her job.

Stay in tonight and start reading *David Copperfield*. It's like meeting familiar faces to read about the characters I've only heard of – Tommy Traddles, for instance, Mrs Gummidge, Barkis, who is Willin', Peggotty, with her Bursting Buttons, the Murdstones, and so on.

Tuesday, November 26th: Letter from Amy Tweed yesterday, dubiously considering becoming an Atheist, and asking my advice . . . Huh! What pose next? Mother declares grimly that she wants a Good Hiding.

The siren sounds at 10.45, and we all leap nimbly and immediately from our beds, and nip downstairs, determined not to be caught out. Fortunately the All Clear sounds about half an hour later.

Wednesday, November 27th: Oh for pay-day! I have 3*d.* in my purse, my watch is at the jeweller's and I can't fetch it back because I have no money, I need stockings and a suspender belt and lots more things.

Thursday, November 28th: Take myself to the English lecture, which is hardly under way before a buzz buzz, buzz buzz sounds overhead and the sirens screech. We hear planes going over almost incessantly, so am rather relieved when the lecture ends and I am free to go home. Find Delia there, and she stays all night because there are planes over all the time. We stay up until the All Clear at 4 a.m. What a night!

Friday, November 29th: Feel limp and somnolent all day, but am roused to enthusiasm in the afternoon by the advent of the money bags. So once more I am free from financial embarrassment.

Delia comes down on a farewell visit. She goes tomorrow to New Ferry on the Wirral. It will seem strange without her.

Monday, December 2nd: An Old Girls leaflet arrives, but I fail to see my name amongst the doings of certain old girls who have achieved fame – matrimonially, socially or vocationally. Clare Hollingworth, now Mrs Vandaleur Robinson, has done great work in rescuing refugees in Poland and Czechoslovakia, and is called a modern Scarlet Pimpernel.*

Also in my post (which sounds very important) is a missive from Doug. Once more I am treated to an account of the latest bombs on Ely, in his own marvellous style. The Poor Old REs exploded a mine there; the old siren had just gone; an old German plane was overhead (though probably it was one of the latest Dorniers). He's been stirring up his old brain about Xmas presents, and he ends by telling me not to forget the Old Cellar. It's a wonder he doesn't sign himself off Old Doug.

Tuesday, December 3rd: News trickles through – that our dear Constance Lavinia Howard, headmistress designate, is to commence her duties at Springfield Road School. Oh dear! I quiver and quake.

My father says glumly that we shall all be like cats when the war is over – after blackout conditions and getting so used to the dark. Lord Woolton broadcasts the latest Food Bulletin – ¾ lb of sugar instead of ½ lb just for Xmas, and 4 oz of tea instead of 2 oz. But we are not to have any more imported fruit or tinned goods or imported meat. Goodness knows what we'll be living on soon. Things *are* coming to a state. Even brides will be marching down the aisle soon clad in tin hats and carrying respirators

*May's old school was Ashby de la Zouch Girls' Grammar School. Author and journalist Clare Hollingworth (now one hundred years old and resident in Hong Kong) achieved a famous scoop when, while working for the *Daily Telegraph* on the border between Germany and Poland in 1939, she saw German armed forces massing for the invasion.

to the gladsome screech of the sirens, instead of wafting down in that anachronism, wreath and veil, to the archaic peal of wedding bells.

Wednesday, December 4th: Freddie rings up to say would I like to go to the flicks. Tell him I'm going to Swanee's to tea, but he says he'll meet me there. Accordingly attire myself in my best and go to Swanee's, then dash out to meet him. See his car parked up the road and him coming towards me. However, feel no uplifting of the heart and no quickening of the pulse, but merely a faint wonder at myself for going. We go to the Ritz, but have not been in long before, to my horror, the lights go up in the middle of the picture for a minute, and the diminutive figure of the manager is seen on the stage. He says that the sirens have just gone, then hops off and the picture continues. However, I lose all interest in it, imagine I can hear all sorts of noises, and am anxious to be gone. Dear Freddie, however, is quite unperturbed and says he doesn't want to go back to his digs yet because it is so dull, so I heroically endure my qualms for another hour, then drag him out. Hear a German plane quite close as he gets the car started and I beseech him in anguish to put out the lights, so he does. However we get home safely and he says he has Quite Enjoyed It. Feel like thanking him very tartly and with sarcasm, for such a concession, but instead I leap out. He is in such a hurry to be off that he doesn't give me time to close the door. Ponder upon the hurry. Either (1) he was afraid of bombs or (2) he found me very boring (very possible and not at all surprising, but very unflattering), or (3) he couldn't control his passionate feelings any longer (Most Improbable, but flattering).

After this unceremonious dismissal, I wander indoors to find the household hovering round the cellar door, the cellar being lit and cushioned ready to receive them. They have already been down twice. They receive me with relief and indignation, asking

Where Have I Been to until Now? though they know perfectly well. During the alert, Barbara and Mrs Gee wander up with Bob, home on 7 days' leave, so we have recitals of Army life past and present given as a duet between him and my father until about 11.20. Meanwhile the All Clear has sounded. And so to bed.

Thursday, December 5th: A recent ordinance decrees that poultry is now on the ration cards, so I hope Dougie doesn't forget to provide my cockerel with a card. I'd hate to think of the poor thing going hungry.

To the English lecture. Mr Addison discusses the characters in *The Forsyte Saga*, and asks whether we think of them as types or really alive. As usual I say nothing. Most of them, he thinks, are just types, but one or two are more than mere silhouettes. After the lecture is officially ended the discussion turns upon which books and authors will last. In Mr Addison's opinion, Priestley best carries on the tradition of the novel. He thinks that the Bloomsbury Set – V. Woolf, T. S. Eliot, Jas Joyce etc – will die out: they live in a rarefied atmosphere apart from normal everyday life, as though in a centrally heated house with air-conditioned rooms. I think Charles Morgan will survive – because he has something in his books besides a story – a kind of philosophy of life. I think E. M. Delafield's *Diaries* will too.

Friday, December 6th: Friday, thanks be! Three letters this morning, from Jack (now in Cornwall), Amy (still running Goldsmiths College) and Delia (feeling very lonely at New Ferry). Delia says there are two Big Bertha anti-aircraft guns behind her digs and a barrage balloon above. In addition to this, they run mobile guns along the streets when necessary. Poor Delia! She'll need reinforced eardrums.

Bitterly cold, with a boisterous, icy east wind.

Saturday, December 7th: Another perilous expedition to Derby, with Joyce, but go without qualms this time, arguing philosophically that if the sirens go we'll just have to take shelter. When we arrive, there is room to move round the shops comfortably, examining the Christmas goods – all the same as in previous years. The usual gaily coloured gift boxes of perfume, bath salts, notepaper, covered hangers, brushes, etc. appear again, but all with increased prices attached. We prowl around, buy several oddments, dart to Marks and Spencer for two carriers to contain them, then go to the Midland for lunch. We hesitate between fish and pheasant, but as the waitress says No to our request for chips with the fish, we have the pheasant.

On arriving home we find Mother and Auntie Nell pacing up and down in a frenzy, having heard fantastic tales of Derby's having been bombed this morning. They ask us with exasperation Where We've Been till this time, knowing full well.

Monday, December 9th: The Day of Wrath! Miss Howard arrives in pomp and state. She has what might be called A Presence, and wafts about the school with swaying stately gait like a ship in full sail. When I go to tell her that Mr Rowley has no savings stamps, she smiles sweetly and says, 'How sad!' Gape at her and make a mumbling exit, wondering if she really thinks it 'sad', or is just being gently sarcastic. She informs Trissie that she Never Uses A Cane, but merely Smacks Them as their Mothers do. Ha! (sardonic). I wonder how long she'll go on being Just A Mother. Some days I feel more like a lion tamer.

Spend the evening with my nose glued to *The Forsyte Saga.*

Tuesday, December 10th: Our châtelaine evidently pictures herself in the guise of Hercules, and Springfield Road School as the Augean stables. Anyhow the new broom is sweeping clean. She has intimated to Mr Wheat that she wants the floor of her room henceforth polished and the wall cleaned. She has had Miss H's boys marching up and down the corridor for 10 minutes, and she has had to suppress Miss Cook's children. Her ladylike tones hardly rise above a whisper – she makes me feel quite uncouth. What a presence! But she thinks now that she'll buy a cane! Miss Clark, Miss H, Miss Peat and I walk home from school indignantly discussing Constance Lavinia's acts.

Wednesday, December 11th: A thrill like an electric shock runs through the school this morning – the first snow of the season! It infects the children with a fever of excitement. They dash along the corridors, pointing and exclaiming with ecstasy, 'Snow!' They would roll in it like puppies, I think, if we'd let them. Quite a heavy fall, but it is over by playtime, and a pale sun comes out and melts it all away.

Stay in at night and continue reading *The Forsyte Saga.* Our peace is shattered by the wailing of the sirens about 7, and we sit up, doze in various postures, and I spend the night on the sofa. The welcome All Clear doesn't sound until 7.30 the next morning, by which time I have fallen into my first deep sleep, so I fail to hear it.

Thursday, December 12th: Miss Howard is on the prowl. I think she labours under the delusion that we didn't do any work under Miss Foster. Spend the day vainly trying not to yawn, but really feel very weary. In fact am in two minds about going to the Eng lec but I do. However, about 7 the sirens blare forth again. Mr Addison makes a quizzical remark about them and continues, but finishes 10 minutes early. Continuous planes over all night, and heavy fire from the Derby guns. Sleep first on the sofa, then in Grandma's bed, then my own. All Clear about 4.30. They were at Sheffield.

Friday, December 13th: An orgy of Christmas activities at school. We spend the afternoon making calendars and cards. Mr Wheat tells me in sombre tones that there are Dark Days Before Us, and adds grimly that it is Nothing to Laugh About, though as far as I can see, no one has the slightest inclination to laugh.

An effusion from Dougie relating, as usual, how many sirens have sounded since he last wrote, with details. During one alert, he went out with his Little Ambulance (have visions of him at the wheel of a toy vehicle) and knocked down the biggest lamppost in The Blinkin' Town. He has been informed by the gas company that they cost £30, but he is prepared to go to prison rather than pay. After this I read something which gladdens my heart – he will, he says, be sending on the Old Bird at the end of the week (not too old I hope).

Amy down from College today, having hitch-hiked – a bold and brazen proceeding which seems to be in vogue among the students. Would never have dreamed of it in my day!

A calm and peaceful night, which we all deeply appreciate.

Tuesday, December 17th: Dougie's Bird comes – a Fine Feathered Creature that will look well on our table. So he really has given me the bird after all this time!

Dispatch Christmas cards.

Wednesday, December 18th: A large parcel arrives for me from Dougie, together with a touching card. In a burst of Christmas good will, I send Mrs W a 10½d. tin of bath crystals, and she sends me my latest frock – the blue, which is Very Fetching. It is made like my greeny one, but has green, petunia and yellow ivy leaves in clusters round the hem, and one cluster on the belt, and two small ones on the yoke.

An afternoon of agony – our little party. We while away the time by reading and stories until 2.45, then it begins. We play Hunt the Thimble etc, and the noise is terrific. Then the children have a little present each – the boys a drawing book and a rubber and the girls a hankie. They look rather downcast at the sight of the hankie. Then they have a bun, a cake, and a mug of lemonade. A London evacuee breaks her Lady's Cup, much to her distress. At 3.45 I pack them off with profound relief, and bike thankfully homewards.

Thursday, December 19th: Arise after an interminable night spent writhing in agony. Have been attacked by pains in the middle, which seriously disturb my rest. The pains make school a night-mare. Go to Miss H for sympathy, and she looks concerned and says she hopes I'm not going to be like That Man in the Bank who died – he only had a stomach-ache too! Immediately feel on the verge of the grave.

Still, there is one bright spot in the day. We Are Paid, and we get our bonus back-dated from April, so mine amounts to £8.8*s.* Feel like Croesus.

Friday, December 20th: Go to school with flannel swathed round my middle, and many jeers thereby from an unsympathetic and flinty-hearted family. Have spasms of aches and pains. And we break up, thanks be!

Have quite a collection of intriguing-looking packages now, all waiting for Christmas Day.

Jack arrives on 7 days' embarkation leave before going to Egypt. Bill Swan is already there. Still, so far we seem to be doing well in that part of the world. So is Greece. Good old Greece!

Sunday, December 22nd: Receive a Christmas card – but nothing else! – from the Dear Freddie. Mean old Freddie! The card is Very Massive, being about a foot square, so my father suggests that he wanted to get value for his money. Scrutinise the interior of the envelope for a 10/- postal order, perhaps, but no! Place the card in an inconspicuous position behind the others.

Go to Grandma's early, about 6.15, and no sooner are we there than the sirens tootle and shortly afterwards the Derby guns start firing.

Mrs M wanders in on her way home from chapel, but full of the most un-Christian sentiments. Mr S makes her Blood Boil, she says. He's a Coward and she'd like to knock his head off. Why should he get out of fighting? If she were fighting, she'd never take any German prisoners, etc, etc. The conversation then revolves round the Scarcity of Onions, Widows with Matrimonial Intentions, Legs of Pork, the German Invasion and the Grim Future.

Bed down on the extended chair, and fall asleep till after 2. Go to bed about twenty to 3, but still hear planes crawling above, and gunfire. Am chilled to the marrow in my cold bed, so lie uneasily and frigidly awake till 4, when I can stand it no longer. Pad downstairs and get a lukewarm hot-water bottle, get into bed in my dressing gown, and manage thereby to achieve sufficient warmth to send me to sleep. Hear the tail end of the All Clear at 6.30 a.m.

Monday, December 23rd: The date is about the only thing that is Christmassy this year.

Catch the 10.20 bus to Burton. I meet Swanee. We dither around and do oddments of shopping and finish off with turkey and plum pudding (each of a sort) at Boots. Thence home to tea. Just as we are all beginning tea at 4, the sirens shrill, and we sit agape, but the All Clear sounds about 10 minutes later, so we relax again.

Go to Grandma's early, and have just sat down when Ivy walks in. Hardly has she sat down than the sirens shrill again – now becoming a nightly occurrence. The foul fiend Hitler and his henchman Goering must be working up for an Xmas orgy. Ivy thereupon leaves hurriedly and I bravely escort her to the bus, feeling truly noble.

Listen in to Mr Churchill's broadcast at 9 p.m. to the Italian people. He outlines why our two peoples are at war, laying the guilt at the door of One Man and One Man Only (he repeats this phrase two or three times) – to wit Dear Benni. Our Mr C is a marvellous man – a true bulldog! – and the scorn with which he charges his voice is really vitriolic. After all this, as the aeroplanes seem to be passing over us instead of visiting, we decide at 10.30 to retire to bed. A wise decision! For I sleep so soundly that I don't even hear the All Clear when it sounds about 1.30 a.m. Have a lovely night's sleep.

Tuesday, December 24th: Christmas Eve: Christmas Eve! – though it doesn't seem at all Christmassy or festive. After tea go to the flicks to see Clive Brook in *Convoy* – very good, and an excellent piece of propaganda. Emerge to find all quiet, and we can hardly believe it when we are told that the sirens haven't gone. Begin to think that dear Adolf must have some better feelings tucked away, after all. And sure enough, we retire to bed sirenless and embark peacefully upon –

Wednesday, December 25th – Christmas Day: Our second war-time Christmas, and a very dull and quiet one too – albeit a peaceful one – no bombs, no sirens, no enemy activity over this country.

Have stacks of presents – an underset from Mother, £1 from my father, handkerchiefs, winter pyjamas, stockings, notepaper and envelopes, scent and powder, a teacher's diary, a darning set, a bowl of tropical crocuses, coathangers, a pot-pourri, and last but not least a marvellous blue-and-gold brush, mirror and comb set from Dear Dougie. Everyone very thrilled by this last addition.

Monday, December 30th: London had a most fierce Blitz again last night, the enemy apparently intending to set it on fire. Several notable churches are down, and the Guildhall. Oh how dreadful! And St Bride's in Fleet Street too.

Text of Pres Roosevelt's speech relayed during the 1 o'clock news. He promises largely and magnificently Unlimited Help for us, and is certain that the Axis Powers are doomed to failure. Good! The sooner the better.

Mamma, I hear, has asked Her Boy when he intends to Settle Down, but he has declined to discuss the matter. He probably thinks that when he has ascended higher on the social and clerical scale, the matrimonial field will be larger, and his choice more extensive. Forgot to mention that he endowed me with a microscopic Christmas card. Took solace from the fact that I had wisely anticipated this and sent him one even smaller.

Tuesday, December 31st – New Year's Eve: Mr Shaw toddles breezily in, with news of the latest bombs in Birmingham. He affirms knowingly that we are perfecting a Device against the Night Bomber, and hints darkly that we are bringing down more bombers lately than we announce. Hope so! But he always seems to have inside information of some sort from some mysterious source – probably his own imagination!

1941

Wednesday, January 1st – New Year's Day: The turn of the year, and the old year merges imperceptibly into the new. Do not speculate upon the possibilities of 1941, they are too numerous and too diverse.

Attend a whist drive at the Baptist schoolroom at 3.30 p.m. in aid of the Soldiers' Fund. Crawl home feeling chilled to the marrow. Thence to Grandma's and Mrs M oozes in. She talks about miserly habits (with instances, e.g. a bit of boiled bacon for Christmas dinner), onions (which in their scarcity exercise the greatest attraction over housewives these days), the hasty temper of her nephew, and tomorrow's Vacuee Tea, then her chances of re-marriage (very great). In the midst of all this we are startled into attention by the sudden and entirely unexpected wailing of the sirens. So dear Adolf is on the prowl again.

Thursday, January 2nd: Didn't stay up last night, as it seemed fairly quiet. Awake this morn, this truly wintry morn to find snow – snow on the ground, snow on each roof, and snow eddying delicately in the greyish-white air, while my father battles with it to keep a path clear to the garage. Find also a letter from Eunice awaiting me, very pleased with life and her lot. She's just moved into a new job, and they have two evacuees from Radford, near Coventry, a boy and a girl whose home has been bombed.

Monday, January 6th: As black as night when I crawl home from Grandma's at 8.30 this morn. Wrap myself in a mantle of self-pity and back to the prison house I go – for another term!

Begin reading *Sons and Lovers* by D. H. Lawrence before I go to bed. Feel as though it needs a breath of fresh air blowing through it, as Priestley's novels have.

Tuesday, January 7th: I fear I shall soon be driven on to a diet. I am waxing grossly fat. In fact so fat that today the fact is borne in upon me without a shadow of a doubt – I burst the zip of my skirt and gasp at the implication thereof.

Spend an uneventful evening by the fire with *Sons and Lovers.*

Letter from Vera reminiscing about our jaunts during our college days to the forbidden Guildhall Library and the questioning smile of the attendant as we signed 'Miss Smith and Miss Brown'. 'Poor dear London!' says Vera, 'but methinks it will rise again to greatness and glory when Hitler's doom is come,'

Another night of peace.

Thursday, January 9th: Go to the English lecture, and Mr A sums up his talks on Wells, Galsworthy and Bennett, none of whom he considers great, because they are each limited in some way – Galsworthy by upper-middle-class traditions and a sense of property, Bennett by the provincialism of the Five Towns, and Wells by his inability to portray refined, sensitive upper-class women etc. Halfway through the lecture, we hear a familiar buzz buzz, and shortly after this Wailing Winnie blares forth. Stacks of Jerries are heard overhead, and the All Clear doesn't sound until 2 a.m. Blow old Goering and his Fly By Nights!

Friday, January 10th: Am worn out when I get up these dark mornings. I lie and battle fiercely with the urge to have Just Five More Minutes in bed, so that when I crawl downstairs I am exhausted with the struggle.

Hear from Amy and read that I am 'one of the best friends anyone could have'! Good for my vanity. She tells me to my grief that there is practically nothing left of poor old Goldsmiths now after the Second Fire of London last week, and the effects of various High Explosives at different times.

Dougie also writes. He's glad I like the colour of the brush etc he sent me because blue is his favourite colour and he always thinks of me dressed in blue. I'd love to see his mental picture. He's looking forward to having a crack at the Old Germans (probably thinks the young ones would be too good for him). Certain recent bombs shook The Old House for about 5 minutes.

News in brief – Amy Johnson, now a ferry pilot, has been killed. A bomb was dropped on Burton during last night's raid. My father has a cold. I have now in my possession several bars of chocolate, Miss Harvey having procured them for me. Chocolate is as scarce as roses in December these days, so I gloat over my 3/- worth like a miser.

Joyce and Eric are getting married at Easter and want me to be a bridesmaid but I think I am going to put my foot down at last. It would make my 7th time – which is a bit thick. I can't repeat these performances indefinitely or I shall be hobbling down the aisle in blue georgette at the age of eighty.

Monday, January 13th: A complete and perfect blackout prevails this evening for the simple reason that the electricity fails suddenly about 5.30. My father says indignantly but paradoxically What next? – What with the Blazing Blackout and the Blazing Electric Light. Luckily lights reappear about an hour later.

Wednesday, January 15th: A somewhat boring and uneventful period. I eat, I sleep, I work, I rest. As a diversion, I read. No highlights, no bleak depths and no dangerous currents. Just a vegetable sort of existence, and I am even becoming rounded like a vegetable. Soon I shall sprout leaves and roots – but even that would be a little diversion.

Mr Sergeant then comes in to leave catarrh tablets, and says reassuringly, 'Nothing to worry about tonight – only odd ones going over!' We all trust that his optimism is well founded. He repeats 'Only odd ones on reconnaissance', and strides out.

Bomb damage in Derby

However, after this, the optimistic theories are all exploded by the sound of bumps and bangs in the distance, the noise of doors rattling in the house, and the boom of the guns pounding forth. Some of the bombs sound too near for comfort, so we sit up (or rather I sleep in the chair) until the All Clear at 1.30. Thence to bed, but the siren sounds again at 3.30. Lie and endure bumps, bangs and zooms, so eventually crawl downstairs with my pillow and eiderdown, and doze fitfully until 5.30, when the All Clear sends me crawling back to bed again. We all oversleep.

Thursday, January 16th: Card from Hilda T asking me to meet her on Saturday and Be Frivolous, as she is down in the dumps. Bert is expecting to sail for foreign parts at the weekend. How does one meet and be frivolous? Have a mental picture of myself bounding up to her with a fatuous grin.

The raids were all round us last night. Platform 4 on Derby Station hit, Shobnall Road, one end of Wetmore Road, Branston gravel pits, the outskirts of Nottingham and Winshill, etc.

Letter also from Amy Tweed with a fantastic tale of having tea in Nottingham with two Germans in khaki and an Italian at the same table. The foreigners of course, as in all these tales, asked Many Questions. Sounds very far-fetched.

But the worst (?!) is yet to come – The Archbishop of Buxton has finally made his choice, the lady being Head Masseuse and Chief Lecturer at a hospital in Buxton. She is 26 and very good looking (naturally), and he brought her home for Xmas. Her photograph adorns Mamma's drawing room! I don't mind. She's Scotch. Hope she makes him dance the Highland Fling all the way up the aisle, and finally I hope she massages all the Conceit out of him.

Friday, January 17th: Our kind friends at Derby have been racking their brains for further work for us. Evidently they are repenting not cutting down our holidays at Christmas. Anyhow, a neatly worded and gracious circular arrives today informing us that we are to include Fire Watching in our duties, and must take it in turn to Fire Watch our wonderful building. Huh! If they make me fire watch, I shall encourage the bally bombs to fall and burn out their precious edifice. I'd like to see Constance Lavinia pacing up and down in the small hours scanning the sky for bombs and rubbing her freezing fingers. Or our noted and beloved manager Jas W likewise on the prowl at the dead of night – he wouldn't do it as enthusiastically as he pokes his nose into our classrooms. We hold an indignation meeting, and I hold a further one when I get home.

Lovely morning – the trees are grey and covered lightly with snow and rime, which glitters as the sun shines on it. Outlined against a pale blue translucent sky, they make a lovely picture, the white tops merging into the blue through a soft yellowish tone. These stand in the background, while the flying figures of boys skating down the glassy slides in the foreground complete the scene.

Saturday, January 18th: It snows all day, but I trundle through the whirling flakes to meet Miss Tooth. Bert hasn't gone abroad, after all. After a meal in Boots, we potter round looking at their display of books and we both buy a 6*d.* Penguin. I buy *Captain Scott* by Stephen Gwynn and she buys *Cold Comfort Farm.* Thence we go to the Electric to see two funny films. After giggling spasmodically, we have tea in the Electric café, with two chocolate biscuits each! At one time this wouldn't have merited mention, but now it is as rare as snow at the equator. Dark and snowing as we wend our way to the bus park. Find a carpet of snow in my bedroom – having inadvertently left the window open.

Sunday, January 19th: Find ourselves muffled in two feet of snow this morning.

Monday, January 20th: More snow, with huge drifts. Less than half the children arrive – and those who do come are very foolish, in my opinion. Why couldn't they stay at home?

Tuesday, January 21st: Start knitting a striped glove this evening, and knit so furiously that I knit a hole in my finger with the point of the steel needles. Find no pleasure in this occupation, but am rather goaded on from one stripe to the next.

Wednesday, January 22nd: An easy day – only 22 children, so my classroom seems to have been transported to the celestial regions.

Miss H and I spend the day turning out cupboards and drawers in a general spring clean.

Struggle nobly with the glove, with a bandage over the punctured finger, and finish it. The thought of the other one reduces me to deep gloom.

I am on the rocks – oh for pay-day!

Thursday, January 23rd: Have a mere handful of 28, so potter about bringing odds and ends up to date. Sort out pictures, do notes for two weeks ahead – and, this done, look about like Alexander for fresh worlds to conquer. We finish off the day singing *John Brown's Body* and *Ten Green Bottles.*

Do *The Dynasts,* Hardy's epic verse drama about the Napoleonic Wars, in English this evening. View its 525 pages askance and decide to take Mr Addison's words about it on trust. However, the Southend teacher next to me tells Mr Addison airily that It Isn't Really Very Long, and it is Very Readable.

Friday, January 24th: Still have a delightful 28 at school, so finish off the week feeling free and unfettered. Wash my hair and scan it when dry for golden glints, but find none. Letter from Dougie who has won races in skating. He refers proudly to Young Ladies who have flocked to him for tuition.

Saturday, January 25th: Finish off my striped gloves and start a scarf to match.

Tuesday, January 28th: Children all back in force and the snow has gone to their heads. They're simply wild so I spend the day roaring like a lion.

And what an evening! Miss S, Mother and I group ourselves gloomily round the fire, Mother snoozing, Miss S knitting, and I painfully plodding through *The Dynasts,* which I give up in

despair at page 104. We all moan in unison about our boredom – we even look forward with enthusiasm to supper as the
climax of the evening. Finally Mother and I have a desultory
game of Lexicon, then we migrate to Grandma's. Would accept
with enthusiasm an invitation from dear Freddie to the flicks,
but even he has deserted me in my hour of need. Jilted once
again! – by the faithless Freddie! He should leave the cooling-
off part to me – I could do it with greater skill. Still I am indeed
stricken and broken-hearted to think that he has abandoned
me.

The Budget comes again, having taken since last May to go
round, via Persia and India.

Tuesday, February 4th: Letter from Dougie. He invites me to Ely
for my summer holidays. This invitation comes annually, but this
year it has come a little early. I haven't accepted it yet. He ends by
adjuring me to take care of myself once more, and includes in the
letter Bomb Outrages at Ely and the terrible tale of a fellow he
knew who had a machine-gun bullet through his neck and died
thereby. Oh dear! I do wish he wouldn't tell me these tragic happenings.

Wednesday, February 5th: Mother, Dad and I proceed to the flicks
for a little vicarious excitement and synthetic glamour and see
trivial but amusing comedy called *My Favourite Wife.* Ken
Rowley who showed me card tricks at Jack's wedding and was a
wireless operator in the RAF is missing. Oh dear!

Friday, February 7th: Pluck an aged hair from my head after
washing it this evening – not even a grey one, but one of Pure
White! Old age creeps on apace. See Stuart S home on leave
again, with his mother, who is very anxious to know, for reasons
apparently of her own, if I have A Boy.

Finish reading Priestley's *Postscripts* which I didn't hear when they were broadcast.

Saturday, February 8th: To the Ritz with Joyce to see *Pride and Prejudice* – simply marvellous. The best flick I've seen in years. I could go into raptures over it. I could see it again. I could read the book again – enjoyed every minute of it, but wish the end hadn't been altered to make Lady Catherine unbend. Every part well taken, especially Lydia, who is delightful. Greer Garson and Maureen O'Sullivan are Eliz. and Jane, and Laurence Olivier is Darcy.

Swanee has to return to Wilmslow or else her house and furniture will be commandeered by the Govt. Mr E calls at night and tells me I look well. Oh dear! I simply must diet. He thinks we are Just As Well Dead, as there is simply Nothing To Live For Now. He points out lugubriously that although we are Fighting for the Right, look at the deaths among our leaders – Chamberlain, Lord Lothian, and Metaxas, while Hitler and Co flourish like the green bay tree.

Sunday, February 9th: The Vicar announces high jinks and revels on Shrove Tuesday, in the shape of a Social Gathering. The first item will be a song and dance by our Vicar, à la Fred Astaire. His wife will follow, in the grass skirt of a Hawaiian beauty, to perform a native fandango; then Gladys will pop on as comic reciter, with Bertie in the background dressed as Tarzan. The programme will be concluded by the Wragg sisters crooning popular song hits.

Ha cha cha! As a matter of fact, we are to have a Lecture on Missionary Work in India by the Rector of Hartshorne, who is, says the Vicar, going to be an Asset to the District. It all sounds very inviting.

Stay in all afternoon and read *Testament of Friendship* – very interesting. Vera Brittain and Winifred Holtby both belong to the Feminist Group, followers of Viscountess Rhondda.

Listen in to the Premier's speech at 9 p.m. It lasts until 9.40 – he was marvellous! His withering and scornful references to the two Dictators are grand – He calls Musso that 'nasty, cold-blooded, black-hearted Mussolini'. He rolls his tongue around the words as though savouring their full flavour before releasing them, and almost sounds as though he's going to smack his lips. He's a fine orator and inspires confidence everywhere. He has almost become a legend. He spoke with sober confidence but no suggestion of complacency – said how well the Army of the Nile was progressing, and complimented Gens Wavell, Wilson and O'Connor (I think), then went on to reiterate the warning of imminent invasion.

Tuesday, February 11th: Have a Black Eye to give a finishing touch to my demoralised appearance. A girl in my class hit me in the eye with her gas mask! A pure accident, but that doesn't comfort me.

Even the Duce must spare a little sympathy for Gen Berganzoli – he is between the Wavell and the deep blue sea.

A new type of shelter is out – an indoor one, the size of a dining room table. Gas masks are being examined again to make sure they're quite gas proof.

Thursday, February 13th: Latest date for the invasion is now Saturday, 15th February, so they say.

To the flicks to see *The Private Lives of Elizabeth and Essex* in Technicolor. Quite good, very colourful – naturally! Bette Davies very good as Qu Eliz. Quite a few historical distortions.

Saturday, February 15th: Arise with many croaks, my cold having deteriorated after the stay in the damp shelter on Wed. Sunny day however, so meet Friend Tooth in Burton. See Bella in Marks and Sp. She tells me she is going to join the WAAFs. Meet HT at 11.30. We eat, then go to the Picturedrome to see *Busman's Honeymoon* and a silly Laurel and Hardy flick. Have to wait 1 hr 10 m for a mouldy tea in the Picturedrome café, while the solitary waitress attends with great unfairness to the needs of the soldiers in the café.

Have coffee in the Electric, then home on the 20 to 8 bus. Mother as usual exclaims, 'You are late!' and explains that they are expecting the Invasion – Ivy having said men have been round to find how much petrol there is in each garage.

Sunday, February 16th: Spend the day indoors, writing letters and reading. Finish *Testament of Friendship*. Awfully good, moving in parts, and sympathetically drawn. Finish by feeling that I know Winifred Holtby and could recognise her. Think Vera B sentimentalises a wee bit. She writes to WH saying, 'Darling, you are a joy, and a love. What gave me the miracle of your friendship?' etc. It makes my undemonstrative self wriggle slightly.

To Grandma's early. Discuss Fire Watching, Stirrup Pumps and Hose Pipes, and the latest Housekeeping jobs.

Wednesday, February 26th: The false and faithless Fred has at last abandoned me, cast me off and severed all connections. Huh! What a cheek! He's no right to treat me thus. It should be I who do the Casting Off, not him. Still I can manage very well without him. I've never even been lukewarm. My spirit of independence is roused. Accompany Mother to mid-week service at church at 6 p.m.

Howbeit, when I return from church, am staggered by a phone call from the false Freddie to ask How I Am. Retort curtly All Right. He declares that he's been Very Busy, having interviews with the Admiralty, Air Ministry and what-not, trying to get himself into uniform. His interview with the Admiralty was futile – he didn't know enough – but he has hopes of being taken in by the RAF as a Weather Forecaster – for which job he is supposed to be able to Inspire Confidence and Mix with the Officers. He has therefore been swotting dynamics and will start at £270 a year – if he gets the job! But he'll see me before he goes. How nice!

Friday, February 28th: Paid! My new coat put in an appearance.

Saturday, March 1st: Ivy P's wedding dawns sunny and bright, but the wind is cold and the brightness deceptive. Attire myself grandly – or so I hope, being of unquenchable optimism – in my new black coat, turquoise dress, Ivy's hat (lent), Mother's bag (purloined) and turquoise gloves. Sally forth in this finery, only to find it an inadequate protection against the cold, but I shiver unobtrusively for the sake of vanity. In the church I find myself dwindling into insignificance amongst all the other guests. Ivy, looking very charming and George, pale but composed and well groomed, at last emerge and we all trail into the schoolroom. For a wartime wedding breakfast, it is really marvellous – tongue and beef, rolls and butter, tea (with sugar!), with wine or lemonade for the toasts. The three-tier wedding cake has white cardboard covers to represent icing.

Monday, March 3rd: Go to a billeting meeting at 4.30 – 17 more Birmingham evacuees expected – and thence to the library. On returning I discover Freddie sitting by the fire, having a tête-à-tête with my father. He asks Would I like to go to Burton, so I abruptly say Yes, if he'll wait for me to wash. We move off, while a row of faces at the next-door window peers out with unabashed curiosity. The dear Fred tells me in sprightly tones that he has been offered the job as weather forecaster, to begin his training

(10 weeks) in 3 weeks' time. Fail to detect any strain of melancholy at leaving me ... Still if he'd fallen on my neck in a gush of tears I'd have turned and fled. The prospect of his departure evidently stirs his charitable impulses, for he takes me into the 1/9 seats at the Ritz instead of the one shillings. We see *The Sea Hawk*.

Wednesday, March 5th: Know before opening that Dougie's letter will relate to me every bomb that has fallen on Fen soil since he last wrote. And it does! A few bombs, flares, and deaths comprise three-quarters of the letter, and the last quarter is devoted to a gloomy but touching lament about the imminence of his departure. His time is Growing Shorter and Shorter, he moans. He will be needed any time after March 8, he declares lugubriously, so he's Sort of Waiting. He is filled with gloomy forebodings – not knowing whether Jerry will drop a bomb on his home before he gets back – if he Does Get Back. But he's looking forward to Killing A Few of Those Rotten Blighters, he declares viciously. He adjures me to Keep Out of the Way of Old Jerry – but the warning is superfluous. Shouldn't dream of placing myself in Jerry's way.

Saturday, March 8th: Joyce's wedding. We all have new clothes, although I feel painfully aware of having a borrowed hat on my head. Joyce in white lace looks awfully nice and so do the bridesmaids in their blue and pink organdie over taffeta. The reception is held in the Midway schoolroom – 70 guests and a wonderful feast for wartime, with tinned cream even, and real icing on the cake. Tables laden with tongue, cold pork, trifles, jellies, blancmanges, fruit cakes, biscuits and cheese, tea, wine etc. Sustain the festivities until 10 p.m. Play musical chairs, dance and generally make merry.

Monday, March 10th: Miss Howard and Miss Harvey away. Painful day. Trissie has my top section and I trail the rest into Miss Harvey's class, where I cope with the resulting 64 for the rest of the day. Weary and worn.

Wednesday, March 12th: News announces Slight Enemy Air Activity over this country last night. It didn't sound very slight to us. Bombs were dropped at Clifton and Lullington and near Measham.

To Church, to the Lenten Service with Mother and Mrs Tweed. More planes over and the sirens sound. Oh help! It's going to be a nightly occurrence again. Begin now to appreciate properly the peace of the last few weeks.

Policeman went to Hassells' for Jack on Monday night, saying that he'd overstayed his leave. They told him he'd gone back, so he said he'd phone through and tell the authorities. Have visions of Jack being met off the train by an armed guard, or being placed under lock and key and fed on bread and water or forced to march up and down on fatigue duty – all sorts of direful possibilities.

Thursday, March 13th: See Mamma in Swadlincote, accompanied by a Female in a Grey Fur Coat. Mamma gives me a look of Gloating and Triumph, so I assume the Fur Coat to be Ronnie's Young Lady. I wish her joy.

Friday, March 14th: Ronnie didn't find his Intended until last June. She was 27 last Saturday, is named Catherine, and her father was a shipping director or something. He would be! Anyhow, she's got a bun and looks about 40. (I feel sour, hence these tart remarks.) I gnash my teeth.

Saturday, March 15th: Trot out and billet five of the twelve evac-uees that arrive from Birmingham this morning, then sally forth to meet Mona in Burton. She hasn't changed a lot – except that the fringe has gone, replaced by curls. When she left Guernsey before the Germans came she was given 4 hours to get out and was only allowed to take one suitcase with her so she had to leave stacks behind.

Wednesday, March 19th: Letter from Dougie. I had to explain somehow the non-appearance of the gloves I've been fictitiously knitting him since Christmas, so I told him that when the gloves were finished they weren't big enough. He exclaims that it is Jolly Bad Luck, but adds warmly that it is a Darn Sight Worse for me after putting all that time into knitting them. He says that it shows Real Bulldog Spirit to engage upon another pair. Oh dear! My white lies are causing me acute pangs of conscience.

After this the letter is devoted, as is his wont, to Bomb Damage in Ely, and a reference (now stale) to the imminence of his calling up. He is spending his Last Few Days digging for victory in his spare time. He leaves me suddenly to attend a celebration with some soldiers, and expecting to have a Riotous Evening. I bet!

Go with Mother and Miss S to the Midweek Service at Church. Freddie calls just after we've gone. His call has come! He goes on Tuesday! So he says he'll come tomorrow.

Thursday, March 20th: Freddie arrives to bid me a Fond Adieu, so he bears me off to the Ritz where he celebrates the occasion by taking me into the best seats again. I celebrate the occasion by losing my posh scarf. He asks me once more to write to him, so say affably that I will. Find myself very cruelly treating his departure as a joke instead of a catastrophe. Foresee the possibility of his asking if he can give me a goodbye kiss, and have decided to say kindly but firmly, No. However, am not given the chance, for he suddenly gives me a hasty kiss before I am aware of his intentions. Leave therefore with great haste, and a feeling that I have somehow been Taken In.

Friday, March 21st: The first day of Spring – tra la la. Actually not very spring-like, but cold and dull. Herald the weekend with joy. However, I look like being one of Ernie's Girlies soon, so I shall probably be wishing myself back at the blackboard as I grease cartridges in some far-flung factory. The 20s and 21s have to register in April, so my age group won't be long. Miss S predicts that I shall be adorning some munitions works before the summer holidays. Oh glory! Teaching has its advantages, after all. They're just becoming apparent.

Mrs T at home on my return, glorying in the latest 'lifts' Amy has had. The brazen way she thumbs cars (always men drivers) to hitch-hike home is outrageous.

A family crisis – Mr Skerritt has given Grandma notice that he is leaving. Auntie F cool and calm about it, but Grandma Very Worried.

Monday, March 24th: Letter from Delia. Three of their girls and families were among the casualties during the raids on Merseyside. How terrible!

Tuesday, March 25th: Yugoslavia has signed a pact with Hitler now. Nobody seems at all anxious to flout him except us.

Thursday, March 27th: Revolt in Yugoslavia. Prince Paul has fled and the signatories to the Tripartite Pact have been arrested. King Peter, 17½, has proclaimed himself King, backed by the military. What excitement!

Mr S's goods and chattels departed by lorry (Belfield's) and it looked as though all West Street were removing – 6 or 7 suitcases, a wardrobe, shelves, and numerous mysterious parcels and luggage. End the day engulfed with weariness.

Saturday, March 29th: Spend the morning – and a bitterly cold one at that, with tentative attempts at snow – diving from one queue to another. In fact, the queue fever bites me and I park myself stolidly on the end of the Candy Stores one without knowing what is at the end of it. Eventually find myself with ¼ lb of a concoction called Snowballs, ¼ of horrible pink and green boiled sweets, and a 2*d*. packet of clear gums. Thence I add myself to the throng of people round Harrison's stall, where there are sweets, and feel like a wasp round a honey-pot. It is only when I am so hemmed in that it is impossible to withdraw that I decide it is not worth either the effort, the indignity, the time, the ignominy, or the bruises. However, I reap a harvest of ½ lb caramels and 6 bars of inferior chocolate. After all this I scoot homewards to thaw.

Monday, March 31st: A bitterly cold day, with an icy, wintry, blustering wind with an edge like a knife. The absent Fred bestows a letter upon me and opens by addressing me as His Dear May. But I'm not His Dear May, nor likely to be, so his optimism is quite unfounded. He tells me he is lodged with a butcher, that their class of 20 includes Irish, Welsh and Scottish fellows, ex-secondary school and public school masters, that they have been deluged so far with thousands of codes, that the work is hard and that he won't be able to give me details because he has had to sign the Official Secrets form, that he enjoyed the evening at the flicks immensely, and he adjures me to carry my gas mask as he doesn't want me to be gassed as he wants to see me again. I can't think why either he or Doug thinks I shall willingly put myself in the way of either gas or aeroplanes.

Thursday, April 3rd: Letter from Doug, who has just been to still another of his celebrations. This time it is a pal about to enter the Army. He crawled home at 2 a.m. he says. They brought out bottles of champagne at 1! He now has a slight headache. Serves him right! Told him when I wrote that the Reverend's young lady, a superior being with a bun, was in the district. He says simply at the end of his letter, 'PS: I hate superior girls with buns.' Then 'PPS: I think you're OK.'

Ron's mother has been hiking the young lady around the district, proudly introducing her to all and sundry. My father suggests that she has her trailed round the locality on a decorated cart.

Virginia Woolf presumably dead. Has been missing for days after going for a walk by the Ouse. She left a letter behind, so it sounds as if she has committed suicide.

Friday, April 4th: Marvellous news from the Mediterranean etc. Best week of the war yet, I should think. A great naval victory v the Italians in the Medit with no casualties on our side and lots on theirs, with the loss of several ships, and we are still forging ahead in Abyssinia and Eritrea etc. We are only about 150 miles from Addis Ababa.

Saturday, April 5th: Parcel containing the promised jumper arrives from Delia. Letter couched in the usual terse, direct style, with sentences like bullets, going straight to the point without any circumlocution, and very clipped: 'think I prefer teaching to greasing cartridges'; 'don't much like the idea of a bun on the head!'; 'She must be prim and proper' (i.e. the Young Lady). 'Hope she has to make bombs anyway – and grease them!' That's a happy thought. I'd love to see dear old Kate in an overall and grease-bedaubed, listening with scorn to 'Music While You Work'. But the Bishop would never let her, nor the retired shipping magnate, her father.

Monday April 7th: Another horrid wintry freezing day. And Easter imminent. What prospects! Have my income tax form to fill in, but my wages are so contorted, with the addition of the bonus and subtraction of the income tax that I've no idea of the correct figures.

Budget out – income tax 10/- in the £. Glory! – but no increase in indirect taxation. I should hope not! This is to reduce expenditure. It will certainly succeed. Part is to be credited to us into a Post Office account for use after the war – a sort of compulsory saving. Better than inflation anyhow.

Fierce fighting along the Struma Valley. Both Greeks and Yugoslavs fighting desperately, but the Yugoslavs have had to withdraw to other positions.

Tuesday, April 8th: Hadn't been in bed long last night – though it seemed ages because I'd fallen asleep – when the sirens began to warble. This was about 11.30. Heard them with sleep-benumbed senses, but didn't dream of stirring. Mother went downstairs, then came back to bed as all seemed fairly quiet. Then I must have dozed off again, when a sort of sixth sense wakened me. Heard the whistle of a descending bomb but before I could leap out of bed, there was the terrific crack of its explosion. We all dived downstairs, and learned it had fallen near the greenhouses in the fields along Eureka Rd. Stayed up after this until 2.30, but retired to bed before the All Clear which sounded round about 4 a.m. Heard it dimly in my slumbers.

Bomb damage on the way to school – windows along Midland Road showing holes. The front doors at school were wrenched open, and three of my windows were splintered but held together by the netting we had stuck over them.

Lengthy news bulletins once more, now that there are land operations again.

Thursday, April 10th: To school with a joyful heart, this being breaking-up day. Finish about quarter to 12.

Awakened about 2 by most terrific bumps, bangs, and the roaring of hundreds of planes, but everyone else is snoring peacefully so lie awake and listen in solitary alarm until it slackens a little and I fall off to sleep again.

Saturday, April 12th: Go to Derby in search of a hat and find a nice one – black trimmed with green. Terrible struggle to get on a bus home – a huge mob waiting and we nearly have a fight. Mrs T at home, who bestows the highest praise she can offer upon my New Hat – she calls it Ladylike.

Wednesday, April 16th: Letter from dear Freddie – been home for Easter but very, very busy. Poor, poor thing! He is Desperate when he thinks of the amount of work to be done. He would very much like to have taken me out this weekend, but his car wasn't licensed. Oh, I am broken-hearted with disappointment.

Saturday, April 19th: Joyce had to register for National Service with the 20s and 21s today.

Monday, April 21st: Oh wretched day! Return to the daily round. Struggle through it with a resigned spirit. Go to billeting meeting in the Town Hall at 6.45 p.m. to discuss Extremely Secret Scheme for evacuation in case of invasion. Sounds hopeful! The usual gaslight – yellow like poached eggs, green baize and endless futile discussions dragging on wearily until 8 p.m.

Wednesday, April 23rd: The Greek army has capitulated. Oh dear oh dear! We *are* doing well! Still they couldn't do anything else. They were cut off.

Sunday, April 27th: I fear I grow duller – and duller – and duller.

As cold as Christmas – horribly, bleakly, greyishly cold with skies like lead and air like pincers.

Have to have one milkless day a week now – Sunday. In order to make more cheese, I suppose. Listen in to Mr Churchill on the wireless at 9 p.m. – very good as usual. Positively withering reference to The Striped Jackal Mussolini.

Tuesday, April 29th: Pay-day, oh joy, oh joy. Have £9 a year rise – which is truly acceptable. Letter from Dougie. Miss S has finished his gloves, so stitch them together and parcel them ready for dispatch. I only hope the shock doesn't prove too great for him.

The Great Ice Age still persists.

Friday, May 2nd: Beginning of Swadlincote's War Weapons Week. Much activity in the town. Flags flutter from various buildings, a decorated ladder to announce the progress of the week's savings is set up, and a dray with flags as a sort of platform along High Street.

Walk along the street with Mother, Joyce and Auntie Nell about 6.15 to see the proceedings, and find it lined with people. A few aeroplanes in formation zip over, and one or two odd ones appear and loop the loop. We wait patiently by the dray for the Salute and the appearance of Mr Grenfell, Minister for Mines, who is to open the week. Wait and wait and wait. 7 p.m. comes and goes, likewise 7.30 and 8, and still we wait, grimly determined by this time to see the Salute (about which we're vague). By 8.15 our patience is rewarded. There is a stir and things begin to appear. First comes a baby tank and Army lorries along High Street, then contingents of Sherwood Foresters (very smart) and a drum major (also very smart) and the man with the drums and leopard skin, then the Home Guards, ambulance men and ambulances, AFS and fire engines, wardens, women ARP workers, policemen etc. In short a grand and representative turnout.

Saturday, May 3rd: A glorious warm day – spring at last. 3 cheers! Go with Joyce to Derby on the 1.15 bus to buy a frock. Buy the green one I tried on at Bracegirdles before. Like a red one with white flecks better, but it is 6 guineas.

Another raid over Merseyside. Sirens go but don't get up. A lot of activity, so only sleep in snatches.

Put another hour on, making double Summer Time.

Tuesday, May 6th: Three letters for me today – quite a shoal – from Delia, Dougie and Freddie. Delia writes poetically of daffodils and narcissi nodding in the halcyon breeze, and a chorus of birds performing in the trees. She refers to the previous two nights' raids – terrible experiences when she and her landlady just lay flat wrapped in blankets under the stairs, while the houses nearby were razed to the ground. She likes *How Green is My Valley* and is going to have her racquet restrung.

Dougie's is a paean of praise and thanksgiving for the gloves he mistakenly supposes me to have knitted. Miss S, real author of Dougie's gloves, makes sardonic comments over this. He doesn't know how to thank me. I have made a Jolly Fine Job of them, and he appreciates the time and trouble I must have put in (pangs of conscience smite me). He's sure he doesn't deserve it. Not only is he awfully pleased, but proud also. He really does Think The World of Them, and Please Write Soon. There's one thing – Dougie is nothing if not grateful.

Freddie's letter is full of technicalities like isobars, wind pressure, charts and codes connected with weather forecasting. Though he shatters me by calling me May Dear during the course of it. Oh dear! That is terrible. He wonders who takes me to the flicks these days? Will certainly not enlighten him that nobody does. He has to get his own supper tonight as he is alone and he wishes I were there to join him. Glad I'm not! The rest of the letter is about complex differential equations, plotting synoptic, a definition of isobars and general weather forecasting. That's the most interesting part.

Freddie (left) with a colleague at the meteorological office

Cooler today. Connie on the warpath and has suggested to Miss Peat that she marks in ink: Even if the children's books are untidy, she needn't make them untidier! Gosh, sarcastic woman!

Wednesday, May 7th: Cold again. My dress arrives from

Bracegirdles and my father states that it is The Worst I've Ever Had and he doesn't like The Colour.

Sirens after we have gone to bed, but don't get up. Raid over Merseyside. But we brought down over 24 enemy planes. We're doing well lately with our night fighters.

Friday, May 9th: Great rivalry between my class and Class I about War Savings, Miss S leading this morning, then by a super-human effort in the afternoon we forge ahead by 1*s.* 6*d.* to £26 5*s.* Miss S says she'll put the 1*s.* 6*d.* to her total and adds contentedly, 'Then we shall be equal, shan't we?' Whereupon in his furious indignation my Geoffrey G leaps up and exclaims in anguished accents, 'Yo Wunna!' Manage to splutter 'Geoffrey!' in scandalised tones that I don't feel at all, and he subsides looking sheepish and abashed. Barbara calls in. She tells me about the raid on Nottingham. I begin to wish I were not going after all.

Saturday, May 10th: Catch the bus to Ashby, where I am just in time for the 10 a.m. bus to Nottingham. Miss Tooth is already there in patient pose. Find that almost everyone has been inspired to go to Nottingham this morning, on the same bus, for there is a crowd to get on, including the female of the Eng lectures and three other Southend satellites. Find myself seated in the midst of a contingent of Birmingham women at the back of the bus. They turn and twist in their seats like acrobats, taking a keen interest in the scenery. A shop containing cakes elicits a 'Coo!' of wonder from them. A lovely morning with the sun shining and the fresh young leaves looking very green. We pass an elephant on the road.

At last we arrive. Wander around and find every other shop window out. See damage to Burton's and that street. Buy a hat in the C and A for 5*s.* 11*d.* very misguidedly. Go to get some lunch and find everywhere crowded, so we have to grab the only available seats in the Kardomah and have a measly lunch of sardines on toast and coffee.

Then we queue to see Owen Nares in *Rebecca*. Pay 2*s*. 3*d*. and sit in the row next to the back in the Upper Circle, which is crammed. Quite good, though Owen Nares seems to lisp as though having trouble with a new set of false teeth. Arrive home at 7 and consume a massive meal. The hat doesn't receive much applause.

Forgot to say what happened this morn before going to Nottingham. Parcel arrived from Doug, containing a cockerel! A reward for the gloves, I suppose! Oh dear! More pangs of conscience. Everyone at once eager and willing to provide Dougie with a complete set of woollies, in hopes of similar remunerations.

Tuesday, May 13th: Startling news! Rudolf Hess, Hitler's deputy and second on his list of succession, is in England, having descended by parachute in Scotland from a German plane. All sounds very fishy. Everyone debates the whys and wherefores of it – a great scoop for the press.

Connie is still snooping round on the warpath. She comes upon Mrs B, Miss Cook and me gossiping when we should have been on our lines, sends Miss C packing, looks greatly incensed and sends a little note later in the morning to Miss Peat, Mrs B and me, saying that we are to accompany (underlined) our classes into school.

Tuesday, May 20th: Glorious fine night. Go for a walk with Joyce. War in the Council Offices about 3 nights a week overtime without pay. All threatened with the sack. Letter from Dougie.

Wednesday, May 21st: Connie springs a vile arithmetic test on my class and they get an average of 2 and a bit out of 7, which is terrible. Oh lor'! Go to the library with Miss S. The shelves seem to have burgeoned with yellow jackets – hosts of new ones, mostly detective ones with lurid titles.

Sunday, May 25th: Our biggest battleship – the greatest in the world – HMS *Hood* sunk off Greenland by the German *Bismarck*. Little hope of survivors. Terrible. Have a gloomy note all through church – sing 'Brief life is here our portion' and such-like strains.

Tuesday, May 27th: Whoopee, whoopee! We have sunk the *Bismarck*, after a hectic chase. Crete is still holding out, but German parachutists are still landing and German planes are still dive-bombing. I'm sure we shan't be able to hold it.

Letter from the dear Freddie, who scatters 'dears' about it again, but am not at all thrilled. He doesn't know whether I like him or not! Not surprising considering that I don't know either. He feels that he has done a good paper in the exam. What self-confidence! But he would like to come over and see me when he has a day off if I'd like him to. Don't mind either way.

Thursday, May 29th: Class I has done the arithmetic test that we had and got even less than we did. Feel an unholy joy at this. Wash my hair and have it set. Break up tomorrow!

Sunday, June 1st, Whit Sunday: Shattering news. Clothes to be rationed from now onwards. All to have 66 coupons only, and a coat alone takes 14 of these, a frock 11 (if woollen) or 8 (other-wise), stockings 2, a blazer 11, blouse 5, pyjamas 8, nightdress 6, petticoat 4, tennis socks 1, shoes 5, and so on. Oh dear! Why have I put off for so long buying essentials?

Lovely hot day. Go to Tweeds to tea in my new muslin dress and last year's sandals. The new curate at church today. He seems very conscientious and anxious to please.

Awful news on the wireless. We're evacuating Crete now! Very heavy losses. 15,000 evacuated.

Saturday, June 7th: My birthday – my 27th anniversary. How terrifically old and decrepit that sounds.

Monday, June 9th: Cards from Bella and Swanee and letters from Delia and Freddie. The latter is at an aerodrome near Portsmouth, in the officers' mess, a large country house converted, and has a room of his own, a batman and good meals including fresh salmon, green peas and tomatoes. What luxury! He wants a snap of me. What a thrill for him.

Thursday, June 12th: A parcel arrived from dear old Dougie containing asparagus and lettuce. So we have the asparagus for dinner. Great controversy and mirth about how to cook and eat it.

Tuesday, June 17th: Have a wonderful present today – the three ringleaders from Class III with whom Mrs Baker is unable to cope, so I'm to have them till the holidays. Begin with a firm hand.

Another summery day, so to tennis with Swanee. Not a man there except the young Osborne.

Wednesday, June 18th: To tennis with Miss Clarke. Weary by the end of the first set so come home at 8.30. Only females there. What a thrill.

Letter from Dougie, who is going to send More Garden Produce When the Time Comes. When and what?

Friday, June 20th: Connie is pleased with the way I'm managing Billy L and Co, says Trissie. One has asked to go back to Mrs B.

Letter from Freddie, who thinks my photograph sweet. He is now at an aerodrome near Nuneaton, and has bought a bike to travel to and fro on.

Thursday, June 26th: Billy L tries the effect of smooth words on me and tells me he is Trying Ever So Hard Miss, etc. Ha!

Saturday, June 28th: Bike to Lullington with Hilda T and take sandwiches but fail to see the German bomber that came down there.

Tuesday, July 1st: Letter from Doug, saying he hopes the eggs arrived OK and I'm not to spend half a page thanking him for them. Couldn't very well as they haven't arrived, much to our grief. In any case, he says, he has plenty of Eggs and Things (what things?) and if he can help me (or us?) in any way, he Jolly Well Will. Good old Dougie! The rest of his letter is taken up with his Home Guard activities – repulsing mock paratroops and he exclaims optimistically Heaven Help Old Jerry if he does make a start!

To tennis. Boiling hot. Nobody particularly good there tonight, so mouldy sets.

Thursday, July 3rd: Dash up to Mrs W's after school to have my tennis dress fitted, then dash to the bus and just scramble on the 5.20. Buy embroidery whatsits for my tennis bolero then Hilda T and I go to the Ritz to see *You Will Remember.* I shan't, because we only manage to see the very end, then whole of the supporting picture, then a fragment of the beginning.

Saturday, July 5th: Had a letter from Freddie. Says he likes the work and is hoping for a day or two off in which case he'd like to come over for a game of tennis. Still bestrewed with Dears which sound odd coming from the pen of the dear Freddie.

Wednesday, July 9th: This spell of unbroken sunshine and heat is almost too good to be true. It is simply glorious, wonderful and marvellous. I love it, and wish it would go on for months and months and months. It gives me a really contented feeling to wake up to the prospect of another hot bright day.

Friday, July 11th: Dougie writes to say that he hopes the eggs have arrived OK – a forlorn hope, for not a trace of an egg have we seen and he sent twenty. Oh misery! The rest of the letter is about Home Guard duties, which seem to fill up most of his time now. There is the usual grim note – two of their men got killed by a train and one by a motor bike during their activities with the paratroops.

Saturday, July 12th: Shattering news reaches my ears today. Freddie, the false and faithless Fred, is not constant to me, but divides his attentions between me and Another. He writes to her! – and he had tea with her in Derby when he was last over! Oh treachery! What monsters of deceit are men! And only this morn I received a note from him saying he'll be home on Monday night and will I go to Geary to tennis on Tuesday and will I be there by 6. He ends deceitfully 'Cheerio for the Present, May dear, I'm very much looking forward seeing you again.' Huh! Probably my rival is booked on Tuesday evening.

Sunday, July 13th: We are told to stand by for an important political announcement to do with foreign affairs at 2 p.m. Conjecture the entry of the USA into the war, at least, or a declaration of war on us by Japan, but it proves to be neither. It is an announcement of the signing of an agreement last night between us and the Soviet Union, for mutual help in the war v Hitlerite Germany, with neither side to conclude an armistice independent of the other. It is to come into effect immediately, without ratification.

Tuesday, July 15th: A holiday, and St Swithin's Day. And I might have expected what would surely accompany it – rain, loads of it, torrents, bucketsful, gushing down from leaden skies. A wash-out of a day. All plans frustrated. Garb myself hopefully in tennis shorts when I get up, but no sign of the weather clearing up, so potter around aimlessly, make tarts and clear up the mess in my bedroom. Then the phone rings, and Freddie dear is at the other end, in great woe because his cousin's car has broken down but could I get over to Derby? Magnanimously stifle my grievance and say kindly Yes. Go to Derby in stockings, black shoes, mac and gloves and meet the dear Freddie at 2.45. It still looks threatening so we make straight for the flicks. Then we have tea at Boots and find ourselves with two hours to spare before Freddie's train leaves, so we go for a walk. I catch the 8.10 bus home.

Wednesday, July 16th: Freddie said he might come over to tennis if the car was mended, but couldn't promise, so wasn't surprised when he didn't come.

Thursday, July 17th: A letter from Swanee awaiting me. She is still deputising for the Registrar. Bill was in the Crete evacuation after the Greek business. He hasn't missed a thing. Swanee writes just as breezily as ever.

Go to Geary and manage to get in some good games as there are quite a lot of men about.

Friday, July 18th: A note from Hilda Tooth saying we can get in at Blackpool either the 2nd or 3rd week of August but only for bed and breakfast. Oh dear! Don't relish the idea of mooching around Blackpool in the keen sea air with an empty stomach, tortured by visions of Food. Reply evasively and hope for the best.

Sunday, July 20th: Victory Day, according to Col Britton. See a large V on our door and on the pavement etc as I bike belatedly to church at 8 o'clock. See Vs sprouting and blossoming in chalk and paint on doors and fences all through the day.

Monday, July 21st: Brightens up after tea, but I am to be cooped up in Miss B's emporium, to have my ends permed. Go through the usual processes with the usual minimum of patience. Don't get home until 20 to 8, after going at 4.30. Hilda Tooth awaits to arrange about holidays. Suggest we go to Delia at Corwen, and Miss T agrees very obligingly, so say I'll write to her.

We've had some tomatoes this week for the first time – oh luscious! None to be seen in the shops.

Tuesday, July 22nd: Oh dear! Feel well-nigh bald. Keep pulling and stretching my little curls, but they provokingly spring back again. Feel a sight. In desperation comb my hair savagely, and this does not mend matters, but only induces frizz.

Wednesday, July 23rd: A lovely day. Letter from Delia, who thinks she'll come to us on August 2nd if we'll have her (our letters have crossed). And a letter from Freddie saying how disappointed he was not to be able to get over for tennis last week. Also he wanted to kiss me at the bus station but I looked so Embarrassed he spared me the Ordeal. Thank heaven. I didn't realise what an escape I'd had, or I'd have looked more than embarrassed – positively panic-stricken. He hopes to get over before going to Portsmouth next Tuesday.

Thursday, July 24th: Glorious hot day again. My perm has descended from the corrugated-iron stiffness into a brief and frizzy mass. Like wool. View it despairingly.

Freddie rings up at dinnertime, being at home, to say he has no means of getting over, but could I get over to Nuneaton for the afternoon on Sunday? Oh dear! Can't cope with this ardour.

Brief letter from Dougie, evidently rather peeved because I'm going for a holiday but not to Ely. (In any case, it looks as though I shan't move from Swadlincote after all.) He was hoping, he says, that if I went anywhere I'd go there but I don't seem very keen on it. Too true! Anyway, he hopes I have a good time and make the most of it (nice of him!) because we've some Pretty Tough Times ahead (gloomy of him!).

Friday, July 25th: Mr Sergeant, the Baptist Minister, comes to give our two top classes a talk on keeping fit. We sit assembled in the hall, and he enters in a bathing costume. Nearly die – agony to keep my face straight. Feel my mouth quivering horribly and bite my lips vigorously. He mounts the platform and stands displaying his skinny frame and stringy arms to all, clad in a black bathing costume with a skirt. Then he smacks his diaphragm vigorously, shows his muscles, walks up and down, bends etc, waves his arms about, then shows how he walks at 6 miles per hour, by striding with waving arms and clenched teeth round the room.

Ring up Freddie who says he could get to Burton by 4.20 today so could I meet him for tea. Stammer and say Well I promised Amy to go to the flicks, but he says Put Her Off. Weakly agree to do so, but feel very mean.

Meet Freddie at 5 p.m., go to the Ritz for tea, then to the flicks. Walk with Freddie to the station and he says Will I Go to Nuneaton on Sunday. Hesitate and demur but finally say weakly that I'll go. Don't relish the prospect.

Saturday, July 26th: The rain beats down steadily all morning. Go to Burton to meet Hilda T. Prowl round the shops, have fresh salmon for lunch in Boots, then ring up home to find out if the tennis match has been cancelled. Get my father on the phone and he replies so politely that I interrupt to tell him that it's me. And oh – what a change! He asks me What the Devil I'm Doing? Find out after all that the match *is* cancelled.

Sunday, July 27th: Yank myself off in muslin frock and bolero – no coat or hat – to Nuneaton to cast a ray of sunshine into the life of the dear Freddie. Train late but am not perturbed. Freddie is waiting on the platform and he tells me I look Pale (with excitement, I presume). We get to his digs just after 4 and have tea almost immediately. His landlady is awfully nice and shows me round the garden afterwards, and the air-raid shelter. Freddie then exhibits his notebooks on meteorology, but am not keen on this as it brings us into too close proximity. Happily it is almost time for the bus.

Monday, July 28th: Pay-day – oh joy!

Tuesday, July 29th: Dull and gloomy. However a feeble glimmer of sun appears about teatime, and I trustfully get ready for tennis. Then it grows duller and duller and about 5.40 it starts to rain gently. However Mr Harris appears stating with undue optimism that it is getting brighter and he thinks we'll be able to play. Disagree silently. Halfway there the gentle rain turns to a vicious squall. Able to have one set when we arrive, then it rains, so we stop. The Harris discards his usual sarcastic vein and begins to dish out flattery. He says it's a wonder a nice girl like me hasn't been Snapped Up (oh, lor'). Tell him with dignity that I have no intention of being Snapped Up but would rather Choose (this very optimistic of me!). From this he becomes quite eloquent and says I'm Streets in Front of anyone who comes to Geary, not only in looks but in disposition (nearly ask him if he wants to borrow something). In fact, he says largely, if he were not already married he'd have a Jolly Good Try himself. Can find no reply to this so merely say that he would be very Foolish then. Oh no, he says generously, anyone who has me will be Very Lucky. This becomes too much for me to cope with so say Oh, I think it is Brightening Up (actually it is raining as much as ever). The rain eventually stops and we have 2 or 3 more sets, and the Harris becomes sarcastic and jeering again. Mr Moody shows me Poems He Has Written. Not very impressed, but tell him that I Don't Know How He Does It.

Wednesday, July 30th: Play tennis on the Park from 7.15 to 9.15 with Mr Harris. Not bad, but would heaps rather play at Geary. The Harris says if I'm going to tennis tomorrow what about going early and going to Bretby Nurseries for some tomatoes. So I say All Right, I Don't Mind.

Thursday, July 31st: Rains all day nearly, and am relieved at this because not keen on going to Bretby with the Harris – he's becoming too friendly. However, he arrives despite the rain, so after a weak protest which he dismisses, I have to mount my bike and go. After all this we get a meagre ¼ lb each, and I am subjected to more flattery. He has never met anyone since he was married that he's liked as much as me because I'm So Nice. He won't think so in future because I'll have to be Rude.

Friday, August 1st: Card from Delia to say she'll arrive tomorrow. Break up at 3.45 for 3 weeks' holiday. Have a letter from the dear Frederic, now at Thorney Island in Hampshire.

Saturday, August 2nd: Lovely warm day. Delia arrives about 5 and we go to tennis. We spin for partners and blow me! I find I have to play with the Harris. Am rather brusque, while he looks moody.

George and Ivy ask Delia and me to go mushrooming, so we

adjourn to a nearby field and pace solemnly up and down in strips, scanning the grass for the pearly blobs. We get a small basinful between the two of us. When we get back, find the Harris still lurking, but he says Goodnight when we arrive and sets out for the gate, looking back (so Delia says) 3 times. About five minutes later, we depart, and have just turned out of the gate when the Harris comes riding behind us, but doesn't stop, thank goodness.

Sunday, August 3rd: Have our mushrooms for breakfast. Go for a bike ride with Delia in the afternoon. Have a festive tea of raspberries and a home-made sponge sandwich – rare occurrence these days.

Bank Holiday Monday, August 4th: It rains in spasms throughout the day, with grey, dull skies. Delia and I go to Nottingham. Go in search of tea, but every café except two is closed and these have long queues, so we catch the bus home. Eat a huge tea and supper combined when we arrive. Delia cuts out two brassieres for me from my old college blouse, and we proceed to sew.

Tuesday, August 5th: Vile, beastly weather. Delia and I venture forth to Derby, wander around the shops, have coffee, buy a yard of Viyella material for bolero, a belt, cream and powder and a lipstick refill. Then have plaice for lunch at Boots. No possibility of tennis.

Wednesday, August 6th: Wander along to see Rayney this morning who is over from Nottingham, and she tells me about the blitz there, reciting to me with gruesome morbidity all the sad cases she has heard of connected with it.

Letter from Dougie. He is getting on well, he says with satisfaction, in the Home Guard now, and hit the Old Bull twice at

200 yards. They seem satisfied with his effort, he says, for he has been put in charge of an anti-tank gun. He is going to keep me to my promise about a holiday after the war – that is, if he manages to come through OK, he adds morbidly. He hopes to get in the Army before many more weeks (he has hopefully been anticipating this since the outbreak of the war) and he'd like to go abroad and take a look at some of the places that only the Army can help him to see. (That'll be nice!)

Go to tennis. Quite a few there, including the Harris, with whom I have to have 3 sets, to my inward annoyance. He mumbles to me while playing that it is a long time since he saw me, and adds hopefully, When is Delia going back? I say evasively, I Don't Know, so he says Oh. About 10 he says Am I Going soon, so I say Yes, Soon, so a minute later he gets up and mutters Am I Coming as he wanders off. Say Mmm, and Delia and I sit for about half an hour after that, until he is bound to be gone, then have a safe journey home.

Thursday, August 7th: Letter from Freddie, enclosing minute nail file that I suggested he might acquire for me. Otherwise the letter wasn't too exciting. He's coming home on Friday for the weekend and would like to see me in Derby on Saturday.

Go to tennis after tea, as George has rung up to say that he and Ivy are going. The Harris unfortunately is there, and he nips up at once to say Will We Play. Beseech Ivy privately not to make me play with the Harris, so when we spin, Ivy says Rough she'll play with the Harris. She spins and gets Smooth, but says glibly, 'Rough, so I play with Mr Harris.' He gives her a Queer Look, having seen the whole of this little performance. I do have to play with him later on, and during the game he tells me that I am Very Distant, he thinks, and has he done anything to offend me? Say Oh no, and whang a vicious ball back. The conversation then subsides, but when we come off, everyone else has gone, so I have to bike home with him. He renews the topic and says Yes, he thought I was Very Strange, in fact he was Quite Upset about it last night. Feel very mean at this, because he hasn't done anything to me except try to be Nice, so say breezily, Oh, he must have imagined it, and change the subject. Then he says that he won't see me many more times now, will he? So say No, tennis will soon be over, whereat he says he has enjoyed it very much. Relieved when I get home.

Friday, August 8th: Goldsmiths Old Student Association Handbook arrives, in which is the marriage of Freddie Stoneman last Easter, but it doesn't say to whom. This revives memories of my Dreadful Treatment of aforesaid Freddie.

Saturday, August 9th: Ring up Freddie and arrange to meet him in Derby, but warn him that I must get back on the 6 o'clock bus to play my singles. Garb myself in my new blue frock and navy bolero, with navy shoes and gloves, a combination in which I imagine myself to be Quite Smart, but Ivy shatters me by remarking that I look Like A Schoolgirl. Go to the Gaumont, but the programme not too good. Freddie very daringly holds my hand – a feat which must have required great courage and initiative. Let him, having no alternative, but make no response. He says he wishes I hadn't to go back so soon, but say I must, with firmness.

Monday, August 11th: Set forth hiking with Hilda Tooth. Meet Miss T about 11 and we just manage to scramble on a bus to Sheffield as it is leaving. Arrive at Sheffield about 12 and see lots of bomb damage. Terribly grim to see the shells of great buildings in the centre of the city.

Wednesday, August 13th: An awful day. A torrential downpour all day long without a break. We thank heaven we are bound for

Buxton, where we'll be able to scurry into the flicks. Go into Boots for lunch and sit at the same table as two soft females of about 35, both married and both very lah-di-dah and shallow. One is about to leave Buxton for Bradford and the other is so sad about it: 'My dear, oh why must you go?' etc, etc. The maid of one isn't going to register for Women's National Service. She is simply going to refuse, out of sheer devotion to her mistress, I suppose! One of them exclaims that she is growing 'so tired of this terrible war: really, my dear, I don't mind who wins'. At this I sit bolt upright in disgust and give her a look of concentrated hatred, whereat she amends her remark to, 'Well, I do, I suppose, really,' and offers me a cigarette. I refuse with curtness.

Thursday, August 14th: Determine to wander round Buxton before leaving. Explore the gardens and the Museum, scour round the Reading Room, and see that an announcement of importance is to be made at 3 p.m. by Mr Attlee. This leads to many conjectures.*

Saturday, August 16th: Pack my bag and get ready to go to Skegness with Barbara. Arrive at 9.45 to find her Bob pacing about, looking worried. Put up at the Red Lion in Burgh. Go to a dance. Hear four bombs just after getting into bed, and learn that twelve were dropped within a radius of two miles.

Sunday, August 17th: Go into Skegness. See the sea for the first time in 2 years. Lovely tea of salmon mayonnaise and slab cake in a café.

---

*Clement Attlee, the deputy Prime Minister, announced on the radio that Winston Churchill had met President Roosevelt (on a battleship off the New England coast) for three days of conferences.

Monday, August 18th: Up early, and start back at 8.15. Stop for coffee outside Nottingham and Barbara loses the ignition key and we have an officer and a waitress both helping to look for it when B finds it in her bag. Stopped by a policeman who asks B how she'd immobilise her car in case of invasion.

Lovely evening. Go to tennis. The Harris there, but have nothing to say to him. Oh goodness! He'll tell me I'm being Distant again.

Saturday, August 23rd: Oh, the most vile, awful, wretched, horrible, miserable, depressing day. Nothing but uninterrupted rain. Can't settle down to anything. Can't read, because it's too much like anticipating the winter, and I dislike the winter too much to anticipate it. Letter from Freddie, now back at Nuneaton in his old digs.

Monday, August 25th: Wailings and gnashing of teeth. Assailed by the most terrible feeling as I trail miserably into school. A drizzly, dull morning, with a new class to get accustomed to.

Tuesday, August 26th: A lovely day again, just because we're cooped up in school. My material arrives from Austin's – 2 lots, so bang go 15 coupons! Also have to borrow the money to pay for it. Still, it's quite nice. A mauvy-blue crêpe and a turquoise with little white leaves painted over it. Go to tennis and am free from the Harris menace, thanks be, as he doesn't come. Quite a relief to be able to walk about naturally instead of playing hide and seek and exercising various little dodges.

Thursday, August 28th: Hoped we might be paid today, but we weren't. Go to tennis. Have to make up a set with the Harris, then shun him for the rest of the evening. Ivy and George come, and George warns me to have Nothing To Do with the Harris – People Talk!

Friday, August 29th: Receive a letter from the dear Freddie with 2 discreet little crosses at the bottom underneath his signature. Suppose they're meant to be kisses – silly thing! The weather forecaster before him, an MA, BSc, has not proved satisfactory and has been placed on a further 3 months' trial, but Freddie is sure he's doing well. Pay-day today, thanks be!

Tuesday, September 2nd: Go to Geary. Ivy and George there, also the Harris, whom I studiously avoid, though I feel very mean about it. Discretion often means rudeness and hurting people's feelings. What a business!

Wednesday, September 3rd: Two years ago today since we declared war. Remember the first thing Amy and I did when we heard the announcement at 11 a.m. on the wireless. We dashed helter-skelter to the shop up the road and bought a ¼ lb block of Cadbury's whole-nut milk chocolate, because we said there'd be none, intending to store it. And I ate mine that same morning. Then the sirens at night! – absolutely terrified when Mother and I sat snorting in our gas masks. What a time!

Letter from Dougie dear saying that his time expires on October 1st so he'll Soon Be Gone Now. Oh dear! He's been moaning about it for long enough. He adds that one of his pals was torpedoed and drowned last week. Poor boy! And that Bert is home on survivors' leave. But he says nothing about sending us any more garden produce. Had hoped he might send us some apples.

Saturday, September 6th: Go to Derby in search of a new coat. Go to Bracegirdles and I buy a sort-of air-force-blue plain tailored coat, like last year's in style and cloth. Leave a deposit, having no more money except £1 to live on until we're paid.

Bike to tennis. Mr Moody produces with pride the poem he

has written about the Home Guard, that I have already read twice and I have to read it again, then he reads it to the assembled company and says he wondered whether to send it to *Punch*. He also sent a poem called 'For Freedom' to his sailor brother, and it was put on the ship's notice board, and then published in the ship's magazine.

Sunday, September 7th: Day of National Prayer. Also anniversary of the first big air raid on London. President Roosevelt is to broadcast an important statement to the world on Tuesday morning (our time). Wonder what that can be? Probably a statement of American policy. Forgot to say that I had a bright and breezy letter from Swanee yesterday, saying that she's expecting me in October, and that Bill is going to send her a pair of silk stockings. He's still at Port Said.

Tuesday, September 9th: President Roosevelt's announcement was about American warships firing on enemy submarines when necessary.

Wednesday, September 17th: Run expectedly into Mr Harris on my way home at dinnertime so have to dismount and say Did He Have a Nice Holiday? He says Yes, and adds that he wondered whether to send me a card and decided not, because I Was Mean To Him when we played tennis. Oh dear! Stifle a groan. The man's always got a grievance. He says I hardly spoke to him. Break away from him exclaiming that I must get off to my dinner.

Friday, September 19th: Letter from Freddie asking me to meet him on Monday. Have to play the Finals of the Ladies' Singles, so cautiously check my prowling this afternoon so as not to Exhaust Myself beforehand. I found it much easier than I had expected, by some fluke. To my surprise – and everyone else's! – I win, 6–1, 6–2, so have now won the 1st prize of 12/6, with which I think I'll buy a book. Everyone pleased with my Staggering Result. Have never won a tennis prize in my life before. Really Amazing.

Monday, September 29th: Grandma's birthday but not much to buy her because (a) she can't eat anything (b) I'm hard up and (c) no coupons for anything wearable. Decide to buy grapes later on when her present ones are exhausted.

A mouldy sort of day. My class are an awful, tempestuous crowd. Find myself snarling and snapping. Would hate to hear myself. Am sure I sound most objectionable.

Contrary to my expectations, the Ardent Fred has not written since last Monday's meeting, so I must have frozen his Ardour. Don't mind. That would be the least of my troubles. My chief trouble at the moment is a pecuniary one. Although it is Pay-day, I am still in the most dire financial straits. After paying all my dues, demands and liabilities, I shall have an utterly insufficient £2 on which to subsist for the rest of the month. Moreover, I have broken four strings in my racquet, torn the sole off my best shoe, lost 2 savings certificates and also a library book.

Tuesday, September 30th: The ardent Fred deigns to write. His salary has been increased to £300 a year with an extra 5*d.* an hour for Sundays and hours between 8 p.m. and 1 a.m. He ends with three small discreet crosses beneath his name. I propose to ignore them as usual.

Letter also from Swanee to ask will I come next weekend. Shan't go now because I can't really afford it.

Thursday, October 2nd: Wend a diligent way to the WEA English lecture which has just begun again. A very sparse assembly. The lecture is on 'The Art of Expression' and is interesting.

Salts have some silk stockings. Acquire a pair, but they cost me 5/11 which is shattering in my present impecunious plight.

Friday, October 3rd: Breaking-up day. Experience the usual glow of well-being at the thought of a fortnight without school.

Mrs Tweed comes to Grandma's with us and asks for the umpteenth time what my father thinks of the war now, but he gives an evasive answer. Mrs Tweed optimistically asserts that we shan't get the bombing again as we used to have it. Huh! I wonder! A foolish hope, I think. It's only because Germany is busy with Russia that we have this lull.

Saturday, October 4th: Have my hair moulded into entrancing undulations, but as usual by bedtime the luscious curls droop sadly.

My coat arrives and it is Miles Too Long and I think I like my Yellow One better. Oh dear! What a disappointment, what a waste! Have had no time to display it to the family yet.

Sunday, October 5th: Don my new coat, after warning Mother that it is Miles Too Long. She gives one look and asserts decisively that it is Much Too Long. Say I Know, and she adds, It's So Long that It Makes You Look Fifty. Say I shall have it shortened, and she continues, Much Too Long, and can't think Why I Had It So Long. Repeat that It Can Be Shortened, and she asks Didn't Anyone Notice It Was Too Long? Take it off in despair and pack it away.

Grandma very ill.

Monday, October 6th: Hilda and I arrive in Buxton at 4.30. Have to get our own meals at Sherbrooke Lodge, so have a sumptuous tea-cum-supper of bread and butter and cheese and biscuits and an apple. Dive off into the nearest flicks after this to see Marlene

Dietrich – as glamorous as ever – in *Seven Sinners*. Out by 8.30 so we drink milk in the nearest milk-bar, then back to the Hostel. About 8 others there, so we sit in a group round the fire, knitting, reading and chatting in desultory fashion. One girl remarks with sagacity that in Finland They All Have Baths Together – Steam Baths, she adds, as though to condone this Strange and Primitive Custom. They also have Double Glass in the windows, she remarks further.

Tuesday, October 7th: Marvellous to relate we actually do what this holiday was intended for, and hike. Only a miniature hike, compared with the efforts of Veteran Hikers, but a hike it is, nevertheless. I feel a certain sense of relief in leaving Buxton. While I'm there I feel impelled to slink along the streets like a murderer

Hilda Tooth

revisiting the scene of his crime, in case I bump into His Reverence.

Reach the Hostel just after 5 to find that we are the only 2 in, but I don't feel any discomfort at that, but rather a sense of relief, as we can spend a comfortable evening without having to make conversation and appear friendly to strangers. Which is quite the wrong attitude really, I suppose.

Wednesday, October 8th: Breakfast most amazingly on fried eggs, bacon, bread and butter and jam – and plenty of sugar! Then proceed to Hike, really Hike. The Warden suggested a good walk to us last night of about 14 miles, but we strongly deprecated this horrifying idea so he put forward an alternative one of about 8 miles. And that proves Quite Enough.

Friday, October 10th: Get to Derby just after 11, so we prowl through the shops, then have lunch at Boots. Go to the flicks to see Joan Crawford in *A Woman's Face* – quite good, and tea at the Midland. Have a lovely sundae with strawberry jam and chopped nuts. Home by 6.30, to find that Grandma died on Wednesday and is to be buried tomorrow. Oh dear! Knew it was bound to happen, but that doesn't make it any better when it actually does. Consequently everything very subdued, with funeral arrangements in progress and a general sense of loss.

Saturday, October 11th: The day of Grandma's funeral. It rains very early in the morning but clears by breakfast time and is bright but rather cold. The morning is spent in making preparations, receiving wreaths and so forth. A Mrs Lunn appears from nowhere, and seems to be taking charge in spite of deafness. She silently and methodically cuts innumerable sandwiches for the afternoon, being very sparse with the fillings and buttering only one side of the bread. The usual assembly trickles in for the funeral. Uncle John treats it as a convivial social gathering, as usual, and after the funeral, when we are back home, he distributes his latest products – not ornamental match boxes this time, but gold and silver Vs for victory. He adds meaningly when we all have one that he sells them for the Fund. At this, several of the assembly make hasty efforts to pay him, but I feel that I have been tricked, so I brazenly stick to mine and pay nothing. Besides, I have no money on me. The talk turns on the scarcity of petrol – amongst the men – and bits of scandal and gossip amongst the women.

Still no news of Jack Whetton who sailed out east 11 weeks ago. Everyone anxious.

Monday, October 13th: Confer with Mrs W about Styles for my frocks, but arrive at no satisfactory conclusions. In the end say Well, I'll Come Again.

General consternation this morn – Grandma's recent will lost, so a general search in progress throughout the morning. Finally an old one, substantially the same, is substituted.

Thursday, October 16th: My tardy reply to Freddie's last letter has evidently brought him up to scratch, for he bestirs himself to reply by return, says he really does Appreciate My Letters (I should think so!) and will Let Me Know The First Time He Can See Me (I'm not worried), and begs me Not to Be Annoyed because his letter is So Short, He Really Will Write Again (I'm not perturbed). The small crosses reappear very hopefully beneath his signature, but once more they will Be Ignored. He also asks hopefully Isn't It Nice of Him to reply by return? Not particularly. I shall just ignore the query.

Friday, October 17th: War news very grave again – the Germans have now penetrated one sector of the Moscow defences. But as usual, until it comes to our doorstep, we remain sublimely untroubled and unconcerned. Oh, what an awakening there'll be.

Go to Mrs W's and bring back my new coat which has been shortened. Hope to see a Great Improvement when I try it on, but am doomed to disappointment. Don't like it as much as my old one. My father says bluntly that It Isn't a Patch on my Green One (which is 4 years old). Oh dear.

Saturday, October 18th: The countryside is assailed by a most boisterous wind – a miniature hurricane in fact, which swirls and swoops about, stripping the last lingering leaves from the trees and tossing everything moveable madly about. Venture forth, however, to Burton to pay for the wreaths, and recklessly decide to plunge on a Jaeger set of vest and pantees for the winter, 17s. 10d. and 6 coupons, but beautifully soft and warm and small. Hate large, bulky, cumbersome things. Also buy two patterns.

Sunday, October 19th: I have lots of odd jobs to do before starting school tomorrow – oh repugnant thought!

Monday, October 20th: The shades of the prison-house close round me once more.

The day opens with the long-expected apples and pears from the faithful Dougie, who is nothing if not generous. It is really awfully good of him, because he gets very little in return. That's what I call Real Generosity.

Wednesday, October 22nd: The Sword of Damocles falls, after an interval of months of peace, and the sirens suddenly blare forth. However, after various ejaculations and speculations we sink into resignation and listen to the planes chugging over with the all-too-familiar drone, while Auntie F unwinds a bed-jacket, Mother knits and my father and I settle down to snooze. The guns thud away until after 11, but about 11.30 the All Clear sounds and we retire to bed.

Thursday, October 23rd: Mr Wheat reports that a man was killed at Hartshorne last night by an anti-aircraft shell.

Friday, October 24th: Jack has arrived safely in the Middle East and is in the desert somewhere. He has sent airgraphs and cables.

Saturday, October 25th: To Derby to take the Unsatisfactory Blue Coat – confound it! – to be altered. Wish I'd never bought it. However, plunge on a new dress while I'm there. A startling affair in black, with a red corsage with gold spots and very protruding shoulders. Have tea at the Midland.

Sunday, October 26th: An offer for Grandma's house has been received from Mr Ward, which it is deemed wise to accept. Oh dear! It *will* seem strange when Grandma's is in the hands of strangers.

Mrs Tweed says that it was Derby's Perfect Blackout that saved it from a blitz last Wednesday, and adds that it had the Purple on Friday and last night too. She seems very concerned about this. She is also going to knit herself a balaclava helmet for cycling in. What a vision!

Monday, October 27th: Freddie's burst of enthusiastic letter-writing has soon ebbed. He hasn't written since his reply by return.

Present of apples from Delia's mother. Dougie has offered to send more apples, so think I shall let him. He tells me sadly that one of their Home Guard Blokes blew his brains out the other day, and that they have had several sirens.

Grandma's house finally and irrevocably sold to Mr Ward.

Tuesday, October 28th: The usual query – have we done the right thing in selling the house – crops up again, and we take down the dinner service to wash and divide it. Reminds me of countless Christmas dinners and family occasions when it has shone forth in the glory of its blue and white. Oh, it does seem awful to have to break up things like this. It isn't just the house that's going.

Wednesday, October 29th: A letter from the erring Fred. He had Intended to ask me to meet him in Burton yesterday, but the poor little dear has a Cold. It is a Great Pity, he says, because he is Very Much Looking Forward to seeing me again. He is also due for 3 days next week and would like to see me, but he doesn't see how it can be arranged. I do like his enthusiasm! Still, it's on a par with mine, so I can't very well complain. Am merely piqued because of the blow to my conceit. He thinks I ought to have a correspondence in Economics. Am puzzled.

A most vilely cold, bleak day. We have a fierce little snowstorm at dinnertime. Snow already! Hang round the pipe at school and the fire at home.

Thursday, October 30th: Buoyed up by hopes of being paid, I spend the day in pleasurable anticipation. Accordingly, when Connie summons me at 10 to 12, I speed thither on nimble feet. Alas! She wants to discuss a Proposed Dancing Lesson. Wander home suffering pangs of acute disappointment and distress.

Am also distressed, upon fetching home my purple coat which has been dyed black, to find that is Ruined. It has shrunk so that it will not meet, there are 3 bald patches on the fur of the left pocket, and the lining is a horrible puce colour. Simply Ruined. I do seem to be having a lot of trouble with my coats lately. The trouble is, I'm gaining weight rapidly and am 8 st 10 lbs, which is Colossal and most disturbing. Am advised to Take Back the Coat to be stretched, so I do, but without much hope. When the assistant measures me, she makes me feel like The Professional Fat Lady, and asserts with an Odious Smile that I don't look as though I'm living on rations. Tell her with dignity that I Don't Eat Much At All. But it's getting very serious.

Friday, October 31st: Pay-day, tra la la! Buy a new writing pad to celebrate. What more blessed day is there than a Friday and Pay-day combined? Letter from Delia, who remarks desolately that the fire is almost out and no more prospect of fuel although it is only 7 p.m. She adds that there's no one to talk to there, and goes on to say she's sure I'd Love It. Why? Am I of a Morose and Taciturn Nature? Or is she being Sarcastic and Implying the Opposite? Would like to know. The faithful Harry is still on her trail.

My father sells some Scrap Brass, and shares the proceeds with me, so I receive £1, to my joyful satisfaction.

Saturday, November 1st: Catch the 20 to 1 bus to Derby with Mother. Buy some black suede shoes with red kid trimming to match my dazzling and glamorous new dress of black and red. We scout around the Midland Drapery until the café opens for tea at 3.15. We are lured by entrancing visions of plaice and chips, but black disappointment awaits us – No Plaice, No Chips. I have a sundae. I don't mind – it will benefit my waistline to forgo the chips. And I have lost a pound this week – praise be! Great indignation gushes forth when chips are later seen, and Mother declares her intention of Telling That Girl, but doesn't.

Monday, November 3rd: Am now clad in stockings once again. Was determined to do without what is now a luxury until the end of October. Now that November is here – and horrible cold weather – I can wander forth fully clad again.

Mr Skerritt calls in the evening while Mrs Merchant is here.

He has hardly gone before she bursts forth that she could Throttle Him! She Hates Him! She hasn't patience to talk to him! He ought to be fighting for his country. She is exceedingly wrathful.

Wednesday, November 5th: In the old days this would have been the signal for bangs and cracks, flames and stars and shooting rockets, and bonfire toffee. But now even the smallest unscreened light brings a fine of 30s. or £2.

Thursday, November 6th: Letter from Dougie who is now playing football again, so I expect his next batch of letters will be all about matches. At any rate it will give the Home Guard a rest, thanks be!

Sunday, November 9th: It is Remembrance Sunday, so the usual wreath of poppies is propped up against the altar in church. The Vicar is having trouble with the choir boys who make merry during the Curate's sermons, so today he gravely leaves his chair at the beginning of the sermon and seats himself in the front pew where he fixes the recalcitrant boys with a stern eye. They sit like mice. The Curate's sermon is all about something incomprehensible.

Monday, November 10th: Semi-darkness at 8 o'clock and torrents of rain. Would much rather remain in bed until conditions improve, but with a silent groan I grope for my clothes and awkwardly try to lay the foundations of my attire in bed.

A Communication from Freddie. He was most hurt by my insinuation that it was a trouble trying to arrange to see me, poor dear. Actually, he says, he was very anxious to see me. Now I can sleep with a quiet mind! But he hopes to have a Really Good Day or Two together at Christmas – would I like it? Oh lor'! Would I?

The idea fills me with panic. One Really Good Day would completely finish me off.

Send a cake to dear Dougie in return for his gift of apples and pears (and in all honesty must confess that it is sent in hopes of inspiring him to a further consignment – what wretched greed!).

Tuesday, November 11th: Remembrance Day is scarcely observed this year, except for poppy-selling last weekend.

This evening we talk about about Spiritualism, Stepping Falsely out of Trains in the Black Out, and Friendly Societies.

Saturday, November 15th: Miss B informs me as I have my hair set that there will soon be no more perms as there are to be no more sachets made. Well, nature will soon be visible in the raw again. No perms, no cosmetics, even a shortage of clothes.

Sunday, November 16th: Mother falls asleep during the sermon and starts to snore gently. She spends the evening dozing over a novel, but wakens to ask abruptly what we'd do if the Germans suddenly came in and ordered us to clear out.

Monday, November 17th: Dougie hasn't written yet to thank us for the cake. Hope it arrived safely.

Miss S comes back after the weekend with a fabulous yarn of how her cousin to whom she was once engaged, and whom she hasn't seen for years, suddenly reappeared this weekend and asked her to marry him, before he goes out east. What excitement! My father sits unmoved throughout the tale, and makes no comment but says later very decisively that he Didn't Believe a Word of it. Am inclined to echo this.

Tuesday, November 18th: A letter from Dougie at last, announcing the safe arrival of the cake, and his latest HG exploits, to wit, anti-tank practice, a church parade, and nearly dropping his gun.

To Mrs W's to have my black (dyed) coat fashioned into shape again after its maltreatment. She tells me how her father was Gored by a Bull at 81. How terrible! And he never lost consciousness. His clothes had to be cut from him. He was Covered in Blood from Top to Toe and half his ear had gone.

Wednesday, November 19th: Our last night at Grandma's. Didn't like going at first, and now I shan't like Not Going.

Thursday, November 20th: For the first time for well over a year, I sleep in my own room. Auntie F shares my bed and I toss and roll about all night and get very little sleep.

Friday, November 21st: The Home Budget reaches me, with all the doings of our gang. Maretta is still at Blackpool, playing mixed hockey and badminton, and doing PT and dancing. Kath, says Maretta, is delightfully happy in Abadan, loves housekeeping and plays a lot of golf and squash. Woody writes of Royal visits to Hull, during which the Queen broke down, and of Churchill's comment that he had never imagined that such devastation could exist.

To Grandma's, to find everything looking very bare, as what is left of the furniture and carpets is all placed ready for the sale tomorrow. Home again to sleep.

Saturday, November 22nd: Freddie writes and tells me Not to Expect a Long Letter Dear. Oh no, Darling, I won't. Also he has just started his holiday and goes to Scarborough for a week. Do Drop me a Line, he says, to let him know I'm not annoyed with him. The Line isn't going to be Dropped until he's back again. He's looking forward to seeing me at Christmas. I simply Can't Wait!

Sunday, November 23rd: Communion is at 8.30 now because of the blackout, which lasts until 8.13. The Curate preaches this afternoon about Running the Race that is set before us, and he is very prosy. He is just a younger, and if possible, more earnest and verbose edition of the Vicar.

The first Sunday night at home for years and years. Luckily we can't sit brooding over it because Mrs Tweed trips in about 6.30 and stays chatting and gossiping until 8 o'clock.

Monday, November 24th: An occasion for praise and thanksgiving – today we start school at 9.30 a.m., and this wise and providential decree is in force until the end of January.

Auntie F departs rather pathetically to take up her abode with her daughter-in-law. Feel very sorry for her really. No one's home is the same as your own.

Tuesday, November 25th: The Blue Coat – ill-fated creation – is a Problem no Longer. Have sold it, at a reduction of course, to Miss S. She looks much better in it than I did.

Wednesday, December 3rd: Letter from Freddie, now back from his week at Scarborough. He would like to meet me in Burton next Tuesday. And he has been officially recognised by the Air Ministry and posted permanently at Bramcote.

Thursday, December 4th: Dear Dougie announces the imminence of his departure once more. He will have to go any time after Dec 15th, he says. Oh dear! I've heard this tale so often! Then he adds ominously (for me) that he might Pop Over and see me one of these days after Xmas because he would like to see what I look like again, if I don't object. I do! But I can't very well say so after accepting his cockerels, asparagus, lettuce, apples and pears. Oh dear! Then he continues morosely that once he gets in the Army there is no telling where he will get to, or when and if he gets back again. But he predicts a Merry Hell of a Splash before the war finishes (oh dear!), but adds that we shall Beat the Blighter in the end.

Have perforce to go into Lisle Stockings – oh monstrous! They look terrible. But I can't keep going with the silk ones.

Saturday, December 6th: Go to Derby. Meet Hilda T and we have lunch at Boots – steamed halibut – then make our way to the theatre to see Vivien Leigh in *The Doctor's Dilemma.* Have a simply super seat, right in the middle of the front row of the circle. Awfully well done, and a very good show indeed. Vivien Leigh is lovely. She wore a beautiful purple velvet dress at the end.

Pouring with rain when we emerge, and get soaked. Manage to get on a bus immediately, and get a seat into the bargain. Am just sitting down when someone pokes me, and looking up, I see – the Harris! Haven't seen him since tennis, much to my relief. He hovers around my seat and turns a deaf ear to the conductor's plea to those standing to Move Down Please, and eventually the wretched man manoeuvres so that he has the seat next to me. At first he talks casually about The Blackout, The Play, Tennis, Christmas and so on, then he suddenly demands why I was so Distant in the summer. Reply evasively, then the silly cheese is spurred to confess that he Never Meant to Tell Me, but he fell Hopelessly in Love With Me, and lost hours of sleep when I was so mean to him. He says he has Got Over It Now. Silly ass.

Weigh myself in Derby, after a week's dieting. Nimbly mount the scales with hope in my heart, and watch with horror the needle swing round to 9 st. Gasp, blink and look again. 9 stone! Crawl off in black despair. Have never been nearly so heavy in my life. Can't understand it.

We have declared war on Finland, Romania and Hungary. No matter! Let 'em all come!

Sunday, December 7th: Much excitement in the news. Japan, after many manoeuvres and concentration of troops recently, has raided American bases in the Pacific, and the Hawaiian and Philippine Islands.* Everyone therefore on tiptoe of expectation. The King of the Belgians married again, to a commoner.

Monday, December 8th: Speeches today by Mr Churchill and Pres Roosevelt, both declaring war on Japan. Ordinary BBC programmes therefore much put out and interrupted.

Tuesday, December 9th: Telephone call from Old Friend Fred to say he has to work today, so can I meet him tomorrow instead. Say Yes.

Wednesday, December 10th: Bad news. The *Prince of Wales* (one of our latest battleships, on which Roosevelt and Mr C met in the summer) and the *Repulse* sunk by Japanese bombers in the Far East. 2000 survivors, but Adml Sir Tom Philips reported missing.

Meet Freddie in Burton at 5. Go to the Ritz for tea, then into the flicks to see *The Lady Eve*. Freddie opens his heart and takes me into the best seats, the half-crowns, so sit in luxury. Esme G has volunteered for the WAAFS.

Thursday, December 11th: Germany and Italy have now declared war on the USA.

Wallow in a sea of decorations at school. Despite war conditions and a shortage of paper, the children have brought loads of garlands, so have the job of putting them all up.

Friday, December 12th: Large parcel of apples and nuts arrives from Dougie. Good old Dougie!

*Pearl Harbor 7 December 1941.

Letter from dear Freddie saying he enjoyed seeing me very much on Wed (how touching!) and wishing he could see me more often (I don't!) and ending with Five Crosses. He wants to see me next Sat in Derby.

I am now 8 st 10 lb – a loss of 4 lb! Thanks be! But I had only my thin costume and thin shoes on.

Thursday, December 18th: Stunned to receive a letter from the Bishop of Buxton. Find a bold announcement of his engagement, and the credentials of the lady in question. So what? Shall ignore it. Do not feel either like giving my blessing or alternatively writing in sarcastic vein. So shall do nothing. In fact, there is nothing I can do, if it comes to that. He must have written as a sop to his conscience.

We are galvanised by the wail of the sirens just after 7.30, but the All Clear sounds about 8.

We Are Paid.

Friday, December 19th: All women between 20 and 30 to be called up but with a few exceptions, school teaching being one. Break up. 3 loud and prolonged cheers! We have decided as a staff to dispense with presents this year.

Saturday, December 20th: Catch the 20 to 10 bus to Derby to meet Freddie. Am vastly intrigued by a conversation that goes on behind me in the bus and am dying to glance round to see what the females conducting it are like. But have to possess myself in patience till they get up to get off, then see that they are both earnest and bespectacled young women. They talk about cod fishing off Norway, Eskimos and Lapps, *Tell England*, and *We the Accused*. One describes in detail a book she has read about a surgeon who conducted cancer research. The woman next to me talks about the weather and the war.

Collect Freddie at 11 a.m. and trail him round while I buy frilling, a book, notepaper, and Christmas cards. He carries them for me with a look of patient resignation and suffering nobly borne. Then we have lunch at Boots – at his expense – and go to the flicks – also at his expense! – in the best seats. Tea at the Midland Drapery, and I catch the bus home. At my departure, bequeath an inferior pair of cuff-links upon him, but he doesn't seem very surprised at this burst of generosity on my part.

Arrive home to find the resuscitated Budget from Lil in India. Thought it must be at the bottom of the ocean by now. It has passed through the hands of the censor, and bits have been clipped out of Maretta's and Joan's letters.

Kath describes life in Abadan, Iran. They have a lovely bungalow with company furniture – plain and modern – but with their own trimmings, carpets, glass etc taken out from England. Their day begins at 5 and until 7.30 they play golf, or swim or walk or wash or iron. Breakfast at 9.30, and until 1.30 Kath stays indoors with shutters down and fans and cooler going because it is about 120F outside. They sleep or rest in the afternoon and at night go for moonlight swims etc. They have oleander and eucalyptus plants in their garden, and grape vines laden with fruit, and pomegranate and fig trees. The native cook and boy speak a mixture of Farsee and Arabic and the native quarters are really squalid – flat-roofed mud huts. They just had a marvellous time in Basra. What an exotic flavour! It makes me envious. Lil also tells of the heat, which is a humid one in which one's skin is never dry. Joan has had a Terrible Experience, having been assaulted by a soldier while cycling down a lonely road on her new sports bike. The man got 3 years!

A surprise gift from Dougie today – a Cockerel, which is worth its weight in gold this Christmas, as poultry is so scarce. Good Old Dougie.

Tuesday, December 23rd: Arriving home find Maurice, having been there for tea. He is home on survivors' leave from the *Ark Royal* and relates his experiences until 7 p.m.

Christmas Day, Thursday, December 25th: Up in time for Early Communion. Back to open my presents, but know what they all are this year except Dougie's, which proves to be 3 pairs of Super-Silk Stockings, fully fashioned – whoopee, whoopee!

The first year we haven't been able to get a Turkey, but we have a goose instead.

Wednesday, December 31st: Meet Freddie in Derby. Lunch at the Midland then to the flicks. Am endowed with Xmas present – a silk square. My word! Freddie is becoming very generous.

1942

Monday, January 5th: School – oh, awful! Plod grimly through the day. Bitterly cold.

Speech by Mr Eden after the news last night, after his return from Russia – very good.

Tuesday, January 6th: Receive a letter from Dougie. He had a grand time at the Home Guard Dance at Christmas, he says. He bets some of the people there had Thick Heads the next morning, and remarks that he didn't feel too good himself. He also says he has plenty of coupons and can give me some if I wish. Gosh!

My father reads fictitious items from the *Burton Mail* – an announcement of the Viper Ron's engagement, which produces a speech of wrath from my mother, and a statement that we have made an advance in Syria, led by Jack.

Wednesday, January 14th: Day overclouded by the shadow of the wretched man, His Majesty's Inspector Booth, who descends upon the hapless C of E. Quiver and quake, fully expecting the blow to fall upon us, but it doesn't. He stays there all day and is most critical and not very pleased.

Friday, January 16th: Hapless day. Drop a bottle of ink at my feet upon reaching home at dinnertime and it smashes and splashes all over my boots and stockings and seems to have penetrated everywhere. In a terrific mess, with dark blue legs and hands, and stockings ruined beyond repair. Boots also unwearable until thoroughly cleaned.

Saturday, January 17th: Draw out £2 from the bank and flip off to Burton in search of crêpe-soled shoes. No more are to be manufactured, so get some while the shops still have a good stock.

Arrive home about 5. Find the Home Budget waiting, but it has letters in it from Kath (to Maretta) and Lil (to Vera). Kath describes the occupation of Iran by our troops as it affected them – warships on the river, gunfire and bullets etc.* Then Iranian officers demanded their car, to make a getaway, and they found it in a little village later, stripped of every available part and fitting.

Tuesday, January 20th: Snow – inches of it. Have to dig ourselves out. Huge drifts.

Wednesday, January 21st: The phone rings – a long-distance call which I answer. After a lot of helloes, a voice says, 'Is that May?' and then says two or three times, 'This is mumble-mumble-mumble.' Can't make out the name, then finally decide it is Freddie, so say cheerily, 'Oh, is it Fred?' A brief pause, then the voice says, 'No, this is Doug.' Wilt and say deflatedly, 'Oh, hello.' He wants to know why I haven't written and mentions that he is coming over one weekend. Oh lor'! Thought he'd forgotten.

Saturday, January 24th: Travel to Derby and meet Freddie. We prowl around, have lunch at Boots and then go to the flicks to see a long but mediocre programme. Tea after this, then catch the bus home. Am paralysed in case Dear Freddie attempts to kiss me in the bus park, so when he lays a hand on my arm, I leap on the bus in a panic, and leave him looking rather puzzled. Probably no such thought had entered his head, but wiser to take no risks.

---

*After the Shah refused to expel German nationals, British and Russian forces invaded to secure the oilfields and supply routes.

Thursday, January 29th: Letter from Swanee bluntly asking, Why Don't I Have Freddie (as though she's handing him to me on a plate ...! Good old Swanee!). She thinks he's Jolly Decent. Mmm! Good advice!

Friday, January 30th: Today we meet the full blast of Increased Income Tax. My hopes of a new coat, new ankle socks and new underwear fade. I have to face a reduction of £3 14s. 2d. a month from this day forward.

Dear Freddie deigns to write. He has a feeling that he will be posted very soon, but hopes they won't send him miles away so that he can't see me. He would be Most Upset if they did, he confesses.

Spend the evening by the fire unpicking my last year's tennis dress to be remade, in the interests of economy.

Saturday, January 31st: Activated by the Principles of Economy, I tell Miss T when I meet her in Burton this morning that I intend to have a frugal lunch. Accordingly ask for Something on Toast, but the waitress says coldly that they only serve The Lunches. Considerably dashed by this. So have the cheaper of the two and moan silently. Hilda shows me effusive telegram from her Bert, thanking her for her Christmas parcel, and telling her that she is Always in His Thoughts Darling. She thinks he is just off India.

After this we take a bus to Derby, where I am sufficiently demoralised and weakened to buy a pair of yellow ankle socks, so finally cast the principles of economy to the wind and spend all I have (which wasn't much, however!), except for a shilling. Having chosen and paid for the socks I am engulfed by a minor catastrophe, for I find I have no coupons, having left them in my other bag. After much debating and the assistant's dashing to and fro in search of the voice of authority, she says she'll put them by until I have sent the coupon – but I'll have to leave postage on them!

Write to Dougie, telling him that he may come either of the two following weekends (with much inward reluctance and misgiving), to Delia, World Books, and the Midland Drapery enclosing coupon.

Wednesday, February 4th: Letter from Hilda T saying she will trot over on Friday. She looks forward to hiking at Easter, when she says we will show the world great strength, great stamina! Poor Bert, she says, is now existing on corned beef, very dry biscuits, and three thin slices of bread a day. Letter from Freddie suggesting that I go to Birmingham with him on Saturday.

Friday, February 6th: Letter from Freddie changing Birmingham to Burton because of a difficulty with connections.

Saturday, February 7th: Go to Burton to meet Freddie. Go to the Ritz to see *Married But Single* which has amusing incidents but is silly and not my type of picture. Freddie seems to be thoroughly amused. Have tea at the Electric, then the bus home. Freddie wants me to meet him again on Tues. Oh dear! This is getting too thick. Will have to put a stop to it.

Tuesday, February 10th: Trek to Burton to meet Freddie, who comes attired in natty new trilby of the type I dislike – viz squashed flat on the top, like a pork pie. Far too dandified. Am not therefore half as concerned as he is when a strong gust of wind sends it rolling along the damp and dirty road. He scuttles feverishly after it, while I stand and giggle. When retrieved, he doctors it tenderly with his handkerchief.

Wednesday, February 11th: The blow has fallen – all those cockerels are coming home to roost, and the dear Dougie is about to appear.

Friday, February 13th: Renie thinks Dougie is coming over to propose . . . In that case I'd better start packing at once, ready to return to Ely with my intended. Gosh! What a prospect!

Dougie writes to tell me that he'll be here at the appalling hour of 1.47! It's a pity he can't travel overnight – he'd be here even sooner then! He got in the Dickens of a Row with the football secretary for dropping out of Saturday's Cup match, he says, but he's Jolly Well Coming to see me now he's got the chance. Nearly send an urgent note telling him on no account to drop out of the match. Oh dear!

Saturday, February 14th: Get all prepared to receive Dougie at 2 p.m., but he doesn't put in an appearance until 4 o'clock. He brings dressed chicken, ham and 20 eggs, and a purple butterfly for me! Carry him off to the Empire after tea, then we play Lexicon with Mother until bedtime.

Sunday, February 15th: Doug anxious to go to church, but am equally anxious not to take him, so yank him hurriedly off for a secluded walk around Cadley Hill. Go to Auntie N's to tea and home in time to hear Mr Churchill's speech. Singapore has fallen! No evacuation, either. Oh dear!

Monday, February 16th: After accompanying me to school, and badgering me vainly to promise to go to Ely, Doug returns to Ely at 10 a.m. Well, that's that, thanks be!

Letter from Freddie – typewritten most appallingly. Says if I go to his home in the summer, he'll give me some trout. What a hope! He also rings up to see if I'll meet him in Derby tomorrow, but I'm not in, so I drop him a brief note saying No, I have already promised to go out.

Thursday, February 19th: A letter of thanks from Doug arrives by the morning's post. He says sadly that he only wishes I were as pleased to see him as he was to see me, but that would be impossible. True, too true!

Icy cold, but brighter today, and the general brightness results in a conflux of visitors – Auntie Nell, Auntie Frances, Mrs Tweed and Brenda here for tea. Mrs Tweed announces with pride that Amy has had a job offered her at £4 15s., then weeps in case Amy will take it and so remove herself from home. She could also have a job at Woodville, if she'd only accept it.

Auntie Nell thinks Dougie was very nice and was ashamed of the way I treated him!

Saturday, February 21st: Trail to Birmingham in very disgruntled frame of mind, owing to the bitterly cold weather, with snow. Would rather stay by the fire.

Arrive about 12.15, so after I have shivered pointedly, dear Freddie takes me for lunch. As it is still bitterly cold when we emerge, I shiver again, and we trek towards the nearest cinema. Have tea there afterwards. Freddie gives me some fuchsia-coloured felt flowers on a band, apparently for the hair, but I decide later that it is intended to be a necklet. Peculiar. The train is late, and I shiver and turn rapidly blue and pink-nosed. Arrive in Burton at 7. Attempt a hurried dash off the train, uttering an airy 'Cheerio', but he seizes me firmly by the arm just as I am sliding away and attempts to kiss me. Tear up the platform in a panic. Home about 8.

Monday, February 23rd: Am reading an Agatha Christie after tea – *Murder on the Links* – when my father brings home a real mystery-cum-murder story. A body has been found in a field at Gresley, with the face battered in, and teeth, hair and muffler – plus blood of course – strewn around. What an event for the district! Tongues will be wagging, conjecturing, relating and debating tomorrow. There seems to have been a fight and this man was knocked down and viciously kicked to death. Then he was dragged under a hedge. Ugh!

This leads to the story of the murder of 'Mexican Joe' – an unsolved murder that happened before the last war in Swadlincote, when my father and grandpa sat on the jury. We have all the gory details paraded, including the body in the wheelbarrow, and the suspicious action of the night-watchman in having his shoes unnecessarily soled and heeled a day or two later. Retire dubiously to bed after wallowing thus in crime, but have no gory dreams.

Tuesday, February 24th: The local murder still uppermost. There are columns about it in the *Burton Mail,* including the deceased's Sunday School record. My father has been summoned to appear on the jury at the inquest – evidently his fame on the Mexican Joe jury must have spread, and they are anxious to avail themselves of his Sherlock Holmes touch.

Wednesday, February 25th: My father sits on the jury, and a verdict of Death By Violence, due to haemorrhage and shock, is brought in by the coroner. We have a lively account of this at teatime.

Thursday, February 26th: Lots about the murder in the *Burton Chronicle.* A fellow of 23 has been apprehended and says he did it in self-protection. It didn't prevent his kicking the other poor boy's teeth out and his ribs in, and stealing his watch and money.

Friday, February 27th: Bike to Miss B's to have my hair set, and she asks if I've heard about the murder. (What a question!) She offers to fetch me the paper to read all about it, but she comes back to say that she must have lit the fire with it. We pool our knowledge about this terrible happening.

Saturday, February 28th: Bike to Swanee's. She agrees to come to Derby with me, Mother, Auntie Nell and Joyce in search of a coat. The expedition is doomed to failure. Five is too many to take to choose a coat, and the day we have chosen happens to be the opening of Derby's Warship Week, and the town is crowded. It is impossible to walk down the street without pushing and jostling and being violently elbowed in return. Bracegirdles is crammed and every cubicle full, but at last we are shown into the smallest, and a young, inexperienced girl shows me horrible coats that I hate on sight. Take them from her disconsolately and say Hasn't she Anything Else? She wanders forth and returns with even worse concoctions. They aren't even anxious to make a sale either these days, knowing that people will buy anything and pay anything. Dally over a blue tweed edge-to-edge which isn't bad, but frightfully ordinary, and finally say Well, I'll Leave It.

Sunday, March 1st: Wireless announces that Utility Clothes are shortly to be on sale, to exclude (almost) the other sort, and to be limited in price, style, and materials, with no pleats etc. Am wondering whether to phone and say I'll have the blue edge-to-edge coat.

Monday, March 2nd: Phone to say that I will have the blue edge-to-edge. So that's that! Anyhow, it isn't too dear – 7 gns, which is cheap nowadays.

Letter from Freddie saying he's working very hard, and had to feed himself with his left hand while he wrote forecasts with his right hand the other day.

Battle for Java going on. We're outnumbered, as usual. The Burma Road abandoned too.

Wednesday, March 4th: More Government changes, including our Emrys-Evans this time. He is Under-Secretary of State for the

Dominions. Good old Emrys! Anyhow, he does stick up for his convictions.*

Thursday, March 5th: My stars! It snows fiercely from morning till night, and we are enveloped once more. This is awful! Go about rampaging like a bull – albeit with a nasal accent and many snuffles and sniffs. It is now to be an offence to destroy waste paper, and civil servants in Whitehall are to write with blunt pencils to preserve them for longer use. My word! We're actually beginning to waken up. And food rations are to receive a further cut shortly I believe. Also all aged officers are probably to be removed – a list is being made and overhauled of all who have reached the age of 45. The trouble is that we never start until the battle is almost lost.

Saturday, March 7th: See several zealous members of the profession wending a diligent way to an NUT meeting, as I proceed in the opposite direction towards the 20 to 10 bus to Derby. The bus is horribly wet, and oozes moisture, and my feet rapidly grow colder and colder as we proceed. A white-haired market woman with a youngish face carries on a vigorous conversation with all around her, beginning with a dream she had last night. She felt Germans all round her, but no Home Guards. The invasion had started, parachutists were dropping, and all we had for defence were Wooden Bullets. After this she passes on to The Murder – the murderer being well-known to her apparently. A nicer lad never trod shoe-leather, she declares, but what worries her is his Theft of the Watch. She wishes he hadn't done that.

---

*Paul Emrys-Evans, Conservative MP for South Derbyshire, played a part in the replacement of Chamberlain by Churchill. He voted against the Government in the May 1940 Norway debate and was secretary of a back-bench group favouring change.

She concludes with the remark that we're Getting in a Rum State.

Go straight to Bracegirdles and have the blue tweed edge-to-edge fitted, and hanker after a Susan Small navy fine wool dress, piped with white. Go so far as to try it on, but reluctantly have to cast it from me, as it is 8½ guineas.

Wednesday, March 11th: A meeting of exceedingly private nature held today for the Food People (i.e. bakers, shopkeepers, etc.), but my father comes home and tells us all about it. White bread to disappear – no baking after 6 April.

Japanese atrocities at Hong Kong published. Awful!

Would love the navy dress I tried on from Bracegirdles, but my meagre pittance won't stretch to it.

Tuesday, March 17th: Clothing coupons to be cut down by ¼ – only 60 for 14 months! Lovely spring-like day.

Wednesday, March 18th: Letters from Freddie – hoping to meet me in Derby on Saturday morning – and Doug, mostly about Home Guard and football. Bob Tweed has sailed overseas, and Eric sails this week, I believe.

Saturday, March 21st: First day of spring – misty and dubious at first, but not bad later. Go to Derby in tweed costume to meet Freddie. Go to the flicks after lunch, tea then at Boots, and catch the bus home. Freddie darts off in most unchivalrous fashion and leaves me to wait for 25 mins for the bus, but do not mind in the least.

Saturday, March 28th: To Derby with Hilda T. The Birmingham and Southend teachers have had their bonus. Hopes of getting ours now.

Tuesday, March 31st: We Are Paid. But No Bonus! Also a visit from HMI Booth. Am calm and self-possessed while he is in the room, but tremble when he has gone out. Says he intends to return on Thursday – breaking-up day! – the dog!

Freddie rings up to say that he won't come to Burton after all because it is raining. But don't mind.

Monday, April 6th: First appearance of the National Loaf.

Meet Freddie about 11 in Derby. Have lunch then queue to see *Dive Bomber*, which is quite good. Keep my gloves on in the flicks.

Monday, April 13th: School again – with a vengeance. The wretched Booth prowls around, in and out all day.

Monday, April 20th: Letter from Freddie to say that he has been moved to Honeybourne in the Vale of Evesham near Worcester.

Wednesday, April 22nd: Letter from Eunice Lowe. Her boyfriend Eric Roberts is missing from Singapore.

Tuesday, April 28th: A small registered parcel arrives from Freddie, which causes Mother much excitement but not me, because I already know what is inside – his watch to be mended. Also a letter from Freddie saying he'll be home again the weekend after next and would like to see me if I wouldn't be too bored.

Wednesday, April 29th: Go to the Electric to see Walt Disney's *Fantasia* – which is composed of several symphonies played by the New York Philharmonic, and the images and scenes evoked by them. Am simply enchanted and enthralled. It is a Work of Art and a Work of Genius and the best flick I've ever seen. A most successful experiment. The colours are blended most harmoniously, the little animals, shapes, leaves and flowers etc most delicately drawn, and the imagination incredible. The whole thing is simply super – superb. Could see it again. Come home and rave about it to all and sundry. There is a ballet done by ostriches, hippopotamuses, elephants and crocodiles-cum-dragons, who are really quite graceful, strangely enough. There is a dance of the water lilies, and lovely little lady centaurs getting adorned ready to meet their male counterparts, with Cupids flying in between. There are 2 lovely flying horses – white and black, with 4 or 5 babies, all coloured differently. There's Bacchus, Diana, Apollo, Thor, Odin and several other mythical characters, and also prehistoric animals like the Dinosaurs – a section showing their evolution from the amoeba. One highly original piece is the introduction of the sound track, and the patterns evoked by different sounds – from the harp, violin, drums, cello etc. One symphony is represented merely by shapes – cloud forms, geometric patterns and so on. Simply marvellous.

Thursday, April 30th: O Day of Days. Pay-day – with additional bonus, increment and £7 10s. back bonus, so that I draw £21 9s. 9d.

Friday, May 1st: Arrange to go to the Sadlers Wells Opera when it comes to Derby on May 16th to see *Madame Butterfly* and book accordingly in the 6/- stalls, still feeling affluent.

Saturday, May 2nd: To Nottingham with Hilda and Joyce. Have a vegetarian lunch cheaply at the Savoy. Then I splash wildly on striped pyjamas, white satin underskirt, and pantees. Have tea at the Savoy among the troops – figs and ice cream – then out to Boots where Hilda's sister works as a dispenser and have three jars of cleaning cream and cleansing tissues from under the counter where they are kept for the privileged. Then have milk in a milk bar, then have to stand on a crowded bus as far as Donington. Lovely warm day.

Monday, May 4th: See Mr Wheat daily like Prometheus carrying fire to the shelters, which are now heated. Talk about luxury! We also have hurricane lamps for our enlightenment.

Saturday, May 9th: Meet Freddie at Derby at 10.45, and proceed to Nottingham, where we pick up the tickets for *Macbeth*. Very powerful opening – the witches are truly weird, with horn-like creations and picturesque tatters. Macbeth is superb and so is Lady Macbeth, and Macduff too. Duncan forgets his part once and has to be prompted, and he stumbles in several places, but he appears again in a minor part at the end, so perhaps he was understudying. Lady Macbeth's *chef d'oeuvre* was, I consider, the sleep-walking scene. Gielgud was consistently powerful all through.

Tuesday, May 12th: Learn that Eric is in Madagascar, because the names of the companies are given out on the wireless and the Seaforth Highlanders is one.
　　Vile cold day. Cold enough for snow. What a climate.

Saturday, May 16th: Go to Derby for *Madame Butterfly*. Very good, but Madame B, the dainty little child-wife, is a hefty creature of between 40 and 50 with a face like a horse.

Tuesday, May 19th: Dougie has deserted me – no letter since Easter! After all these years!

Wednesday, May 20th: Go to Mrs W's to have pink voile dress tried, but it doesn't look very impressive. Am very disappointed. Am getting tired of home-made clothes.

Friday, May 22nd: Letter from Doug! Yes, he has Jilted Me! He has decided I don't care a darn whether I see him or not, and that I'm not keen on writing, so what point is there? He thought it best to write because we have been Jolly Good Friends. Well, he ends, that's about all I have to say, and he supposes I understand. He is still Mine Very Sincerely Doug.

Whit Monday, May 25th: Worse weather than ever. Nothing but violent winds and heavy rain.

Tuesday, May 26th: This is really a most delightful holiday. A tentative bike ride is promptly squashed by sheets of unending rain which lash down with great and vicious spitefulness.

Friday, May 29th: Looks like being a nice day, but Oh no! More squalls. Meet Freddie in Derby and he drags me round the market buying celery and marrow plants. He brings me flowers . . . my my! A nice bunch of tulips and lilies of the valley.

Saturday, May 30th: After a dubious opening, the day blossoms into a really warm, bright, sunny, summery day, the best of the week. Go for a lovely bike ride. The countryside is looking beautifully fresh, with the young light green of the trees, the creamy-white of the hawthorn blossom, and the rhododendrons and bluebells in the woods.

After tea bike up to Geary. The Harris has his wife and two children there, to my great joy.

Thursday, June 4th: Glorious hot day, with a temp of about 86° in my room, and the tar dripping from the verandah roof.

Saturday, June 6th: Letter from Freddie. Simply boiling hot again, with not a breath of air. Go to Burton before dinner and buy shoes and a brassiere, with difficulty. Also buttons. Dad gives me 10/- for my birthday. To Geary and have a good set. Afterwards there is thunder and rain, but it clears up and we have another set.

Sunday, June 7th: I have been impressing the date on all and sundry for weeks now, but it doesn't seem to have aroused much activity or excitement. Cannot detect any rejoicing or thanksgiving upon this occasion of my nativity.

Much cooler today.

Monday, June 8th: Horrible cold north wind blustering about. Mother has a box of asparagus from Doug. A peace offering or just to show that he harbours Mother and Dad no ill-feeling, whatever he feels towards me? Too cold for tennis. Huh!

Thursday, June 11th: Nice night, so bike up to tennis. Have a grand set with Mr Harris, who largely affirms that it's the best he's had this season. Attempt to steal off home while he is talking, but he catches up. Still, he seems quite normal again. Thank goodness!

Friday, June 12th: King's Birthday. Go to the Electric to see *Dumbo* – another Walt Disney (his latest). The flick is simply marvellous, and Dumbo is positively sweet, and so is his little manager, the mouse, in his red uniform. Poor little Dumbo is most pathetic when all the children laugh at his big ears and pull them. Mrs Dumbo surveys him with the most marvellous look of maternal pride.

Most puzzling behaviour from Dougie. Another parcel addressed to Mr & Mrs C. Smith, containing a Dressed Chicken, New Potatoes, Gooseberries and Asparagus! Luscious! But he still hasn't written to me!

Saturday, June 13th: Dull and cold. Catch bus to Derby to meet Freddie. Lunch at the Midland Drapery. He has just had a rise of £11 a year. Go to the flicks – a song and dance affair with not a very powerful plot. Have tea afterwards and catch the bus home.

Go to Geary. Quite cold, so when we retire for a drink all have a port and lemon. Even that makes me lightheaded.

Sunday, June 14th: Have a most sumptuous dinner of chicken with stuffing, bread sauce, asparagus and new potatoes, and gooseberry and rhubarb tart. Lovely. For once cast all thought of my waistline to the winds.

Wednesday, June 17th: Still cold and grey. The first match of the season, but it will be the last I shall be picked for I fear. Play rottenly. Don't finish until 10.30, so it is 11 by the time I get home, and am so tired that I toss and turn in bed, and when I do sleep, am playing tennis in my dreams.

Sunday, June 21st: The fall of Tobruk – oh gosh! Things get worse.

Monday, June 22nd: The Libyan news is very bad. 25,000 prisoners and 3 months' supplies captured.

Wednesday, June 24th: To tennis. Ivy and George there, and Ivy tells me full details of a Rumpus on Saturday from the lips of an eye-witness. Mabel D – the snake – apparently said Well, she knew there'd been a lot of talk last year about Mr H and me and didn't know whether there was any truth in it, but *this* certainly makes people talk. 'This' being two sets with the blinkin' man. Scandal-mongers! Give them whiskers, claws and a tail. Shall certainly tell Mabel D. Fed up with all this gossip and malice and slander.

Retire to bed fairly early. In the midst of peaceful slumbers we are aroused by the sirens, which have lain dormant for six months. Mother immediately dresses, but none of us gets up. Alert lasts from 1.15 to 2.30. Learn later that they were at Nuneaton or thereabouts. My windows rattle alarmingly, but the bomb thuds themselves are hardly discernible.

Thursday, June 25th: Class is depleted a little after last night. Connie brings back our comprehension test papers and professes to be quite pleased with them. Waiting for the day of doom – viz our arithmetic ditto. She'll be horrified.

Monday, July 6th: Terrible bombshell. Schools to be open all through August. So have a meeting about it at school, but Connie very reasonable and will champion our cause, I think.

Tuesday, July 7th: The managers have decreed that we open all August, but we're to go in turns to dish out dinners, milk and entertainment, so it will only mean two or three days each. Might be worse.

Wednesday, July 15th: St Swithin's Day – and an odd shower or two during the evening, but then it usually rains on this holy day, and even if it doesn't we get the allotted 40 days of rain.

Connie more or less compels me to attend meeting about the Holidays-at-Home Programme. Just evade being put on sub-committee to arrange sports.

Thursday, July 16th: Oh calamity! A letter from the Harris, holiday-making at Blackpool and therefore apparently at a loss for something to occupy his idle moments. Says I am the loveli-est and sweetest girl he has ever known. Oh hush! Also the usual type of letter from Freddie.

After all this, spend the evening washing my hair.

Saturday, July 18th: Another pouring wet day. Brave the elements and go to Nottingham. See a marvellous turquoise coat which I would love in the Jaeger shop, but it is 15½ guineas. It would be! Nearly get squashed to a pulp boarding the bus. Arrive home to be greeted with the fact that that Blasted Man has been hanging about outside. He's mad.

Wednesday, July 22nd: Lousy weather. Rain all day. Letter from Dougie yesterday saying he has booked a cockerel for us for Christmas, and not to be surprised if he walks in on us one day as he knows someone who drives a lorry to Burton.

Thursday, July 23rd: Have the sirens during the night.

Friday, July 24th: Mrs Tweed here with the news that Amy is fixed up with a post at the Council School after all and won't therefore be leaving home.

Sunday, July 26th: Mother squanders her fortnight's sweets points, and we indulge in a 2 oz bar of chocolate and 2 oz of Mintoes between us. This gargantuan feast is disposed of in a matter of minutes.

Monday, July 27th: Rudely awakened at 6.30, as it is raining heavens hard, by the wail of the sirens. Hear two muffled bumps but little else, so go to sleep until the All Clear about 7.15. Compose myself for slumber once more, and manage to achieve a few winks, when lo! The warble tunes up again and shatters all repose. Get up this time, as it is just after 8, but hopefully anticipate a late start for school this morning. No good! The wretched perverse All Clear tootles merrily at 8.30, so to school as usual.

Have to represent Connie at the meeting for the Holidays-at-Home arrangements. Find that most of the other zealous and dutiful heads have had the same brainwave and have delegated unfortunate members of their staff to do their work for them.

Tuesday, July 28th: A disturbed night. Another air-raid warning lasting from 1.30 until just after 4. Hear planes and muffled bumps, but fall asleep before the All Clear. Learn later that Birmingham was the chief target. Feel quite out of gear for the rest of the day. The Rolls-Royce works were hit yesterday morning with some casualties.

Wednesday, July 29th: Spend the morning on the playground and part of the afternoon on the park running off heats for the children's sports. Somewhat energetic, but quite a pleasant change from the usual routine. Hope for a restful night, but this hope shattered by another raid on Birmingham from 1.30 until nearly 4 a.m. Try vainly to sleep through it but remain wide awake much to my exasperation. I always feel so washed out after these night watches.

Thursday, July 30th: I really think the weather has picked up. Today the sun shines and it is quite hot, and the sky is almost cloudless. Plod to the Rec with our Winners – 18 in all – to run off the Inter-School Sports, and for once Springfield Rd manages to shine. If we can't win the Salvage Cup at least we can run!

Home from tennis about 10.15, and retire to bed, worn out. And blow me – another raid! Am so dead-beat that I hear the siren half-consciously and think it is the All Clear, so lie abed quite happily, then I grow more and more anxious and realise the horrible truth. Raid lasts from 1.30 till after 3 but we don't get up. We are paid.

Friday, July 31st: Oh happy day! We break up, so have a terrific turn-out of all cupboards etc to mark the end of the school year.

Everybody of course wants to help, so we all fall over each other and I get peevish and irritable and begin to snap and snarl, and the noise gets louder and louder. Thank goodness for 4 o'clock! Shake the dust from my feet with profound thankfulness – although it isn't like having a clean break for 3 weeks, having to go back and dish out dinners.

Am still hankering after a new racquet. They have a solitary Dunlop at Lobbs.

Buy my month's chocolate ration today – four 2½*d.* bars! Still, it's a pleasantly exhilarating feeling to be able to choose from an assortment, instead of being presented with a bag of Take-It-Or-Leave-It, and accepting it, whatever it may be, with a feeling as though one has just received a magnificent favour. It's amazing how the shops have suddenly blossomed forth with sweets and chocolate after, 'Sorry! We haven't any!' Some people must have been having a terrific amount, but anyhow the points system should equalise that.

Saturday, August 1st: And a lovely hot day. Am hot on the trail of a tennis racquet, but I draw a blank at each shop, and a look of faint astonishment at most, that I should have the foolishness even to inquire for what is now almost unobtainable. Give up the chase therefore, and after weighing myself and discovering to my joyful surprise that I am now a mere 8 st 1 lb, I catch the bus home. Stacks of people with cases despite Govt's plea to keep railways clear and not to travel.

Sunday, August 2nd: Retire to bed fairly early, thinking optimistically that after all this rain we must be due for a fine Bank Holiday tomorrow. The sirens sound during the night, about 3 a.m., and for about the first time I sleep through, but the All Clear wakens me for a few minutes when it sounds about half an hour later. Nothing happening.

Bank Holiday Monday, August 3rd: And what a Bank Holiday! Cast a speculative eye towards the window upon awakening, but am considerably dashed to see rain and general greyness. It rains steadily until evening, thus effectively and without question biffing all idea of tennis on the head. Am thus stranded, with nothing to do, so potter around disconsolately. The only break to the monotony is the siren – which isn't as desirable a break as could be hoped for. We hear the loud and raucous wail about 2 p.m. and immediately smile at the incongruity of it. If it had sounded in the night there would have been no smile – and no incongruity. However the alert lasts only half an hour.

After tea, Joyce and I queue at the Empire. We see Wilfrid Lawson in an old Edgar Wallace thriller *The Terror.* After this comes *The Big Blockade* – a propaganda flick with a lot of wishful thinking put into it but quite interesting.

Shortly after the programme has begun, hear a sound resembling the siren, and find when we emerge that it really was the siren again. Apparently the canteen at Donisthorpe Colliery was hit at dinnertime, one man killed, several houses demolished.*

Tuesday, August 4th: Hear from Vera and Eunice this morning. Eunice has still had no news of Eric. They have just bought a horse and trap now that petrol is so inadequate.

Wednesday, August 5th: Freddie rings up to ask when he can see me, as he is now home until Sat. Huh! I suppose he thinks I'm sitting waiting. Tell him it's awkward, and that I'll have to see whether I can change the time for my hair and let him know, and add that he should have let me know sooner. Whereat he says

*Fortunately the colliery was not working because of the bank holiday.

aggrievedly that he didn't know till Sunday – it's this New Fellow in charge.

Thursday, August 6th: Ring up Freddie to say generously that I'll see him tomorrow after all, in Derby. He asks me about tennis, but before I have time to tell him, he starts to tell me about the marvellous tennis he has been having lately with County players and what-not. That's just Frederic all over. He's too selfish.

Now Dougie is not the least bit selfish. Hear from him this morn. He's been working very hard, making ladders. He'd like to pop over and see me again before the year is out. Oh dear, oh dear!

My duty day at school. 30 children turn up for milk and a mere 8 for dinner, so give them an early meal at 11.45 and bundle them off just after 12.

Friday, August 7th: Go to Miss B's to have my hair set, then to school to dole out milk and dinners, but am home just after 12. Attire myself very grandly in my black-and-red dress and black coat and journey on a hot and overcrowded bus to Derby to meet Freddie. Have tea early at the Gaumont then to the flicks to see *Uncensored.* Awfully good – about the publication of a free newspaper in Belgium during the Occupation. Home and pack ready for tomorrow. The Harris appears to see if I'll play in the tournament with him next Sat, but tell him No. So he says will I go for a bike ride with him next Friday, but again say No most decidedly.

Saturday, August 8th: Arise with the lark ready for the expedition to Wilmslow. Although the trains are full, we manage to get a seat all the way. Swanee is waiting on the platform, and we are soon at Windsor Avenue. Take a trot into the town before tea. Put the clocks back an hour before going to bed, and have just retired when the sirens sound, but can hear very little going on. The All Clear follows about ¾ hour later.

Sunday, August 9th: After breakfast we go for a 2½ hour walk through the woods belonging to the National Trust, by the river. Lovely and quite decent weather. Write letters during the afternoon, while we recuperate our energy for another 6 or 7-mile walk to Alderley Edge. We crawl back almost too limp to drop one foot after the other. Shortly after we are in bed, we hear the sirens. Then planes, then gunfire. Swanee affirms later that the alert lasted for about 3 hours. A raid made on Liverpool.

Monday, August 10th: We journey to Manchester, where our first move is towards the Tudor café for lunch. Then we begin to trail around the shops and see most marvellous things but at colossal prices. Have a lovely ice and jelly mixture at Marks & Spencers, then sit in some gardens until it is time to go to the Opera, where we have booked to see *Gaslight*, a thriller I have heard twice on the wireless and seen at the flicks and enjoyed each time. Out about 9. An undisturbed night.

Wednesday, August 12th: Have a comfortable journey and are in Burton by 11.20 and home in time for dinner. Gorge on stewed blackberries and apple and custard for tea, while Mother flips off to a Whist Drive in my best stockings, and returns with them laddered ...

Decide to Go to the Dance, not having been to the Rink since the days when dear Freddie took me. Attire myself after due deliberation in my black-and-red dress, but am not unduly staggered by the result. Find it quite a nice change, though compared with the old dances it is a sober affair. No decorations or bunting. Retire to bed about 12.30.

Thursday, August 13th: Get my bike fitted up with new batteries again, as the nights are beginning to draw in. Go to school, to find that the Scheme has been abandoned and I needn't have gone. Apparently everyone else has been notified by card. Why not I? Anxious to get away, but Mr Wheat has to show me the Hall, which took him 2 days to clean, and although he says it himself, there isn't a school in the district better kept than ours.

More rain, so I can't go to tennis. Instead go with Mother to the flicks to see Joan Fontaine and Cary Grant in *Suspicion*. Quite good.

Saturday, August 15th: Up early again, bath, grab a packet of sandwiches and a very heavy suitcase and catch the same train as last week but bound for the sea this time – Llandudno. Am not wildly excited by the prospect, being rather deterred by the £10 I shall have spent by the end of the week, and the fact that I shall miss the tournament today. I manage to get a seat. At Crewe I unearth my package of food, but seem to be the only one with anything substantial. The others eat plums and chocolate, but I wade solidly and hungrily through 7 cheese and tomato sandwiches and 7 biscuits. Journey seems endless. Miss Vera at Crewe, so grab her on Llandudno station. A man takes our bags on a lorry to the Apsley for 1/6, and we follow on foot as it is only a 5 min walk. The place seems at first rather small, but very clean, and we are on the 3rd floor. Go out for tea, and walk around to get our bearings, then in for dinner at 6.30. Lovely – soup, roast duck, stuffing, beans, potatoes, and mincemeat tart and custard. Find our way into Happy Valley and listen to the tail end of a concert party, another walk along the Prom where we hear the tail end of the Town Band, and in about 9.40. A peaceful night.

Sunday, August 16th: A lovely warm day. After a good breakfast of porridge, sausage, and tomato, and toast and home-made jam, we bask in the sun on deck-chairs on the beach. I write letters to Swanee, Freddie, Delia and home. The sea is almost without a ripple. It is a lovely day with the two Ormes on either side. The sun shines, children are paddling and building sand-castles. The beach is well filled with deck-chairs, but not crowded – there is plenty of Lebensraum, and it seems hard to believe that it is wartime. Have a lovely lunch after this – lamb, green peas, mint sauce and potatoes, and trifle – then walk about 4 miles along the Marine Drive and back through the town by tram, which takes about 2 mins and costs 1*d*. After this, Vera bathes, but I prefer to sit lazily on the beach, as the water is still rather chilly. Change then, ready for supper at 7.30 – meat roll and salad, salad dressing, bread and butter, and a most marvellous sweet – a sort of grapefruit tart with lots of fruit, and a sort of cream on the top. After this we go to the Orchestral Concert at 8.15 on the Pier, in the cheapest seats. Sleep very soundly.

Monday, August 17th: Most astounding weather – touch wood! Another bright, hot, sunny, summery, seaside day, and I get quite pinkishly burnt. After a wondrous breakfast of egg, bacon and toast, we make for Colwyn Bay by bus – 1/- return. There we bask on the beach until lunch, then have a snack at a café called the Blue Bowl, then we walk along the prom and into Eirian Park. Play miniature golf. Back then to Llandudno, where we bathe, and the water is fairly chilly but lovely.

Change into my blue costume and go for a short stroll until nearly time for dinner. Very tired after our exertions, but we return to a most marvellous dinner – boiled chicken with white sauce, cauliflower and potatoes. I have at least half the breast I should think, very thick and simply luscious. We have to dash away after this to the Pier, where we see a Clarkson Rose Variety called *Twinkle* which is very funny.

Tuesday, August 18th: Really hot again. After buying the morning paper, which announces Mr Churchill's visit to Moscow, writing paper and cards, we clamber up beyond Happy Valley in search of the miniature golf course which is advertised. Finish the 9 holes about 1.30. After lunch, proceed to the beach to bathe. Really lovely. Swim about quite happily for longer today. A man is solicited to take a snap of us. Leave the beach about 5, change ready for the evening. Very, very hungry, and we have another good dinner of soup, beef, beans and potatoes, and damson tart and custard. We shoot off after this to the flicks to see *One of Our Aircraft is Missing*. Quite good.

Wednesday, August 19th: Letters from home this morn. We awake to wet pavements and a thin drizzle of rain. However it is fine by the time we amble forth, and by lunchtime the sun is shining and it is really warm. We tram to the top of Great Orme and look around at the view. Then swing a nifty club at miniature golf. After lunch, we have an ice and a milk shake in the nearest Milk Bar, then get ready for bathing. Go to the Swiss Café for tea and cakes, then to the putting green, and return just in time for dinner – soup, fish with a very nice sauce, peas and potatoes, and charlotte russe. Nip off immediately afterwards to the Arcadian Follies, which is weak and simply mouldy. We trot out condemning it roundly and lamenting the sad fate of our 2/10.

Coffee when we get in and a chat with some other girls. Apparently, so Vera tells me, one of them, who is just over 30, lost her boy at Dunkirk and is only just recovering, and it has sent her quite grey. She has to rest in the afternoons.

Thursday, August 20th: A big Commando raid on Dieppe yesterday lasting 9 hours, we read in our papers this morn.

Dash out after breakfast bound for Bangor. We get as far as Conway, and find that we have just missed a bus. When the next one comes, we can't get on, and we can't get on the next either, so we give it up as a bad job and go to the nearest café for coffee and biscuits. Proceed with a bag of tarts for our lunch to Conway Castle. There is a square Norman window which has only one counterpart in the whole of the country.

Seek out then the smallest house in the country, which has 2 diminutive rooms, where a fisherman of 6′3″ used to live – or crouch, I should think. We arrive back in Llandudno in time to bathe. Go to the Swiss Café for tea, then to miniature golf. Go to the flicks after dinner – *Good Morning, Doctor.*

Friday, August 21st: A duller morning, and as there are oddments to be done, like buying a loaf for tomorrow's sandwiches, weighing ourselves, and exploring the Pier, we decide not to go to Rhyl. Find my weight to be still 8 st 2 lbs, thank goodness. After my massive meals, I fully expected a great leap upwards. Have lunch at the Dutch café, where there is an abundance of sugar – whereat we gasp in incredulity. Two middle-aged women share our table and are very jolly and chatty, so we laugh a good deal and part with a glow of good feeling. The woman opposite me had her purse taken out of her bag in Liverpool last week while buying fish, and it had £15 in it. She states this in sorrow but with imperturbability. With me it would have been a major calamity, but still, it would also have been a major miracle if I had had £15 to begin with.

Vera and I then walk along the Prom towards Rhos-on-Sea, but there is a tearing gale blowing. We retrace our steps looking dishevelled. After wrenching a comb through our locks, we venture forth again towards a café for tea. After this we pack and pay our bill, and feel much depleted.

Saturday, August 22nd: Vera drags me forcibly from my bed just after 8. Letter from Freddie saying it was sweet of Swanee to send her love, but he'd be more thrilled if I sent mine . . . ! What optimism! We have breakfast promptly, then leap into our taxi and are at the station by 9.30. Am home by 20 past 5. Have a large tea, then bike up to Geary. Mr H thanks me very sarcastically for the card I didn't send him. Tell him that his wife wouldn't have liked it.

Sunday, August 23rd: Clatter late into church clad in an assortment of garments – the first that came to my frenzied hands on my belated rising – and No Stockings. And there among the faithful few kneels His Reverence the Bishop of Buxton, with Mamma and Dadda! Whisper to Mother to Let Them Go Out First, but she whispers back that they are Still Praying, so I dive out, mount my bike and speed away.

Auntie Frances here to dinner. No chocolate to eat afterwards, as our month's ration has long since vanished, so make do with plums instead. About 10.30 the sirens tootle, but we don't get up, as it is only a short alert, though lots of gunfire. Incendiaries dropped at Stretton and a hayrick burnt.

Monday, August 24th: Oh vile and loathsome day. I return to the grindstone, and struggle through a long weary day, feeling as though I have never had a holiday. Have a new class up, but they seem better than the last and I have only 40.

Our Morrison table shelter has arrived, thick with rust and looking like a collection of scrap iron. It will make the front room look like a junk shop.

Thursday, August 27th: Our English summer has arrived with a flourish! We taste the joys of hot sun and a miniature heat wave. Folks go about lightly clad, complaining about the Closeness. But I fling open all the doors and windows at school and rejoice. The heat arouses all the wasps and flies of the neighbourhood too, from their early hibernation, because we have shoals of them buzzing about in school all day. The children keep waving corpses aloft and exclaiming in triumph that they've Killed One, Miss, and asking, what shall they do with it? Try to smile a patient smile.

About 20 lbs of luscious Victoria plums arrive from Dougie, bless his cotton socks! But it makes things very awkward. Still – the plums are really super.

Scramble into another frock and dive into Burton straight after school to meet dear Freddie. To the flicks, but it is very close and airless inside. Freddie opens his heart and takes me into the best seats, now 2/11, and even produces a bag of Mintoes, though I would much have preferred chocolate. Leave him at 8 o'clock to catch his train, and so home.

Wednesday, September 2nd: Oh shocks! O terrific shock – which makes me feel quite queer, though I don't know why it should. Have just come home from the flicks when the telephone bell rings, and who should it be at the other end but Freddie – home again. He rings up to say he has been posted – to West Africa! It seems incredible. Oh dear! Have treated him most casually and have put no end of things before him, but it will seem queer when he's gone. In fact (startling thought!) I shall miss him! This thought again gives me a shock. Anyhow, spend quite a restless night after all this. Don't know quite what to think except that it's Jolly Rotten. Freddie sounds quite gay, and treats it as a joke. So that's that! I'm to lose him after all these years!

Thursday, September 3rd: After all this, am awake very early, and present myself at 8 o'clock Communion on the dot, as this third anniversary of the war is to be kept as a Day of National Prayer. Amy whispers to me, 'You look awful,' and asks me how I feel.

Am forced to confess that I feel decidedly queer, but this passes off towards the end. Nevertheless feel very washed out for the rest of the day.

Dash out of school for the 5 past 4 bus to Burton, 4.30 bus to Derby to meet Freddie off the 6 o'clock train. It feels like the Last Supper when I see him now (no irreverence intended). Anyway, the saying 'You never miss the water till the well runs dry' comes home, though I'd never have thought it somehow.

It has stopped raining by the time we leave the station, but it still looks doubtful, so decide to spend the next two hours in the flicks. On the way and during the picture, Freddie tells me as much as he knows, about the posting. Another fellow named Francis is to go with him. Am presented with A Red Rose, and am very touched.

Collect Isobel and Miss S on the way from the bus. Apparently everyone is agog, fully expecting an engagement. What optimism! Have never considered it, nor am I in the least likely to rush into anything of that sort. Most impractical.

Friday, September 4th: See Dorothy Adams in Swadlincote and learn that Geoff is home on embarkation leave. Poor old Swanee! It might be years before they all return.

Had a most curious dream last night about The Last Days of Sir Walter Raleigh. Nothing happened in it, except that I saw dear old Sir W pacing up and down in his doublet and hose, and learned that all the members of his expedition were to die with him. I do have peculiar dreams.

My horoscope for this week, as predicted by the *News of the World* (awful rag): 'Midweek the most vital period. You will be brimming over with new ideas which will involve substantial readjustments. Rather a restless week, but your efforts turn the tide in your favour.'

One good bit of news, which has paled into insignificance

beside the events of the week – our War Bonus is to be increased
£19.10s. to £36 a year, as from 1st July.

Letter from Doug, thanking me for the invitation to come over
(which, however, was his suggestion; I merely politely said he
might), and saying he'll come some time before Xmas. He will
stay at a hotel, as he couldn't possibly stay at our place again. It's
not Playing the Game. Good old Dougie! That's the spirit. His
brother John is about to celebrate his last night at home, so (in
Dougie's graphic language) 'a flood of young women and boys
have rolled up and are holding a dance on the tennis court'.
They're always celebrating something or other.

Saturday, September 5th: Joyce has heard from Eric – in India.
Mouldy day. Depressing weather. Very bored. Think I shall have
to accompany Freddie to W Africa for a change of atmosphere
and a nice sea voyage?! Still can't believe he's going. It doesn't
seem possible. Haven't reverted yet to my usual attitude of sub-
lime indifference, but probably shall when the shock has worn
off. Can't tell yet. Only know that I wish he were not going and
regret having treated him so badly so often. Wish I'd been nicer.
Of course it may be because he's become inaccessible that his
stock has suddenly risen. Have noticed so often before that I
hanker after things when they seem unobtainable, then as soon
as they're in my grasp, my feelings change completely and I no
longer want them. I've always been like that. Silly! Also most dis-
concerting.

Showery and dull all day, with lashings of rain after tea.
Nothing at all to do. Write a spasmodic letter or two, the clock
seems to drag, the evening interminable. Finally wickedly decide
to practise the Art of Smoking – which I have never acquired, for
beyond the odd cigarette or two at school, when it seemed highly
daring, it has never appealed to me. Puff away, feeling like a des-
perado, very rash, very bold, and very much steeped in vice.

Unfortunately, keep having to stop to detach grains of tobacco from my tongue, cheeks and mouth. Still, I win through to the end, though I consider it highly overrated. Play Donkey with Mother, Auntie N and Joyce. Have an early supper, then read, while Mother indulges in highly imaginative and lurid speculations such as what we should do if Hitler suddenly walked through the door? and: 'Suppose Freddie asked you to meet him in Derby when Doug was here?' Consider both of these very improbable so continue to read.

Sunday, September 6th: Today's horoscope tells me firmly that of One Thing I can be Sure – things will not run just as I plan. Where I expect to succeed I'll probably flounder, and the doubtful issues will result in triumph. A confusing week, but a good one.

Mrs Tweed is here for the day, as Amy is away for the weekend in London for the college reunion. Amy arrives, having waited until the 6.20 train and having had to walk from Gresley. There were stacks of people at the reunion, she says. Afterwards she and several others trekked out to New Cross to view the remains of the poor old college* which must have had several direct hits. Amy bears back a piece of charred wood as a precious relic from the shrine.

Monday, September 7th: Quite an affectionate letter from Freddie, who has now progressed from Dear to Darling, but unfortunately this causes me to retreat a little. The more inaccessible the more attractive is always the foolish case with me. He has applied for his trip to W Africa to be either postponed or cancelled on account of his father's poor health etc, and there seems a fair possibility of this coming off. He asks when my next holiday is, and hopes to see a lot of me. I wonder!

*Goldsmiths

My father is in the garage with Mr Greaves, busily erecting the Morrison shelter, which he vows obstinately he will put up in the front room. He's not going to have That Thing cluttering up his garage.

Tuesday, September 8th: Another missive from Freddie. I remain in the Darling status, I see. He has had his medical and has been passed fit, and also inoculations against typhoid, tetanus and malaria, but is now awaiting his reply from the Air Ministry. Together with this comes a letter from Dougie, looking forward to his weekend here, and asking if he can't take me to a dance while he is over, and telling me to get ready for late nights. Not me! – or rather, not I!

Between the photographs of Jack W in the Army and Jack B in the Air Force on the sideboard, has suddenly appeared a third – my father in the last war, in slouch hat and looking like Wild Bill Hickock or Hopalong Cassidy. He doesn't see why he shouldn't be there, he says, and adds that he belonged to the Real Army. When Joyce asked who the handsome man in the middle was (knowing full well), my father replied delightedly 'That's me!'

Wednesday, September 9th: Have a letter from Swanee this morn. She thinks Geoff is coming home on embarkation leave, but, she says, she will have to put up with it . . . !

Tuesday, September 15th: The arrival of the Budget. Joan's letter gives me a shock – a most funereal affair with black edges. However, discover to my relief that this does not denote mourning but merely economy, as it was given to her.

Still bright, but a nip in the air. Collect Amy and take her to tennis. Then home and eat a colossal and plebeian but most enjoyable supper of fried cheese and onions. Still, onions, the once despised and rejected, are a delicacy these days.

Wednesday, September 16th: Receive a Handsome Donation from the govt for services rendered (or rather Income Tax cheerfully paid), to wit, one Certificate of Post-War Credit for the amount of £10 12s. 7d. It will just about pay my Post-War Income Tax, I expect.

Also a short letter from dear Freddie, who would have me believe that he is exceedingly hard worked. He hasn't heard from the Air Ministry yet about West Africa.

Am cast into a frenzy by the discovery that my precious fountain pen is lost, stolen or mislaid. Whirl about in desperation, looking under cushions, beneath chairs, even in the bath, becoming speedily more frantic, as fountain pens are now unobtainable. Finally a spark of genius causes Miss Sanders to suggest My Blazer Pocket. And there it nestles. Profound relief.

Read an Inspector Maigret – most entertaining.

Thursday, September 17th: Mother spends the morn gloating. She saw the Bishop of Buxton in Gresley, and vows he looked at her to speak, but her opportunity came! – the opportunity of Showing What She Felt About That Devil (her description!). She's often wondered what she'd do, and now she knows. She Ignored Him!

Tuesday, September 22nd: Letter from Freddie saying that he has heard from the Air Ministry at last, but they say that only in very exceptional circumstances can overseas duty be cancelled. He's also Longing To See Me. The other fellow posted to W Africa has applied for 253 coupons. That will Shake Them, says Freddie with satisfaction! He rings up and arranges to see me in Derby tomorrow.

Spend the evening with Inspector Maigret and eat a Cadbury's Blended Chocolate Bar out of this month's ration – luscious!

Thursday, September 24th: Stalingrad still holding out. Awful street fighting there, no hospitals. The wounded have to be taken to boats under cover of smoke screens.

Tuesday, September 29th: Hear from Dougie, who is still looking forward to his weekend visit and says we can cycle to Burton to a dance – The Exercise Will Do Us Both Good.

Go with Miss Sanders and Hilda to the first of the history lectures (Modern European) at Castle Gresley Central School given by the Rev Clarke from Repton. Hilda T asks with intended humour if it Doesn't Make Me Feel Near to Freddie ... ?* Our Rev lecturer arrives late, with breezy apologies, given in a somewhat clerical voice, but gives a good lecture on German Unification under Bismarck.

Friday, October 2nd: Have two letters from Freddie this morn. Carefully open in their right sequence and find the first to be chiefly about coming home – from next Mon to Fri morn, and he would like to see me on Wed and Thurs, while the next announces that his posting to W Africa has been cancelled after all. He'll be able to get off earlier on Mon and will I meet him at the station in Derby.

Saturday, October 3rd: Awake, oppressed by a heavy cold, but get ready to go to Nottingham with Amy. Am scarcely out of the house before Amy looms into view indicating despair, incredulity and resignation all mixed up. The bus, she announces, is already full, and an overflow of about 30 stands grouped on the pavement. Apparently today and Monday are a miners' holiday.

So we decide to go to Ashby and proceed from there. The

*Freddie's peacetime job was as maths and science teacher at this school (for 11–14-year-olds).

Ashby queue is somewhat lengthy, but we squeeze on, and inquire in Ashby the time of the next bus to Nottingham. Learn with dismay that it is not until one o'clock. So there is nothing to be done but leap on the bus and go back and through to Burton. The queue at Swadlincote for our bus is amazing and just stretches on and on.

Go to Boots for lunch, after reluctantly parting with 3 coupons for a new vest, then decide to go to the flicks. However have 1¼ hrs to wait before the Ritz opens, and we have nothing to do, so in despair we turn into the Museum. Trail wearily and very critically round an exhibition of Edward Lear's watercolours, then pass through rooms full of stuffed birds in all attitudes, colours and shapes – all looking very stuffed and very depressing, and rather moth-eaten, some of them very supercilious. The last room of these creatures proves too much for us. We collapse on the hard bench and giggle at the straits to which we have been reduced. We have this place of gloom to ourselves, except for an earnest boy, and one room of stuffed birds proves enough for him.

Monday, October 5th: Go to Derby to meet dear Freddie, on his way home for 4 days. Go to the Gaumont for lunch, and after this to the Royal to see *The Maltese Falcon*. Freddie produces a bar of Coffee Creme chocolate. Tea then at Boots. Asks me if I'll go to their place on Wed.

Wednesday, October 7th: Have to yank myself out of bed just after 7, in order to be in Derby by 10 to meet Freddie. Set forth arrayed in skirt, blouse and yellow pullover, and blue coat, and arrive to find he has already bought a ticket for me to Whatstandwell, so within 10 minutes we are on the train, and I am feeling many qualms and much uncertainty and craven cowardice. However, resolutely refuse to consider what lies at the end of the journey, and so maintain a cool, composed demeanour (I hope). Have two miles to walk from Whatstandwell to Alderwasley, but the scenery is beautiful and the countryside really lovely.

At last with many inward tremors, I arrive, but am greeted very kindly by Freddie's parents, and we have a cup of tea and a chunk of cake. His father has a habit of sitting silent for a time, then breaking out into a slow and deliberate speech. Go for a short walk and return at 12.30 for a massive but lovely lunch of chicken etc and a tart, and damsons and custard, and tea. Insist on blackberrying afterwards because the bushes are laden with them. Walk through the park after this, then have tea and catch the 5.30 train laden with blackberries, flowers and 3 beautiful brown eggs.

Tuesday, October 13th: Accompany Amy to the dentist, and she imparts a Piece of Horrifying Scandal about The Snake in the Grass, Freddie. On the way to Nottingham, Amy was chatting to Miss V, who was asking after her erstwhile colleague, Freddie. When he was at Castle Gresley, she says, neither the staff nor the children dared enter the room when he and Miss Beardsley were in there – alone! Ha! Only confirms what Hilda T told me she'd heard.

Wednesday, October 14th: The day opens with a letter from the Treacherous Freddie. Miss V had the cheek to say to Amy he seems to be concentrating on me now that Miss B is married! He wants to see me next Wednesday. Think I shall write and say Why? Can't Miss B make it? He says he will come to Burton, as it will give us a little more time together than if I came to Derby. Francis, destined for W Africa, is home on embarkation leave, and he adds deceitfully, 'Wouldn't it have been terrible to have had to say goodbye to each other with no prospect of meeting for 18 months?' I wonder! Then he goes on to say what a good lecture he gave on Ice-Accretion and the physics of super-cooled water-droplets in cloud. My word.

Visit Mrs W with my tattered blazer which she has nobly promised to patch. Amy and I go to the flicks. Write to Freddie when I return, but merely say I've heard a piece of scandal about him and Miss B.

Monday, October 19th: Back at school with many a moan and sorrowful sigh. Make my way to the cheerless place with the greatest reluctance. We now have no heating by order of the Government – and it is not to be put on until November 1st. The children return to school full of beans as usual and amiably disposed to chatter all day long. Unfortunately I fail to see eye to eye with them over this.

Freddie writes to complain of a cold and overwork, but hopes to see me on Wed. When he refers to the scandal I heard about him, he says it is nothing new for Castle Gresley people to gossip about him – or me, for that matter, he adds maliciously, and says in brackets, 'That shakes you a bit, doesn't it?' Huh, not at all, I shall retort stiffly. In any case, if he has heard gossip about me, why hasn't he told me? That's what annoys me – he isn't at all personal, and never comments upon what I do, say or wear. Still, I've never wanted him to, so I suppose I can't grumble.

Listen in to the first instalment of *Nicholas Nickleby* – awfully good. Then write to Freddie, telling him curtly that I Don't Enjoy Scandal, as he seems to imagine, and demanding to be told what he's heard about me. I wonder if it *will* shake me? Am not at all perturbed.

Wednesday, October 21st: Trafalgar Day, I learn from the *Radio Times.* With a scramble I catch the 4.20 bus to Burton and meet Freddie there. To the Picturedrome to see Ralph Richardson (who unfortunately dies at the beginning of the flick), Deborah Kerr, Griffiths Jones and Hugh Williams in a story about the invasion of Norway – *The Day Will Dawn*. Quite good but the general treatment just the same as the other war flicks – loads of propaganda with gross and overfed German officials lumbering through the story.

Inquire of Freddie What He Has Heard about me, but he confesses Nothing Much. Persist until I have extracted the details – apparently years ago his landlady knew that he had taken me out, and she warned him against me. He contradicted her (he nobly avers), and after a time she apologised and said she had been misinformed, etc. Huh! Wish I'd known.

Deign to see dear Freddie off at the station and catch the last bus home.

Thursday, October 22nd: Miss Peat has been paid and has got the bonus!* Whoopee. So shall we then, I hope. The Budget arrives – and news of the first Budget baby expected: Maretta's – due next April. She is very thrilled. Joan still writes on funereal paper – wish she wouldn't.

Go to the first of a series of 6 lectures on European Dancing – Finnish tonight, and awfully good.

Saturday, October 24th: A day of much whizzing about – first to Miss Barnett's to be set, then to Sealey's to collect this month's chocolate ration (12 ounces) and next to Miss Joyce's with my navy material under my arm.

Snatch a hasty bite on my return, then leap forth once more to Burton with material for a jacket (maroon) to be tailored at Gilbert's. Buy *Nicholas Nickleby* at Darley's, then catch the 10 to

*Miss Peat, as a teacher of the Birmingham evacuee children, was paid by Birmingham Education Authority.

3 bus home. Nearly a riot as there are too many passengers standing, and no one will get off. The last on are several workers (all
smelling of beer – and sounding the worse for it) and they bleat
loudly and truculently that the Workers Have Preference, Let
Some of These Others get off! At this a soldier retorts that He's
Fighting for His Country etc, etc, and voices are raised. The
woman shopper next to me says with indignation that These
Workers Have Time to stop and get a Bellyful of Beer, and won't
have a ha'penny after the war, and in the end no one gets off.

Begin reading *Nicholas Nickleby* and get as far as Monday's
instalment on the wireless, then bath and get ready for the dance
at Geary. Renie comes, bringing Uncle Jim's nephew Earl, over on
a visit. He is a sergeant in the American army, stationed at
Cheltenham.

Wednesday, October 28th: Am most annoyed with Margaret C for
giving Julius Caesar a red nose when she coloured him in. Tear up
her picture, then giggle to myself afterwards and feel a bit mean.

Go to German (the second lecture but my first time of going),
with Miss Sanders*. An Austrian – driven from Germany by the
purge, I believe and a teacher – takes it and she is awfully good.
The time passes very quickly and enjoyably. Come home with a
few German words – very few! Pitch dark and we grope our way
down the hill. Do high stepping all the way along Hastings Road
to avoid any possible doorsteps, then have to stop and giggle at
the thought of how funny it must look.

Thursday, October 29th: Entertain high hopes of being paid, but
alas! they are rudely dashed. Meet Freddie in Burton about 4.30,
go to the Ritz for tea, then to see *The Foreman Went to France*,

*Evidently in Swadlincote in 1942 there was no climate of hostility to things
German.

which I thoroughly enjoy. Freddie opens his heart and brings out two bars of chocolate. Kindly go with him to the station afterwards, then wonder if I'm being too gracious and accommodating. Says he is coming home the weekend after this, and wants me to meet him in Derby on the Saturday.

My father reports that the captain at whose cottage he is working is home on sick leave, having by his own report been bitten by a spider 5 inches in diameter. My father is not disposed to believe this.

Saturday, October 31st: Awake with a thick head, which does not presage well for a four-hour session of *Gone with the Wind*, whither I am bound today. Collect Hilda in Burton and we arrive in Derby just after 11. In Boots I succumb to the temptation of *Mr Bunting at War*. Having fingered it wistfully every time I have seen it in Boots since before last Christmas, I buy it at long last, then feel very rash. We thoroughly enjoy *Gone with the W* – awfully good acting.

Monday, November 2nd: A snippet from Freddie, written, so he would have me believe, under Arctic conditions. He could write me A Nice Long Letter, but the writing paper is Like Ice, and his Fingers Just Won't Write. What an excuse! He Thoroughly Enjoyed Thursday, Darling, he says extravagantly, but was shunted into a siding and didn't arrive home until midnight.

Tuesday, November 3rd: Excitedly collect my New Dress from the postman this morn and snatch it from its wrappings. Display it, but it merely looks a crumpled rag, and Mother can only say, It Is Creased. Take it off in disappointment.

Attend to a letter from Doug, which I open in some trepidation, fearing an imminent visit. Am relieved to read however that he's 'still waiting his chance to come and see me'. He relates his

latest Home Guard activities. They held some big manoeuvres
last weekend, and he had an all-night patrol through a cemetery.
He says it was a 'very interesting job stalking marble angels in
mistake for the enemy'.

Wednesday, November 4th: Cold, raw and foggy. Barbara comes
to tea and leaves at 8 to go fire watching. Miss S and I leave at 7
for the German class, where we whirl along at a great rate,
making queer guttural noises and asking each other, 'Wo ist der
Mann?' with great fluency. Plans for a French class are afoot, so
if I go I shall go adorned with the medals for French I so intelligently won at school.

Thursday, November 5th: Mother yodels excitedly upstairs, when
rousing me for my day's activities, that They're In Full Retreat in
Egypt – 9000 prisoners taken, 250 tanks, etc etc. Great excitement, whereby I am late for school. We all ask each other What
We Think about the news? and all profess great satisfaction.

The evening turns out wet, but we sally forth to our Finnish
dancing and frisk nimbly about. Wash my hair when I get home,
and read about 50 pages of *Nicholas Nickleby*.

A brisk reply from the dear Freddie, who must have fallen
over himself almost to reply by return. What dutifulness, what
ardour! Am overwhelmed by such attention, so dispatch a brief
reply to say I'll see him on Saturday. He tells me lavishly that
he's looking forward to seeing me, Darling, and ends with five
crosses again. I always ignore them, and never follow his
example.

Friday, November 6th: Glowing reports of the Axis retreat in
Africa are still coming in over the wireless, whereby we all go
about our daily round with lightened tread and ever-renewing
optimism. Mother falls over herself to put on the wireless

every time the news is due – hoping, like Oliver Twist, for more.

The electricity fails this afternoon, and I am somewhat perturbed because this means I can't have my hair set, and I don't relish the idea of trailing around Derby tomorrow with it all frizzy. It comes on again at 20 to 7, so I go to Miss B's, who greets me with happy laughter and relates how two of her customers had to go home with Soaking Wet Hair.

Saturday, November 7th: Read in the *Mail* while I am on the way to Derby that the Archbishop of Canterbury has decreed that in view of changing conditions, St Paul's decree about the covering of women's heads in church need no longer be observed. Thank goodness for that! Meet dear Freddie at 20 to 11. We go to Boots for lunch, during which I am instructed on how to decode weather forecasts. We go to the flicks, but no chance of tea when we come out, so we return to the Gaumont where I am instructed in the deficiencies of the Milk Marketing Board.

Sunday, November 8th: Keep this as Remembrance Sunday, so go to church three times. Gaze curiously around to see if any of the ladies have availed themselves of the Archbishop's decree, but find them all still respectably hatted. Am myself hatted, but not respectably, as I wear my five-year-old pigeon trap as my grandfather used to call it. My father asks me sardonically if it is a Paratroop hat. Wear my new dress and Dougie's stockings, which are grand and fit beautifully. Fully-fashioned stockings these days are as rare as gold.

Good news on the wireless. The American Expeditionary Force has been landed in French North Africa, and messages have been broadcast to the French by President Roosevelt etc. Looks as though this is to be a preliminary to the much-debated second front. For the first time the Vicar is able to use that prayer from the Day of National Prayer paper, of thanksgiving for our recent victories. This has never been applied before, but after the news of the last few days, the Vicar seems inspired to air it, and we say 'Amen' with fervour.

Tuesday, November 10th: Freddie is 'extremely interested' in the news of the American landings, he says, and adds with superiority that he has been more or less expecting this for days. Tut, oh tut! Why didn't I think of that?

Thursday, November 12th: Awaken from a frightful nightmare, wherein I am hiding among Germans, armed only with a mac, a torch and an umbrella, and am speedily run to earth by an efficient German woman, who briskly shoots me in the back. Am just writhing on the floor awaiting Death when I awake, and am then convinced that I can hear church bells. (Incidentally, the church bells are to be rung on Sunday for the first time in a year or two to celebrate our great victory in Africa.)

A thoroughly wet day, but we turn out briskly to the dancing class and frisk around for 1½ hours doing Scottish and Bavarian dances. One girl attires herself in a green satin arrangement which looks like cami-knickers and she prances around looking quite indecent. Dance with Miss Clark, and we have to attempt all sorts of complicated clutches and grasps, but it is good fun.

Friday, November 13th: Forgot to record that the Germans have now entered Unoccupied France, but we are still pushing on into Libya and have retaken Bardia and Tobruk.

Go to Salts' with Hilda, who is also coming to tea, in search of lisle stockings. The assistant says, 'Oh no!', when we ask for fully-fashioned stockings, and looks faintly surprised that we should even ask, but Mr Albutt tootles up and goes to a cubby hole, beckons us to him, and produces four pairs. But these are silk and

I don't really feel that I can afford three coupons, on such ephemeral luxuries (being in need of Something Hard-Wearing for school), so am dubious, but Hilda decides to plunge. However away trips Mr A again, and returns this time with very rare Brettle Sylkesta stockings, thick but serviceable, and we have these, though at one time I wouldn't have stirred a yard in them. After this he unrolls yards of material for our inspection – though quite unasked, and therefore fruitlessly, for I guard my coupons with care, and make great calculations before I spend even one.

Saturday, November 14th: Set forth to see Amy to commiserate with her upon the loss of her front tooth. When she was biking home in the blackout on Wednesday, she ran into three people walking abreast in the middle of the road. She mowed one woman down and sent the other two flying. They turned on Amy and swore at her. Amy was nearly knocked out herself, and bleed-ing, but they merely left her and she had to stagger home alone leaving her tooth behind her. It must have been a terrific bang.

Home to find a letter from Freddie – though without the Customary Five Crosses! His ardour must be waning! Do some mending and darning at night.

Sunday, November 15th: Ding dong, ding dong! The church bells ring out once more this morning, for the first time in two or three years, and they'll be silent again now unless they're used for invasion or another victory. Bells chime over the wireless, and we hear Newhall's sounding forth, but our own little church bell must have been done very softly because I don't hear it at all. It's two years today since the Coventry blitz, so the Coventry bells are heard over the wireless.

I think it's very premature to start all this. We shall look silly if we get pushed back again now. Have nothing against a gladsome peal over the wireless, but not all this universal merry-making.

The Vicar is soberly optimistic in his sermon, and uses once more the prayer of thanksgiving for the victory of our forces, but warns us that there is still A Long Way to go Yet. Too true! He also hoists the flag in the churchyard, again to celebrate Our Victory.

Dream a queer dream about dear Freddie. Am at a dance where he is, but he is dancing with someone else and so am I. However, fully expect him to take me home, so sit chatting to my partner and waiting. He thereupon prances up, but merely to say, 'Goodnight, Miss Smith'. Then off he pops, leaving me gasping. Perhaps it's an omen!

Have a profound discussion with my father upon the light and shade in an Arch.

Monday, November 16th: A nippy morning, though bright and crisp. My legs are beginning to flinch now from the nippy air but I think I shall just last the month out without swathing them in the highly serviceable if ungainly creations I bought on Friday.

Tuesday, November 17th: Our first Christmas card, from Jack, bearing stuck-on flowers from the Holy Land.

My boys are stricken with grief during football this afternoon, when a violent kick lands their ball high up in the fork of a tree, where it lodges. We gather round and throw things at it to no effect, until at last one boy suggests in all seriousness that We Chop The Tree Down Miss. Have visions of myself armed with hatchet.

Am dubious now about lasting out the month with Bare Legs. They're flinching even more, now that the frosts are getting more severe, and the little hairs stick rigidly upright on them.

Wednesday, November 18th: Dear Freddie writes of Trouble He Has Had With His Bike and wants me to meet him next Monday. But no crosses again. Most perturbing!

Accompany Miss S to German, and we find to our joy that our books have arrived (*Heute Abend*), so we work from them, chanting aloud, supplying words, and answering questions etc. Return to cheese and onions for supper. Mother says critically that I need my suspender belt on – I shall let myself go! And she eyes my Rear significantly.

Thursday, November 19th: Have capitulated at last. Go to school decorously clad in stockings – but not as a concession to the oncoming winter! No – in deference to my Spreading Girth, which needs discipline.

Friday, November 20th: Mr Wheat asks me heartily How I Am this morn, and when I say Not So Well and explain the forthcoming Ordeal of the Dentist's Chair, he says Shall He Come and Hold My Hand (then chuckles delightedly). He is then inspired to further heights of humour and says No, I'd Rather Hold Someone Else's Hand, Wouldn't I? Tell him stiffly, Certainly Not.

Am just about to mark Clifford W's book this afternoon, when I notice it is full of crossings out. Open my mouth to Storm and Rave, but before I can utter, he gazes up at me and says He'll Make Up For It Next Time. At which I meekly close my mouth and say mildly, Very Well.

Trail to the dentist with drooping spirits, and have to wait in suspense for an hour. He mutters ominously, 'Oh, several to be filled here,' and starts work on one of the offending molars. He keeps asking if it Hurts Yet, but I answer No quite truthfully, for he doesn't hurt at all. Breathe with delight when the operation is over and the filling in, and know that I have a fortnight's respite before the next.

Saturday, November 21st: Have a letter from Doug this morn to say that His Turn Will Soon Be Here Now. He has asked for and got permission to join the Merchant Navy, but expects to be here for Xmas. Therefore – the hour has struck, and Dougie has decided to come over in the middle of next month. And could he possibly come on the Friday? And will I *please* book him a room at a hotel, as he can't really come to our place. He'd be very surprised if we did push him into the Granville! We couldn't. He's looking forward to seeing me again – even though it will be the last time for at least a year or two, that is if everything goes on OK, he adds pessimistically.

Read the first hundred pages of Vera Brittain's *England's Hour* after supper tonight. Although it is carefully written and truthfully recorded (in a one-sided way) it annoys me. It is so devoid of humour – and it is partly that that has made the people in blitzed areas so marvellous. Vera B is so terribly self-important and so terribly serious and rather a prig.

Our victorious Eighth Army in Libya has now taken Benghazi, and signposts have reappeared in this country.

Monday, November 23rd: The Russians have pushed the Germans back in another counter-attack at Stalingrad. My father says he hopes they'll Persecute them, the Bloomin' hounds!

Trip to Burton on the 10 to 6 bus to meet Freddie. We go to the Ritz café. Freddie relates the tale of a Hockey Match in which he played on Sat, and a Cocktail Party which he attended later, but from which he returned Perfectly Sober, he says.

Tuesday, November 24th: Nice to be able to sit about a bit before dashing off to school these mornings. Have time to scan the headlines in the morning paper and note that we are still doing well, and that Dakar, the French West African port, has come over to us. Mother affirms rashly that In Her Opinion the Germans will Crumple Up, at which my father wonders whether to start getting the garage ready for the Peace Celebrations. Then his eye falls on my ancient crêpe shoes and he is diverted, remarking sarcastically that I must Cover A Lot of Ground in those, and that they seem to have Expanded.

Friday, November 27th: Have my Calling Up Papers this morning! – or rather an official document from the Ministry of Labour requiring me, as a British Subject, to furnish particulars about myself in addition to particulars already registered, under Defence Regulation 58A.

My father is now resplendent in his new false teeth, but he hasn't taken to them at all, and threatens to take a Big Hammer to them. He has also threatened to take a Big Hammer to the wireless when it crackles or relays a crooner or swing music.

Saturday, November 28th: The French Fleet scuttled itself at Toulon yesterday, rather than fall into German hands.

Sunday, November 29th: Alack for my slight weight decrease. I have made up for it today, and more besides, I fear, for I fling caution to the winds and wallow in lashings of roast pork, apple sauce, onion sauce, sage and onion stuffing, and vegetables, for dinner. Oh luscious! Roll about feeling like a barrage balloon come down to earth.

Monday, November 30th: Connie begins the week by exhorting those children who have not already been immunised (about 2/3 of the school) to be done at once.

Have heard from Freddie this morning. He thinks he's coming home the weekend Dougie's due to come! He would! So send a note to Doug putting him off until the following weekend but not explaining why!

Tuesday, December 1st: The date begins to sound quite Christmassy, so we chant carols twice during the day. The children are beginning to breathe the fateful – hateful – word Decorations. Oh dear! that awful scrambling over desks and chairs, clinging to the wall like a fly and getting cricks in the neck and dust in the nostrils! Shall be patriotic, and do without this year, I think.

I forgot to say that on Sunday we listened to Mr Churchill's speech just before the 9 o'clock news – as good as ever, though with none of that blatant and ridiculous optimism that we slung out at the beginning of the war. He was soberly optimistic, but predicted grave trials etc for 1943. Still, that's what everyone expects. He can certainly make a good speech! He'd have made a good Roman. He referred witheringly to 'Corporal Hitler', and warned Italy of what she might expect.

Wednesday, December 2nd: Dougie writes with regret to say that he is not going in the Navy after all. Am not a bit surprised because I have been hearing this little tale in different forms ever since the war started. When he got to Cambridge, they told him he was reserved, so he took a day off to go to the Admiralty in London. He volunteered for everything from a submarine down to a row boat, he says, but to no effect. Now he's just waiting for the Army, and he knows, he says, that he'll make A Rotten Soldier. After all this he has decided to come on the 11th. Oh my stars! He would! Will have to write again and point out the advantages of the following week.

Small girl in my class drives me into a frenzy. She keeps an eagle eye on my roll, and every time a wisp of hair dangles down (which is quite frequent), up goes her hand and she informs me. Spend the morn therefore clutching the back of my head.

Letter arrives from Freddie at teatime – still very cold, and working very hard, and he has lectured one of the WAAF assistants for not working hard enough. Would like to have seen him!

Friday, December 4th: Letter from Fred. He's still very cold and busy – doesn't know whether he'll get a week off at Christmas yet, because their last male assistant is leaving and a forecaster-in-training has been kicked out.

See Mrs Swan, who says that Geoff has gone abroad without any embarkation leave. Expect Swanee will treat this with the usual imperturbability but it's a bit rotten.

We listen – unintentionally – to an ARP quiz. Two teams, from Norwich and Cardiff, compete. One bright man, when asked how he would stop Bleeding From the Ears, says Plug the Ears, and if this is not effective, put a tourniquet round the neck . . . !!

Monday, December 7th: Contrary to my firm resolutions, spend half the morn scrambling over desks putting up garlands and festoons, and one child brings a small Xmas tree. Dark, damp, depressing day.

Tuesday, December 8th: Letter from Freddie. He's looking forward to spending next Saturday with me, Dear. Have heard from Doug to say that he'll come on the 18th then. Miss S finishes my pretty green jumper – over which I have embroidered red-and-yellow flowers – and I wear same for History, feeling very gay.

Thursday, December 10th: Amy comes to tea and we go to the flicks to see Gary Cooper in *Ball of Fire* but I enjoy a Mickey Mouse cartoon just as well. Pluto saves a little kitten, then is jealous. Grand. I love them.

Saturday, December 12th: Go to Derby and meet Freddie at 11.15, weigh myself and note with joy a further decrease of a pound.

Trek into the Odeon to see a spy flick called *Secret Mission* which is mediocre – the same old theme boiled up again, i.e. a 'secret mission' into occupied France, bullying Nazi troopers and officials who are incredibly stupid, hair's-breadth escapes, etc etc. Tea at the Gaumont and catch the 5 to 8 bus home.

Sunday, December 13th: Dear Freddie's birthday, so ring him up as a great concession. Get my old hat remodelled, but it is greeted with hoots of derision, and I shall never wear it.

Unexpected phone call from Dougie! Poor old Doug! He rings up to say he won't be able to come next weekend as he's had his papers and goes into the Army on Thurs. Feel very sorry. Am not sorry he isn't coming because I think it's as well he shouldn't, but it's jolly rotten for him, especially just before Christmas. Besides, he's been looking forward to coming for so long. Ask him what he's going as, and he says A Tank! He says he'll let me know his address as soon as he gets it and that he's made arrangements for us to have our chicken at Christmas. Oh dear! Coals of fire! I feel really very sorry, because he's so loyal and faithful.

Tuesday, December 15th: Letter from Freddie who has now risen to 10 small crosses beneath his signature, and saying that it was Well Worth the Long Journey to spend such an Enjoyable Day with me Yesterday Darling. And his new sports coat is still Tight Under the Arms.

Wednesday, December 16th: Go to German and learn how to greet everyone at Christmas in German.

Thursday, December 17th: Short note from Freddie, groaning beneath a weight of work – he did 17 hours at a stretch on the first day back. Today he's going to Long Marston aerodrome on his own to do some organising as there is no met service there.

He has, he says largely, Been Thinking About Me A Lot, and is Keenly (strange adjective?) looking forward to Our Next Meeting (sounds like a Board of Directors).

Friday, December 18th: Letter from poor old Doug, who Doesn't know how to thank me for the Really Marvellous Wallet I sent him. It came as a Huge Surprise and was the Very Thing He Needed, and he will take Great Care of it. He Can't Thank me Enough for it, and will Always Keep It. Dougie is always satisfied, and more than satisfied.

He is still Patriotic to the Core and says staunchly that he is at the moment Jolly Proud to be in the position to fight for Good Old England. He expects to be at Colchester when his letter arrives. He also says it's rotten going before his little trip to see me, but I'm to Take it From Him, he will be over as soon as he can manage it. And his mother has just suggested my going there when he gets his leave, but he doesn't expect it's much use asking me. He adds that I've been A Jolly Good Friend to him, and he won't forget it. Oh dear! Poor old Dougie! He's a good sort.

Saturday, December 19th: Our Christmas cockerel has arrived – but a puny little bird – only 6 lbs. Mother has also acquired a Christmas pudding.

Sunday, December 20th: A good slogan for Bevin comes in the morning's lesson – Rise up, ye women that are at ease – Join the ATS, WAAFS or WRENS.

Sir S Cripps gives the postscript after tonight's news – very good. He has a pleasant, flowing, but vigorous style, and his sentences are well balanced. He speaks about aircraft production.

Monday, December 21st: Christmas draws on apace, thanks be. The children are getting frenzied.

Have cards from Rayney, Doug, Dan, etc today, powder from Swanee, and from Doug (dear old Doug!) – three most super-marvellous pairs of fully-fashioned stockings (9 coupons!) – Bondor – two pure silk and one chiffon lisle. They're grand. Also a letter written in great haste from Colchester, giving his address. Letter too from Freddie, now at Long Marston.

Tuesday, December 22nd: Am in a positive whirl. Had decided in the interests of patriotism, righteousness, consideration for the GPO, and economy, to shut my eyes to the existence of Xmas cards, and to spend a stern and austere Christmas without such fripperies. However, the thought of my innocent friends sending me their merry greetings, only to be received in a cold silence, gives me awful pangs of conscience, and makes me feel meaner and meaner. So fling patriotism, righteousness, consideration and economy to the winds, and sail forth in pursuit of Christmas cards. But alas and alack! The cupboard was bare. Hardly a single one left in the whole of Swadlincote, but manage to snaffle a packet of very inferior, moth-eaten specimens from Dytham's, so send these, in a flurry.

Another letter from Freddie, enjoying it at Long Marston. They're to have their Christmas party there tonight. He says it seems Ages since he Saw Me Darling, and hopes to see me in Derby on Monday on his way home. He also hopes – optimistically – that we shall get Lots of Time Together next week.

Ivy comes over after tea with a marvellous present – small leather diary and a large ditto covering several acres from George, and a 7/6 book token from herself. Melt before such generosity.

Wednesday, December 23rd: Most marvellous! – receive a plump young duck from Dougie. It *is* good of him. Makes me feel so mean. Mother rejoices openly.

Dash to the library for Christmas reading and return *Surfeit of Lampreys* by Ngaio Marsh, about which I read conflicting criticisms in *Time & Tide* – E. M. Delafield for it, and Margery Allingham very much against, and *The Longest Journey* by E. M. Forster, whom I like very much.

During the course of the evening, when turning out my writing case and writing box to make more room, come upon a batch of old letters from Freddie. Destroy these, but not before re-reading. He used to write more then than now – in fact I think the case of advance and withdrawal cuts both ways!

Write to Dougie and thank him for the Duckie.

Break up tomorrow, oh joy.

Friday, December 25th – Christmas Day: The 4th Christmas of the War – mild and unseasonable weather, but infinitely preferable to cold and frost in my opinion. No grand unveiling of the presents this year. But Mother and Dad give me 12/- and £1 respectively. Christmas dinner is a very small gathering – only Auntie Frances, and we have chicken etc and a Chivers plum pudding, but it is all lovely. Decide to listen to the King's speech, so tear around getting washed and changed before he comes on.

Saturday, December 26th – Boxing Day: Forgot to record yesterday a letter from Doug. Poor old Doug sounds very down in the dumps and ends piteously, Write soon, as it is the Only Pleasure I get now. He hasn't heard from me yet. He has to be up at 6.30, and they are on until 6 p.m. – with 2 hours' extra 'spud peeling' if they are not careful. They do PT every day and he says he can stand on his head and do All Manner of Funny Things now!

Tales that the girls and women at the Rolls-Royce works and Sharpe Bros and Knight were drunk on Xmas Eve and the police had to be fetched to the latter. One woman attacked the foreman.

Jack B says that all the airmen etc are Red – real Bolsheviks, and sing the Red Flag on route marches and name their tents 'Joe's Cottage' and 'The Kremlin' etc.

A long and quiet day. Spend the morning washing stockings and pressing frocks, and the afternoon reading *Mr Bunting at War*. Continue this into the evening, with two slight digressions when I (a) renovate an old vest and mend an old suspender belt and (b) play Lexicon with Mother. Listen in to an Edgar Wallace thriller. What excitement! Different from pre-war Boxing Days with gay doings at Grandma's and a table laden with good things.

Sunday, December 27th: Superintend the making of a new book-case that my father kindly executes, and he does it very well. Install this therefore, and make many journeys upstairs to view same. No letter from the Dastardly Fred, but I should imagine he's coming tomorrow. Shall Swear with Fury if I voyage to Derby in vain.

Monday, December 28th: Meet Freddie in Derby. He relates What a Good Christmas He Has Had, with parties, turkeys, dancing and singing, and so forth. Find it almost impossible to get a word in edgeways, so finally abandon the attempt and just listen politely but with ebbing patience. Go to the flicks to see Joan Fontaine and Tyrone Power in *This Above All*, which starts off in quite a promising vein but rapidly deteriorates. Am presented with an Orange. Have tea after this, see dear Freddie off on the train, though think it a cheek that he should expect me to, and then have to go to the bus park alone. But just like him – self-centred to a degree. All men are alike!

Tuesday, December 29th: Have a letter from Doug, still down in the dumps. He is cold and doesn't get enough to eat. Poor old Doug!

Wednesday, December 30th: A freezing cold day with (horror of horrors) snow. Scuttle shiveringly around, put on my blue frock and camel hair coat, and catch the 8.15 bus to Burton en route for Alderwasley. Still dark when I get to Burton and very cold, so resort to that low dive, Bargates on the bus park, and have a cup of sweet strong tea in a very much cracked cup. Venture reluctantly out to wait for the 9 o'clock bus to Derby. Girl parks herself by me and begins to chat freely and amicably about her imminent absorption into the WAAFs. She is filled with horror at the thought of the underwear she will have to endure – vests with short sleeves, and woolly pantees! Commiserate with her, then the bus arrives and is draughty and cold. The train is beautifully warm, and I soon begin to feel a little happier. Scan the platform both ways when I alight at Whatstandwell but am disconcerted to find no sign of a welcome. It is deserted except for the ticket collector, so in a moment of panic I ask him if this *is* Whatstandwell. I am reassured, so peer up and down again. Finally wander uncertainly out to see Freddie looming along the road.

It has stopped snowing, thanks be, and we make our way to Alderwasley, where we are regaled with tea and a mince pie. Am taken to see Freddie's car in dry dock for the duration, but still looking quite nifty.

Have a massive lunch of chicken and plum pudding – lovely – then go for a walk and eat chocolate and an apple en route. Back in time for tea – have a super rich cake – then get ready to depart – plus rabbit! Dear Freddie comes with me to Derby and sees me on the bus. Am presented with a Christmas present – a silver pencil, which is very posh but not really useful.

Thursday, December 31st, New Year's Eve: Have my hair set, after making mince pies, ready for Freddie's reception this afternoon.

Meet him off the train at Burton and we proceed homewards for tea. We go to the dance at the Rink about 9. Very crowded. We leave just before the end. Have a large supper and retire to bed about 1 a.m.

1943

Friday, January 1st, New Year's Day: **Find** ourselves having breakfast at the late hour of 10.30, then we set out for a walk but it rains. We play draughts until dinnertime, then catch the 1.40 bus to Derby and go to the flicks. Have tea at the Gaumont. Am very hungry so despite my increase of 3 lbs since Monday I have Welsh rarebit. Ask Freddie if he has made any New Year resolutions, and he says No. Ask him if he doesn't want to improve in any way, and he says cheerfully No, he doesn't want to be any better. He wants to Get a Kick Out of Life. Tell him righteously that it depends upon what he calls Getting a Kick Out of Life, but he says vaguely Oh, Enjoying It. Don't agree with his way of thinking at all – he is a Disciple of the Flesh-Pots. Go to the bus then and agree to see him off from Derby on Monday.

Saturday, January 2nd: Renie voyages in this morn and tells me with an air of surprise that she thinks Freddie is nice, and that he is A Smart Fellow. My goodness! Have a vile monstrosity on my upper lip – a Cold Spot that looks hideous. Write to Doug.

Sunday, January 3rd: My cold spot is making rapid progress and will soon cover several acres. We feast on Freddie's rabbit which is very nice, but my father is disposed to be unduly facetious and supposes we shall get A Lot of Rabbits Now.

Monday, January 4th: Still freezing. Go to Derby and meet dear Freddie outside Boots. Then I wander round the Central Ed in search of books in exchange for my book tokens. Resort to Boots again for lunch, and thence to the station. Catch the 3.10 bus home.

Wednesday, January 6th: A note from Freddie, safely back at Honeybourne, written at 1.30 a.m. while he was on night duty. He feels Dreadfully Tired, having just completed A Couple of Charts. Apparently he is writing to me to keep himself awake! He is also Missing Me Very Much!

Thursday, January 7th: Letters from Fred and Doug. Freddie writes with frozen hands but is afraid he has Very little News for me, My Dear. He wants me to know that he's been thinking about me a lot, and wishing he were with me again. Which is very nice of him. Poor old Doug writes from the depths of gloom still, after being inoculated and vaccinated with a knife by someone who, poor Doug vouches, must have been a butcher in civvy life. He doesn't think much of Cold Showers in winter, either. He writes of icy conditions, and says how cold he is, but he did Pretty Well on the firing range last week and finished top of two platoons, with 60 out of 65. Apparently he has taken two of the younger lads under his wing, because it's a Pretty Rough School At Times. Spend the afternoon making sausage rolls and tarts for him, and send these off immediately after tea. Also write to Freddie.

Friday, January 8th: Amy trundles in bringing awful news. A Church School teacher has been torpedoed and lost. She was going to Africa to marry a curate. The ship went down with no survivors. Her family are in a terrible way. How awful! Can hardly believe it.

Hilda wanders in. I get the tea – we have a poached egg on toast each – my first egg since last October.

Monday, January 11th: Oh ominous date! I tank along to the place of my Daily Break this morn. Behold when I arrive a complicated system of blackout, with lengths of rope dangling all over my room. Shall have one or two deaths from hanging, I'm sure. Mr Wheat proudly demonstrates this latest contraption.

Letter from Freddie, rising to two pages – a rare occurrence!

Tuesday, January 12th: Am wallowing in very stormy waters financially, having disbursed today £3 5s. for my new Slazenger racquet, so now have barely a pound.

Oh added affliction – now that my original cold spot has reached the scabby stage, find a second one appearing at the other side of the same lip.

Mrs Tweed comes for supper and tells me roguishly that she'll have to start saving for a wedding present. Wouldn't dream of such a thing. But Mrs T as usual is dying to Know All.

Wednesday, January 13th: A most grateful letter arrives from Doug, who can't thank us enough for the tarts etc that we sent him. He didn't know I could cook like that! – He can't understand how I can manage it (flour, fat and water!) – and it came as a Gift from Heaven. 'It's people like you who make life worth living for us chaps,' he declares. It has saved his life and goodness knows what. Oh dear, oh dear! He has had another inoculation and expects another on both arms on Saturday, and has put his knee out, and is still cold and badly fed. Poor old Doug! He expects to be moved in six weeks. Hope he doesn't gravitate in this direction (which is very mean, but it would be a problem). They have also been having bayonet practice – which is a Real Blood-thirsty job with Shocking Language, he declares.

Saturday, January 16th: Another letter from Freddie to say that he won't be able to leave before lunch on Monday as he will be lecturing in the morn. He seems to be working very hard, and he also has a cold. He wonders if there will be a letter from me waiting for him when he goes to lunch. Afraid not! And he is Looking Forward to Seeing Me on Monday Dear.

Monday, January 18th: Journey to Burton to meet Fred. When the Derby train comes in, nip along to the steps to scan the alighting passengers. Witness one or two affectionate meetings. At last the final stragglers get off, and I am just beginning to wonder What Now? when I am poked from the rear and turn to find dear Freddie, who has arrived on the Birmingham train. We journey to the Ritz for coffee, and sit and talk. Hear about the Latest Party etc, then see him off on the 8.20 train. And so home.

Wednesday, January 20th: Letter from Dougie, still quite unreconciled to army life. He has been on church parade, and says they Looked Jolly Smart Too and had a posh band to lead them. The ATS went, but they're not His Sort. He has passed out Grade 1 in his medical, and came first in two 100 yard races, and was one of 6 out of 40 to run a mile. He is also going to send me a photograph of their platoon. He has had a Lousy Dinner, and says that according to reports the tea is a Darn Sight worse. He adds a PS to the effect that he has just tried to eat it and failed. It consisted of what looked like dog biscuits. He couldn't get his teeth in them!

To Burton to meet Freddie. Have tea at the Ritz then wander in to see *The Man Who Came to Dinner*, which is good and very witty. Am presented with a bar of chocolate, to my joy. Speedily do away with it. Hike along to the station and see Freddie off. Tells me lavishly that he has enjoyed seeing me etc etc.

Thursday, January 21st: Letter from Swanee. She is Acting Registrar at Wilmslow. She did so many certificates that by Saturday she felt she'd got every Cause of Death ever certified by a doctor. Geoff is in Algiers, after a marvellous voyage. He eats 10 oranges a day, and lemons and onions are plentiful. They won't let him put kisses at the bottom of his letters in case it is a code of some sort.

The Budget also arrives to spread its friendly glow over the breakfast table, though don't have time to read it properly until after school. Go to Amy's to tea. Terrible accounts in the paper about the bombed LCC school – 44 children dead, and 5 or 6 teachers, and about 60 or 70 injured. Terrible! My father mutters that they Want Crucifying, the Bloomin' Murderers. And Mother reads snatches out of the paper in tones of agony, and so does Mrs Tweed.

Friday, January 22nd: Miss Sanders returns from Coalville with an account of a lecture attended, given by an Austrian, an eye-witness to, and sufferer from, the methods of Nazi Germany. Everyone gets very worked up over this.

Tuesday, January 26th: Letter from Dougie to tell me not to write again until I hear, as they go on the move tomorrow. Have a ter-rible feeling that he will be deposited somewhere around here. Oh dear! Can manage him much better by letter. He will insist on going to church with me when he comes over. Oh gosh! Not if I can help it!

Thursday, January 28th: A day of disaster. My dinner day, so I scuttle around, preparing the victuals, and in my haste and bustle I jog the open bottle of red ink off the tray, and it falls to my feet with a bounce, spattering me plentifully with blobs and splashes of scarlet. My dress and shoes are alike bedaubed, while a rivulet runs along the floor.

Attend a Rest Centre meeting at night – 7.15 at the Council School, to make preparation for any potential blitzes. A few per-functory arrangements are made for a rehearsal next Thursday – but no one displays much interest. Then there is a sudden liveliness and burst of enthusiastic chatter when a suggestion of tea and biscuits for next Thursday is put forward. Needless to say all are in favour, and an argument about the kind of biscuit (e.g. digestives, shortbreads etc.) waxes very lively.

Friday, January 29th: Mrs W sends my blazer at long last, neatly patched, darned and mended – a marvellous job. Letter from Freddie this morn. At the moment his Eyes Look Terribly Black through lack of sleep, he says, though not so bad as those of some of the pilots – several of whom have cracked up during these last few days.

Sunday, January 31st: Letter from Dougie, plus platoon photograph. He has been put in the Dorsets infantry, and has been kept at Colchester.

Thursday, February 4th: Ought to have gone to a Rest Centre rehearsal, but feel under the weather, and Mother, eyeing me, says 'You don't look very well, and I wouldn't go', so I don't. But apparently there were fun and games – a bust up between Mr Cresswell and Mrs Moir, ending in the former's resigning and stalking off in a huff. They all had their cups of tea, with loads of sugar, and biscuits.

Monday, February 8th: Dougie writes in anxiety to remind me that he has written to me and sent his address but hasn't had a reply yet. He's still having a Pretty Stiff Time. And he reminds me that he's Coming Up To See Me in two months when he has his leave. Go to French and we read (and enjoy!) *Le Bourgeois Gentilhomme.*

Thursday, February 11th: Letter from Dougie saying, Don't Write, as he is moving again to a different part of the barracks, and is going into the Motor Transport section.

Friday, February 12th: Amy and Mrs Tweed come to tea. Am set upon after tea by all and sundry, on a charge of 'philandering and leading young men on'. Mother says it Worries Her to Death, while Father says he is Sick of the Subject, and after announcing that he'd rather have Dougie than This Bloke (i.e. poor Freddie), marches out in disgust. Have no supporters at all, though I am entirely innocent and blameless of offence, having led neither of them on, but this doesn't stop the argument. Oh dear!

Saturday, February 13th: Attire myself in blue dress, old pigeon-trap hat and new coat, and journey to Burton to catch the 11.19 train to Birmingham. Freddie has got on at Derby. Go to Pattison's for lunch and Freddie asks how my morale is: tell him that it is normal. Go to a News Theatre for an hour.

Ron's mother has informed Mrs T that she has heard about Freddie, and that lots of people have seen us in Derby (who?). She condescends to say she is Very Glad. Ron is to be married this summer. The news leaves me cold. Am not affected nor disturbed in any way – at long last! Goodness, it's taken a long time but at last I'm immune, I think!

Monday, February 15th: Ethel calls at teatime and thereupon ensues a conversation about Doug and Freddie – and optimistic speculations about my marrying either. However these are quite unfounded and I do not propose to change them from Theory to Fact.

Tuesday, February 16th: Amy calls at teatime with the news that the Booth HMI is prowling around the district again, having been to the C of E this morning and the Council School infants this afternoon.

Go to History. Mr Clarke talks about Hitler's rise to power and the years 1933–35. He seems to favour the idea that Hitler is a tool in the hands of the military leaders but the Austrian woman disagrees. We rely entirely on her for the discussion tonight, as the mainstay, Mr Cowley, is absent and the rest of us merely sit in an uneasy silence.

Thursday, February 18th: An epidemic of whips and tops has broken out at school, so there is much frantic lashing of tops and whirling of whips each playtime.

Letter from Freddie – he's still on night duty and is feeling very tired. And it has been finally decided to put all Met officers into uniform after April 1. I expect that will mean cutting down the number of times he comes home. Wash my hair after tea, do my German homework, and generally make myself busy. Am just reading – being in alone – when the telephone bell rings. It is Freddie. He says that he has Bad News and I immediately anticipate that he has been posted abroad again, and go a bit weak at the knees. However, it isn't that – but he has been sent for to his father who is seriously ill. He has had a seizure, and has blood pressure too, so the doctor advised his mother to send for Freddie, who came this morning.

Friday, February 19th: Ring Freddie about 7.30 this evening – his father seems worse today, he says, and is delirious, and they have had hard work to keep him in bed. Oh dear! What a worry! But if he's able to leave his father tomorrow, he says he'll come to Derby in the afternoon.

Saturday, February 20th: Quite expect a phone call from Fred this morning saying that he can't get out. However, hear nothing, so catch the bus to Derby and meet the train which arrives at 2.30. Freddie seems very concerned, naturally, but says that his father seems more himself today, though very weak. We go to the Odeon, where we have to queue for about half an hour to see

Basil Rathbone in *Sherlock Holmes and the Secret Weapon*, which could never have sprung from the pen of Conan Doyle. Then we go to the Gaumont for tea, followed by a little walk. Feel very sorry for Freddie.

Sunday, February 21st: Ring up Freddie about 7, but he sounds very upset and says that they have had an awful time with his father, and that he had to get two others to help him to keep him in bed, and that the doctor has advised sending him away. Freddie seems to think that there is no hope for him, and is staying until Thursday.

Wednesday, February 24th: Go to German, but ring up Freddie before I go, and he says they have decided they'll have to let his father go away, as his mother won't be able to manage him. They're taking him tomorrow.

Friday, February 26th: Catch the 20 to 5 bus to Derby and meet Freddie off the 6 o'clock train. He seems more cheerful now that things are more settled and goes back to Honeybourne tomorrow. I am wearing yellow pullover, gloves and ankle socks and Freddie tells me, with lamentable facetiousness, that I look like a crocus.

Saturday, February 27th: Am just in the bath, when the phone rings, and as there is no one else in, I drape my old dressing gown round my dripping self, and go to answer. Am amazed to hear Freddie, but he tells me that his father died in the night. What a shame they took him away, poor man! Still, there was no choice. So Freddie is to get three days' compassionate leave.

I bike up to Auntie Nell's to see if she will go with me to Burton to buy a hat. She tells me that Mrs Tweed has been questioning her – Did She Think I'd Ever Marry Freddie? etc etc. Wish she'd ask me.

Auntie N and I go to Maggs' where I buy a ravishing hat in navy blue at a colossal price. When I ask my father what he thinks, he just makes comments about using it to carry bricks up a ladder.

Write to Freddie and to his mother – with some difficulty.

Sunday, February 28th: Dream that I had a letter from Dougie, severing all relations with me. Mother asks Barbara if she likes my hat, whereat she eyes it critically and says, Well, to be Quite Candid, she's seen me in better.

Monday, March 1st: Letter from Vera, who says she thinks Dougie is trying to wear me down by his persistence, and probably believes a long-established friendship to be a safe basis for marriage.

Tuesday, March 2nd: Letter from Doug, who has been home on a 48-hr leave. He took Pip and Joan to a dance and had great difficulty in hanging on to his badge, because none of the girls there seemed to have a Dorsets one, and all coveted it. Also – will I go over to Ely when he gets his 8 days' leave? He knows he's asked me before, he says, and I've always refused, but things are a bit different now, and if I'd go he could see me and those at home at the same time. He also predicts not many more leaves before the Grand Offensive, so please will I try and make it and Please Him For Once.

Wednesday, March 3rd: Freddie's father's funeral this afternoon, so ring him up when I come in from German. He goes back to Honeybourne tomorrow.

Monday, March 8th: Have a nice, calm, sensible letter from Freddie. He hopes I'll be able to spend Tuesday with him, and is longing to see me!

Tuesday, March 9th: Fred can't get home, as he has been posted to Aston Down in Gloucestershire and goes on Thursday, so today he has to go to Oxford for his medical. He'll probably be in charge there, he thinks.

Thursday, March 11th: Another missive from Fred – he's doing well this week! He's been passed perfectly fit by 4 doctors – part of the process consisted of tapping most of his body with a little hammer, he says. He is also definitely going in charge, and will probably remain a civilian while he's there, and will have a WAAF officer on his staff.

Saturday, March 13th: Letter from Freddie. He was met by a car driven by an ATA girl at Chalford, when he arrived at 4 o'clock – and there was no room in the mess nor at the other fellow's digs, so he was spending the night at a posh country hotel about six miles from the aerodrome. He says the country is marvellous, and has been thinking how lovely it would be if I were there! He thinks he'll have to be on duty most mornings at 7 o'clock. He still doesn't know whether he's to go into uniform or not. Ends with All His Love (?) and 5 crosses and a PS to the effect that it's getting time he had some real ones.

Monday, March 15th: The Ides of March! Opens with a letter from Doug, who has been out on a 200-mile convoy. He drove the last truck, the Most Important of all, he says. He has also had a 30-mile march and an assault course before breakfast. And his brother John is home on embarkation leave. Then he asks about my going to Ely, and says if I really don't want to go he can't make me, but he'd like me to, and his mother is expecting me etc, etc., so it is Up to Me.

Letter also from Freddie by the afternoon post, still living in luxury at Moor Court Private Hotel, until he can get fixed up. He hopes to get home this weekend for a long weekend, and might manage it once a fortnight if he remains a civilian. His staff consists of a WAAF officer and 4 WAAF assistants. Ahem! Among the ladies, it seems, so he should be all right.

Wednesday, March 17th: Another letter from Fred! He has managed to get fixed up with digs – a Mrs Gibbons, whose husband, a Squadron Leader, is overseas. She has 3 children and lives at a house called 'Eight Gables', which is apparently quite handy.

Saturday, March 20th: Up early to catch the train from Derby to Alderwasley. Freddie meets me at Whatstandwell, and we have a cup of tea when we arrive. His mother seems to be settling quite well. Go out after lunch for about 2 hours. Freddie comes back with me to Derby, and we walk again and get entangled in a maze of back-streets. Freddie's mother has given me six luscious eggs, which are well received.

Tuesday, March 23rd: Go for a bike ride with Amy. She says if I don't go to her 21st she'll Never Speak to Me Again. And Freddie wants me to go to Alderwasley for the weekend. Query. What to be done?

Tuesday, March 30th: In the throes of Vile Cold. Letter from Freddie. He says Have I Dropped the Bombshell to Amy yet? – and Of Course he thinks I ought to come to see him – after all, I can see Amy any time, and he Does Get the First Claim, doesn't he??? Then he says calmly that if he has to get his uniform in a hurry, it will mess up the weekend. It had better not – not if I'm going to face the wrath of Amy and Mrs T.

Wednesday, March 31st: Shirk the nasty job of telling Amy about the weekend, but Mother broaches it, and neither Amy nor Mrs T like it. Don't know what to do.

Thursday, April 1st: Letter from Doug, hoping to see me in a few days' time. Oh lor! So I'm expected there the weekend after this, and he says Couldn't I Get the Monday Off, and possibly the Tuesday? Oh no! His mother is looking forward to seeing me, and says I can stay as long as I like! Wonder how long that would be?

Ring Freddie up and agree to meet him off the train at 2.15 on Sat, so will have to break the news to Amy tomorrow.

Friday, April 2nd: Amy's 21st, so bike there before school, plus present and poem, to wish her many happy returns. Tell the news, which is received calmly (impossible otherwise after accepting My Present). Spending the evening pressing various odds and ends ready for My Weekend.

Saturday, April 3rd: Discover the sad truth when I arrive in Derby that I have come without a powder-puff, and they are now unobtainable in velour. Get some cotton-wool as a substitute. Freddie's train is late. Buy a Penguin *Outlines of Eng Lit* while I wait, but proceed to lose it before the day is out. Also lose my powder compact.

Freddie having presented himself, we wander into the town and have to queue until 4 o'clock to get in at the flicks. Have tea at the Gaumont – pilchards on toast without butter, then catch the train to Whatstandwell. Arrive at Alderwasley about 9.30, have supper and retire to bed about 11.30. Take some time to go to sleep – strange bed, strange room etc.

Sunday, April 4th: Don't get up very early, so it is about 10 before we have breakfast. We go out for a little trot before lunch. A most lovely day – more like summer, with a bright sun. After lunch we journey forth again and get back in time for tea about 5. Very enlightening, and causes me to think. Am afraid that dear Freddie's affections don't run very deep. Tell him he is Most Self-Satisfied, and Has No Conscience etc etc., but this merely causes him to grin – quite happily and contentedly. Strictly materialistic, I'm afraid. Also confesses quite honestly that he's never been deeply in love, otherwise he'd have got married years ago! This is a great blow to my vanity and I am somewhat peeved. Asks me if I ever have, but I don't feel disposed to divulge. Says he's had one or two girl friends but that is all. Huh! So I suppose I'm the Girl Friend of the moment. He also resurrects the occasion when he brought me home from a dance and I refused to kiss him and says do I know what he went home thinking? That perhaps One Day I'd change my mind.

Which provides Much Food For Thought.

Monday, April 5th: Oh dear, oh dear! The alarm gives me the most awful shock at twenty to five. Breakfast before 6, then we plod in the darkness over the fields (single file) to the station to catch the 10 to 7 train.

Very weary all day and keep yawning. Debate whether to conduct a strategic withdrawal before it is too late, but decide to leave it over the weekend before I reach this momentous decision. In any case don't intend to be merely standing by for Freddie's gratification. My father says he isn't A Patch on Dougie.

Tuesday, April 6th: Letter from Hilda – asks if I had a good time this weekend. Am discovering many many likenesses between Freddie and Ron – many alarming ones which are still causing me to think.

Wednesday, April 7th: Letter from Freddie. He says that Our Time Together went Far Too Quickly, or Didn't I Think So? and goes on to say that he thought I looked a Wee Bit Fed Up at times, but he does hope I wasn't. He loved being with me. Mrs Tweed and Amy come to supper. Amy unnaturally polite.

Thursday, April 8th: Letter from Fred – my letter was welcome, he says – he had been missing me very much indeed and thinking about me a great deal. Things have been happening at Aston Down. He has had his commission confirmed, but he is not to be mobilised until or unless he is transferred either overseas or to an operational command. He has also a new WAAF assistant, a small blonde.

Saturday, April 10th: Set out for Ely on the 5 past 10 bus. Take the 11 train to Leicester from Ashby. Travel with three soldiers from Leicester, then when they get out another gets in at Market Harborough and tells me what an awful place it is. He is a Cockney, and went through the Norway invasion, so has much to relate about it. His party was sent as a Decoy.

Change again at Cambridge and collect yet one more soldier as I'm running down the platform for the Ely train, which gets to Ely at about twenty to five. Doug – in khaki – is hovering on the platform, and tells me he didn't think I'd make it. He has a taxi waiting for me, and his mother stands at the front door to welcome me. Joan and Hilda, his sisters, and Joan's little boy Michael, aged 3, and Doug's father are within. We sit down to a great feast of salmon, pineapple, choc biscuits etc. Am shown round the garden after this, and a friend of the family named Denny comes, and we all sing, then sit and talk.

Sunday, April 11th: After repeating many times, No I daren't take the day, nor the week off, I finally manage to leave about 10.40. Doug's mother tells me I can go whenever I like etc, etc. So bid them all a fond farewell, and go to the station. Have to come back via London. Dougie travels as far as London with me. Take a taxi from Liverpool Street to St Pancras, where we get a cup of tea and eat our sandwiches, then I decide to get on my train, so tell Dougie not to come on the platform but he does. However, having snaffled a solitary seat only with great difficulty, shake hands and tell him I'm going to sit down. Which I do. But Dougie remains outside the window (although I am on the other side of the train), and I have to keep looking and smiling. Finally he comes in the train again, shakes hands with me once more, tells me to take care of myself, and goes.

Friday, April 16th: Glorious hot day. Journey to Burton on the 5 past 4 bus to meet Freddie, who says he's Glad To See Me. Have a letter from him this morning too, saying he's surprised I didn't tell him I was going away last weekend, and adding that Perhaps He'd Better Start Being Inquisitive. (Perhaps not!)

Saturday, April 17th: Lovely day again, though feel somewhat tired. Catch the 10.10 train to Whatstandwell, where Freddie meets me and thence to Alderwasley. Freddie tells me during the course of the day that he has Missed Me, and that He Loves Me Very Much. I wonder! – and tell him so. Whereupon he says How Can He Show Me? But that's just the point – he shouldn't need to. It should be self-evident. Don't think I really believe it. Still, have a lovely day, and catch the 5.30 train to Derby. Freddie sees me off and tells me that that is the fourth time he's made that journey today, and that once he wouldn't have done it for 40 girls! Very honoured!

Bring back 6 lovely new-laid eggs, purple-sprouting broccoli and some lovely daffodils and narcissi from Alderwasley, much to Mother's delight. Forgot to say that a cockerel arrived too this morning, addressed to Mr and Mrs C. Smith – from Doug.

Freddie keeps referring to last weekend, so tell him I went the other side of Cambridge, and what I did, but omit to mention

Doug (concentrate on Joan and Hilda, which is very deceitful but excusable I hope).

Tuesday, April 20th: Ban on church bells to be lifted. Also Hitler's 54th birthday.

Dash off to Rest Centre rehearsal and am treated for shock, so have to lie down on two desks, with blankets over me, and a hot-water bottle on my tummy. However, we receive a cup of tea to revive us. Auntie Sarah, who should have been treating us, merely sat still and muttered that it was a Waste of Time and a Farce, and sidled off at the first moment.

Letter from Fred. He felt very lost when I'd gone, he says, and was Quite Sad (I wonder!) as he trudged up the hill once more. He looks forward for ages to seeing me, he goes on to say, and in next to no time it is time to say goodbye. He also asks if I Really Enjoyed my day with him – he thought I did. He thought I looked Happy! – and that made him happy too.

Forgot to say too that I had a letter from Doug last week. Next time I go to Ely (he says optimistically) it will be for at least a week, and what is more he's coming to fetch me. He had been looking forward to seeing me for such a long time, but now I've been and gone, and once more he goes back to his old straw bed etc, but he will take back a happy memory with him, and that means a lot. He has just seen Den off to join the RAF – and he's looking forward to seeing me again on his next leave. Anyway – that's a long time away, so needn't think about it yet.

Good Friday, April 23rd: Two letters from Freddie. They now have the Fyffe banana heiress typing there. Asks me to Alderwasley the weekend he's home, and he says Wouldn't it be Lovely if we were spending the weekend together by the sea. The second letter was written later the same day. Says he planted dahlias, lettuce etc. on Monday, tickled a trout, and Thought A Lot About Me. He has been missing me very much indeed and says how awful it would be if he were posted overseas – it would break his heart.

Thursday, April 29th: Letter from Fred. He has been missing me very much – in fact he wished he could snaffle a Spitfire and nip over to see me!

Friday, April 30th: Go on the 3 o'clock bus to Burton and travel with John Ollerenshaw, home on leave from the Army, and stationed at Plymouth in the Bomb Disposal Squad. He is catching the train Fred is coming on, so go to the station with him and stand round chatting. No Freddie appears. Decide to come back to meet the next Birmingham train. Have some tea in Boots, and Mag Whitaker asks me if I've 'seen him off'. Apparently she thought I was seeing John Oll off!

Saturday, May 1st: Catch the 1.20 train to Whatstandwell. Man standing by me on the platform also stands by me in the corridor and nearly talks my head off – all about himself, and his wonderful Knack of Gardening. He just *threw* a packet of aster seeds on the rockery – and lo! he had a wonderful show.

Ladder my new stockings on the way to Alderwasley, so sit down there and then and darn them. After tea go for a little walk and Freddie shoots a partridge (quite wonderfully!).

Sunday, May 2nd: Don't waken until after 9, so it is late before we have finished breakfast. Freddie sets a row of peas in the morn. Go for a walk in the afternoon, and ladder my stockings, irremediably this time. Stay in at night until about 9 o'clock, when we go to the farm to fetch Freddie's mother. Meet his grandmother who seems very nice, and his cousin Eric. Freddie tells me again during the course of the evening that he Loves Me A Great Deal, but I don't somehow believe him. Also that I am Precious To Him, which is very much open to doubt.

Monday, May 3rd: Awaken at 5.30, have a quick breakfast, and Freddie comes with me to the train, plus lovely bunch of tulips. Am at school by 10 to 9, but with a Sinking Heart. Wings for Victory Week, so have to check the £35 savings – and can't get it right.

Tuesday, May 4th: Letter from Doug – in hospital with his knee.

Thursday, May 6th: Walk home through the park and hear the Wings for Victory total announced – £143,000, so we've already passed the target.

Friday, May 7th: Finish off our War Savings Week with a flourish of £110 – having doubled our target. Children all in a ferment, so we go home 10 minutes early.

Letters from Fred and Doug this morning. Doug's anticipates (a) an operation on his knee, though he is going out of hospital now, and (b) posting overseas. Also says he began to think I'd forgotten all about him, but no doubt I have plenty to do without writing to him, so if I can't always find time he'll understand, but it's Jolly Nice getting letters from me! His brother John is at Gibraltar.

Freddie is apparently busy on his Half-Yearly Indent, whatever that may be. He wishes he could come to tennis with me, and hopes that Horrible Creature Harris won't bother me this season – he'll Deal With Him if he does!

Monday, May 10th: Letter from Vera. She writes at length – quite a discourse about her affair with Rick, mine with Ron, and now Doug and Fred. She says I'm in a position to choose either of two husbands (just where she's wrong!) – neither perhaps my ideal

(?) but both friends of some long standing, and their love for me (!!) is more mature. She doesn't think Dougie suitable for my life-partner – not intellectual nor bookish enough. Freddie is more of a good comrade, she says, and I seem more fond of him, apart from my grievances. She hopes I'll solve my dilemma (not mine to solve!)

Saturday, May 15th: Lovely day – a real summer one. Meet Fred about 11.20 and home to lunch. Then go up to tennis, and Ivy and George arrive about half an hour later, so we have a set before tea. Mr Harris asks me if I'll play with him in the Red Cross tournament. Tell him I'll let him know later. Leave about 10.15, and walk home with Ivy and George. Freddie tells me he loves me, but I'm still dubious.

Sunday, May 16th: Lovely day again. Freddie tells me several interesting oddments – that he used to think me a Queer Girl – I used to let him take me out, but I was never enthusiastic, and he wondered why I went. Asks me why I would never let him kiss me – and he says he ought never to have asked me because it was all those years wasted, and that there was One Unfortunate Result – he says if I'd given him any encouragement he'd have taken me home sooner, and then I'd have known his father when he was well. He says too that Ron was a poor sort of specimen. Tells me that I'd have made a good curate's wife – and then giggles. Fear this was made in great sarcasm and meaning just the reverse. Also tells me again that he loves me very much – am beginning to think that perhaps he does, but can't tell yet.

Thursday, May 20th: Letter from Swanee – full of wisecracks about Freddie. Says, 'I should imagine that one of Freddie's characteristics is great patience.' Then she says if I've not made up my mind after all this time, tell Freddie it's not her fault. She's tried to force the pace for him for the last 4 years! Swanee is now a member of the Women's Auxiliary Police Corps.

Letter from Freddie too. He says the weekend passed too quickly and he loved the time we had together – but it only seemed like 10 mins.

Friday, May 21st: Friday, thanks be! Nice little note from Freddie, who says although he hasn't heard from me, and in spite of the fact that he has very little news, he thought he'd let me have a little note to tell me he is thinking about me, and missing me very much. He has just had a chat with a Polish girl pilot with very charming manners – but he says he didn't fall for her! Also he had a nasty moment when a French pilot he'd met before, greeted him with enthusiasm, and poor old Freddie thought he was going to kiss him on both cheeks.

Tuesday, May 25th: Forgot to record a letter from Freddie yesterday. He says would I really like a holiday with him in August – if so we ought to do something about it soon. He's sure he could give me a good time. Also a letter from Doug. His pals are going on an assault course, but he's being kept back for treatment to his knee. If his knee doesn't get well enough for the assault course, he can get in the merchant navy on a machine gun.

Another letter today from Freddie. The ATA are having a party and dance next month, so naturally he will be going – from 10 to 3 – and he wishes I could go. He has also given one of his WAAFs a day off to go to Bristol to buy me a birthday present! He wants to meet me on Friday in Burton.

Saturday, May 29th: To Alderwasley for the weekend. Fred meets me at Whatstandwell. Lovely hot day. Have most luscious thick cream, with pears, for tea. Marvellous! After tea go out and Freddie shoots two young rabbits for tomorrow's lunch. Tells me

he has bought me a hat with a red feather in it for my birthday –
but this proves to be four yards of lovely blue flowered silk. Am
very touched by this generosity.

Sunday, May 30th: Spend the morn pottering about and tying up
plants, and Fred sets a row of cabbages. Call at the farm, and
Freddie's grandmother is horrified by my bare legs and says She
Could Never Go Without Stockings.

Tuesday, June 1st: Got paid! Forgot to say I saw Mr Harris yesterday and he asked me if I was playing with him in the Red
Cross tournament. Told him no, with Fred. So he said I Was
Courting Now Then, Was I? Told him No, whereupon he said it
looked like it at Geary the other Sat. Also his little girl told him
that she's seen His Tennis Partner Courting. He added sourly it
was Time I Settled Down.

Wednesday, June 2nd: Showery. Go to the Rec to run off the heats
of the races for the children's Sports Day in Whit Week. Quite a
nice change. Ivy comes round and says Wouldn't it be nice if she
and George and Fred and I could go away for a holiday.
    A passenger plane from Lisbon, with Leslie Howard on board,
has been lost – shot down by a German plane.

Friday, June 4th: Letter from Freddie again – coping with
teleprinter trouble. Together with this arrives a missive from
Doug – who replies two hours after receiving my letter. Not that
I'm thrilled. He wishes he could pop over and give me a hand in
the tennis tournament. I don't! And will his knee stand up to the
assault course, which is a Perfect Swine? They fire live bullets in
front of them all the time.

Saturday, June 5th: I have a letter from Fred – who is Really

Beginning to think that I love him. It was rather difficult to believe for a long time, he says, because I was so very cold towards him for ages and ages!

Monday, June 7th: Here once more! 29 this year – oh dear oh dear! One step nearer to 30! Still why worry? Have cards, also letters from Vera (with a 3s. 6d. book token), Delia, and Fred. Freddie has just had two WAAF officers sent to him for six weeks' training and he says they aren't half a Straight-laced Pair. After talking to them for half an hour he decided he couldn't stand it any more that day and gave them the day off. He has also interviewed a number of WAAFs who wished to re-muster as met assistants.

Friday, June 11th: We break up – oh joy! Spend the evening preparing for the trip to Corwen to see Delia tomorrow. Go to Mrs W's for my green striped frock – quite nice.

Monday, June 14th: Letter from Fred. Delia and I go to Rhyl. Sit on the beach and paint the sea.

Tuesday, June 15th: Up betimes and catch the 9 a.m. train. Have to stand in the guard's van – about 40 people in there. Awful! Meet Freddie in Burton. Home by 8.30.

Thursday, June 17th: Catch the 10.10 train to Whatstandwell this morning, and Freddie meets me there. After lunch Freddie takes me to tickle trout but after one feel of a clammy, slimy squirming trout I give up. Can't bring myself to touch them. But Freddie catches two, which we later have for supper. Make several dams in the stream in our efforts to catch them. After tea we journey forth again and shoot two young rabbits for tomorrow's lunch. Then call at the farm. Freddie's grandmother very sprightly. Lovely day.

Tuesday, June 22nd: Go to tennis. Mr H is there – says My Word, I Was Making A Fuss of Him on Sunday wasn't I? Silly thing! And have I made up my mind yet? What cheek! He also says we looked as though we'd Been Together For Years??

Thursday, June 24th: Letter from Fred who says the holiday went too quickly – and that it always does when one is happy. Have also had letters from Delia and Swanee this week. Delia supposes it was worth the uncomfortable journey to meet Freddie at the other end ... and Swanee ends, 'Just see that you treat Fred well! Do You hear?'

Friday, June 25th: Mrs T and Amy to supper. Make a nifty brassiere out of an old petticoat, and embroider same.

Friday, July 2nd: Meet Freddie in Burton and come home. Have strawberries for tea – luscious. After tea, Mother fetches my new dress, and we decide that it looks Very Nice.

Saturday, July 3rd: Arrive in Alderwasley just before 5. Go out after tea and shoot a wood-pigeon.

Sunday, July 4th: Was gathering blackcurrants last night when an old lady from over the way tottered along and said Was I Fred's Young Lady? Freddie's mother simply said, 'Yes!'

After lunch we go for a walk by the pond. Freddie says he doesn't believe in a man being tied to a woman's apron strings!

Monday, July 5th: Up at crack of dawn and on my way homewards. To Swanee's for tea. She tells me that George and Ivy don't think I'm really keen on Freddie – and adds that they should know, because I'm far more friendly with them now than with Swanee!

Thursday, July 8th: Keeping a diary is an expensive sport these days – this latest addition having cost no less than Three Shillings and Eightpence.

Day opens with a missive from Freddie. He thinks the weekend went far too quickly. And he feels lonely without me!

Friday, July 9th: The day opens with another letter from Freddie, who has given a lecture, and thinks it went quite well. He has also been to the next aerodrome in a Wellington bomber. Apart from this, he hasn't much to tell me he says, except that he Loves Me Very Much.

Monday, July 12th: We rehearse our concert this afternoon. Our tap dancer clatters up and down along the platform; our two cowboys yodel their ditty; P Badger declaims 'Grey and White'; my four trebles trill 'The White Cliffs of Dover' and our pianist gives her little piece.

Letter from Freddie this morn. If it were not for his father's death, he would feel supremely happy, he says.

Tuesday, July 13th: Letters from Freddie and Doug. Freddie's contains caricature of himself done by the *News of the World* caricaturist, but not a very good likeness, apart from the forehead. Makes his nose look too sharp, and gives him a wholly alien effeminate look. Doug writes to say he expects to be home next weekend on embarkation leave (again!) in which case he'll pop over and see me! Oh dear! Anyhow, he says, he doesn't mind going abroad because, 'the sooner we can beat the blighter, the sooner we can return home and enjoy life once more'. He'll phone me from home when he gets there. Once more – oh dear!

Monday, July 19th: Go to Measham with Joyce to get pantees and vest without coupons. But they are 12/11 and not worth 5/-, so shall do no more black-marketing. Return to find Doug has phoned – 3 times – so ring him up. He is out but his mother says will it be all right if he comes to see me tomorrow, so perforce have to say Yes.

Tuesday, July 20th: Doug arrives this afternoon, as beefy as ever. Take him with me to meet Delia on the 6.15 train, but she doesn't arrive. So we return and Delia comes as I am in the bath, after having had to walk from Gresley. She had a beer in Burton – her first! But she didn't like it.

Thursday, July 22nd: Letter from Freddie, hoping for a week's leave the 2nd week in August and suggesting I go to Cheltenham on the Saturday and travel back with him on the Monday.

Doug, Delia and I go to the Majestic after tea to see a pathetic picture called *Remember the Day* – about a school teacher who had her moment, but lost her man. He was killed in the last war. Delia weeps slightly, but after swallowing a little I refrain. Doug goes to sleep. He has taken Delia for a route-march this afternoon, and had her doubling up and down hills round Bretby. He also has her coming to attention and saluting smartly (in pyjamas and dressing gown!) just before bed.

The curate comes at teatime and Doug rudely goes to sleep, then wakes up to argue with him about telling lies, which Dougie tries to justify.

Friday, July 23rd: Doug, due to return this morning, announces that he will go a little way to school with me. He does – and when saying goodbye on the corner says I wouldn't think of marrying him some day, would I? Say no, I've never thought of that, whereat he says he's no good at making pretty speeches, but he has cared for me more than for any other girl, and he has met lots since he has known me, and it has been good knowing me, or something or other, and he has never met another girl like me. Also that if he ever met another girl half as nice and she cared for him, he'd marry her like a shot. Feel a bit miserable after this for the rest of the morning.

Delia and I go to tennis and have 4 good sets.

Saturday, July 24th: Letter from Freddie – leave cancelled, but he'll try and get home for a weekend.

Tuesday, July 27th: Letters from Freddie and Doug. Freddie is now left alone with 6 women on his staff. One of his WAAF officers has been posted, to his relief. Doug writes to thank us for the Grand Time he spent with us. He says he felt very guilty barging in, but he won't be seeing me for a long time so he hopes I'll excuse him. He will take a very happy memory back with him of a very pleasant 2 or 3 days. He goes on, 'Anyway, May, whatever happens, I still think you're the best girl I've known or shall ever know.'

Forgot to record yesterday an event of political importance – a great surprise but a welcome one. Mussolini has resigned! And the King has appointed Badoglio as PM. Italy intends to continue with the war, they say, but Musso's had it! Reports say that he was arrested while trying to escape to Germany.

Friday, July 30th: Hot day. Letter from Freddie, who's trying to get away next Thursday.

Saturday, July 31st: Most scorching hot day – yet have a letter from Freddie telling me to take my coat if I go for this weekend. Terribly close. Make 2 pairs of pantees, then go to Geary for tea about 4.30 and meet Ivy and George there. Then Ivy and I play off the finals of the Ladies' Singles and I win 6–4, 6–3, to my (and everyone's) surprise.

Thursday, August 5th: Dash to Burton to meet Freddie at 6.30. Freddie asks me why I was pleased Delia came when she did, but feel the moment to be inopportune, so shelve the question.

Saturday, August 7th: Freddie and I go to Alderwasley this afternoon and travel in the same compartment as the august Director of Education, Mr Briggs, deep in pamphlets and papers. Freddie keeps making remarks about him. A lovely day (not climatically though – it rained!).

Tuesday, August 10th: Lovely day. Go with Freddie to chop two young larch trees in the wood, and tell him en route about Doug's visit. Takes it very calmly and says he's not annoyed – but I think he's surprised and he becomes rather quiet. Says I ought to have told Doug that he wouldn't like his coming – and hopes they'll send D to China.

Friday, August 13th: Awful news. Letter from Freddie to say that he has been posted to Banff, right up on the east coast of Scotland, over 600 miles away – to go next Thursday. Oh dear!

Saturday, August 21st: Letters from Fred and Doug. Freddie's was from Edinburgh. He is missing me dreadfully, he says. Doug – oh lor! – is expecting 10 days' leave and wants to pop over for a couple of days again.

Monday, August 23rd: Letter from Freddie to say he arrived in Banff at 7 p.m. on Friday. He says he loves me and is longing to see me again.

Friday, August 27th: Letter from Freddie – on night duty. He says it seems rather surprising that Doug should be contemplating another visit in view of the fact that I gave him No

Encouragement. And he Trusts that I've written to put him off. He says Why not tell him that we are Very Much In Love with Each Other?

Monday, August 30th: Have a letter from Dougie – his last – which is very touching. He doesn't think any the worse of me for my letter, he says.* He realises exactly how I feel about things and says he ought to be kicked for putting me in such a rotten position (not his fault at all):

> But you will have to excuse me that, because I think such a heck of a lot of you and always will. To save you any further trouble I think we'd better part. I've known you and waited for you for ten years, but I really knew in my heart that you didn't care for me, anyway not in the same way as I cared for you. But I wouldn't have missed knowing you for anything in this world and it's going to be jolly hard without you. I'm going to miss your letters too, because I always look forward to them and they sort of give me an interest in life because goodness only knows it's miserable being in this Army. I am sending some chocolate I managed to save and was hoping to bring to you. Well, May, this is the finish, but I shall never forget you and if I can help you in any way at any time just let me know. Goodbye and God bless you, May.

Oh dear! It will seem strange not hearing from old Doug. He's been a good and faithful friend these many years.

Friday, September 3rd: 4th anniversary of the war – my stars! And we have landed forces on the toe of Italy this morning at 4.30. Have a short service in school from 11 to 11.15.

*The diary has not mentioned the sending of this letter.

Saturday, September 4th: Letter from Freddie – asks if I told Doug about him. He says he's missing me every minute and every day we're apart seems like a day wasted.

Go to Burton and meet Hilda. Go blouse-hunting and find just what I want at Herratts – cherry red wool with turned-back collar, but too big. Blow! Buy cami-knickers and stationery. Lunch at Boots, then to the Ritz to see *Talk of the Town* (Ronald Coleman, Cary Grant and Jean Arthur). Not bad. Auntie Nell and Joyce at home when I return. Start to embroider my cami-knickers to make them less Utility.

Tuesday, September 7th: Forgot to record last week that a *dozen* bars of chocolate and five hairnets arrived from poor old Doug. Very touched. Think perhaps he's more considerate and would do more for me than Freddie.

Wednesday, September 8th: Italy has surrendered, whoopee, whoopee! The news was flashed on the screen at the flicks tonight. Letter from Freddie this morning – still rather fed up and complaining of draughts. He cycled into Portsoy on his day off to post his laundry home. His bedsocks have already come into use!

Thursday, September 9th: We begin the day with the national anthem in honour of the news, and I find my bike adorned with red, white and blue pompons. An armistice was signed last Friday! – but we were to choose our own moment for proclaiming it.

Sunday, September 12th: Armistice terms published. We seem to have snaffled every advantage we possibly could – and rightly so! Couldn't have asked for much more, which is what is meant by 'unconditional surrender', I suppose.

Tuesday, September 14th: Letter from Freddie, who has now put in an application for his leave and a travelling warrant. When he does see me he won't want to leave again, he says. I wonder!

Wednesday, September 22nd: Freddie's travel warrant has come through and all is set for his coming home next week.

Friday, September 24th: Have my hair set in a roll at the front. Fetch my frock – black trimmed with blue. Quite nice.

Saturday, October 2nd: Am up quite early and on my way to Derby, en route for Alderwasley. Am considerably – and happily – surprised when I get to Derby station to find Freddie on his way home, having been travelling since 2 o'clock yesterday afternoon. Can't remember now how we spent the rest of the day – stalking rabbits, I believe – but know it was a very happy day.

Sunday, October 3rd: Another lovely day, though looking back, I can't remember any details, except a general impression of happiness.

Tuesday, October 5th: Believe we went tree-felling today, ready to mend the rose-bower – or rather, pull it down and erect a super modern construction. Start on this great project.

Wednesday, October 6th: Have a chicken for lunch. A wet day, but manage to finish the work of construction. Also make some pastry. Freddie says he loves me so much that he wants to keep me all to himself.

Saturday, October 9th: Freddie pays me compliments at which I am sceptical. Also leaves me guarding a mangel field in which there is a pheasant while he dives home for his gun – but in vain. Can't find it. After tea he disappears to the farm, and comes back to ask if I mind if he goes to the Malt Shovel. Know perfectly well he'll go in any case – but don't mind, so he goes, and his mother and I go to the farm about 9. He returns looking very pleased with life at 10.40! When we get home he says I've been a bit Cold today and wants to know why. Says I take life too seriously!

Sunday, October 10th: Freddie's last day! Oh dear! Spend the morn shooting – 3 rabbits and a stoat – and the afternoon gardening, and the evening by the fire, while his mother goes to the farm. Freddie says Will I Be His Some Day, so that we can always be together. He says I'd have a job to shake him off, and that when he wants anything he'll turn everything upside down to get it.

Monday, October 11th: Oh dear! That awful alarm! By 6.15 a.m. Freddie and I are on the way to the station, in the darkness, and I see Freddie steam away on the train with many a pang. Wander back to Alderwasley then. A lovely day, but rather empty. Write to Freddie.

Tuesday, October 12th: Leave at 9 a.m., but have a lift on a milk lorry to Whatstandwell station. Home by 1.30. Spend the afternoon settling in again and reading.

Thursday, October 14th: Italy has declared war on Germany! Is now a co-belligerent, but not an ally.

Friday, October 15th: Note from Freddie, safely back in Banff. Have my hair washed and set. What a scrappy diary this has become!

Monday, October 18th: Letter from Freddie, who is troubled with indigestion, and he has caught his 7th mouse.

School once more, but not too sorry to be back – yet!

Go to History. I get quite out of my depth in parts, and somewhat bored and fidgety by the end. We discuss the repeal of prohibition in America this week. Am afraid that I'm quite at sea where economics are concerned, but the men seem possessed of profound acumen and ask most learned questions. Sidle out at 9, feeling I've Had Enough.

Tuesday, October 19th: Ron is to be married tomorrow, at a small church in Glasgow, and is spending a fortnight's honeymoon somewhere he wants no one to know of. Am surprised he hasn't written to tell me! Mother makes various Catty Comments.

Tuesday, November 16th: Great surprise! – Freddie's mother rings up to say she has had a telegram from Freddie to say he has been posted to Shropshire! Very good news.

Thursday, November 18th: Letter from Freddie, posted to Peplow between Wellington and Market Drayton. He was told he was posted to Italy!

Tuesday, November 23rd: Nice letter from Freddie yesterday. A mouse has chewed a hole in the knee of his best trousers. He says he is thrilled at the prospect of seeing me soon and hopes it won't be long. Tells me he loves me again, and says he doesn't know how he existed before he found that I loved him – my love means so much to him now, he says. It will be a relief when he is settled down again, he says.

Tuesday, November 30th: Couldn't really decide whether I were really anxious to see Freddie or not, but think I was at the bottom, but I have just got more or less settled to not seeing him. Anyway, I feel a calmness rather than a wild excitement during the day, and he seems like a stranger during tea and when I first see him. After tea I feel a little more normal. Freddie is very tired, having come straight from night duty. Asks me if I'll ever get fed up with him, so tell him, 'Often, probably.' Says he wants to be with me all the time, and will be 'one day' (very vague). Says that he has no desire to take any other girl out, and says that he wouldn't love me if I went out with others, like Swanee. Says he couldn't stop loving me if he tried. I wonder! – or rather, I don't, because I know from experience that it is untrue. It is possible to stop loving someone though at the time it doesn't seem so. I wonder if I'm cynical or just somewhat disillusioned.

Sunday, December 5th: Freddie causes a sensation and glitters forth in new uniform, in which he really does look very nice. Spend the morning stitching name tapes on all his oddments.

Thursday, December 9th: Two letters from Freddie, written on his two night duties, on Monday and Tuesday. He has a new WAAF from Derby. Write a short note to him, but somehow feel quite estranged. Don't know why and can only write a bleak little note. But I don't think he'll notice. He doesn't notice things like that.

Friday, December 10th: Disappointed not to hear from Freddie. Would have liked a letter today somehow, because I'm feeling so unsettled. Mother says that she doesn't think we're very thrilled with each other, and that Doug was far more in love with me than Freddie. Amy and Mrs T here for supper. Amy has heard from her new boyfriend, an Australian sub-lieutenant, to say he is coming to spend a week with her at Christmas.

Monday, December 13th: Freddie's birthday. Tells me that he loves me and that I mean everything to him. I don't really think that I do, at the bottom. There are many things in his life of almost equal importance. Amy tells me I ought to be more aloof – that she thinks I'm making a mistake in being always too accessible, and that he takes me too much for granted. Am inclined to agree!

Tuesday, December 14th: No letter from Freddie. Am wondering if he has noticed that my letters haven't been so affectionate. Affairs can be very complicated, and one's behaviour governed by a multitude of things. Don't know quite what to do. Wish I did – but when I do what seems natural to do it doesn't seem to work out right. Complicated!

A miserably cold, raw, dark, foggy day. Amy comes to tea, and we all go to the flicks to see George Sanders and Herbert Marshal in S. Maugham's *The Moon and Sixpence.*

Thursday, December 16th: Find Freddie on the hearth when I arrive home at teatime. Stay in by the fire in the evening. Freddie likes me in the blue dress I have on, he says (the material he bought!). Also tells me that he couldn't live without me.

Saturday, December 18th: At Alderwasley. Freddie announces that he thinks he'll have a drink tonight with Eric. His mother says, 'Suppose May won't let you!', whereupon he retorts that if he wanted to do anything, I wouldn't stop him ... ! Feel the truth of this, and am peeved. In the afternoon he goes off with the gun and about half-past six he goes to the farm. Sit with his mother and knit and grow more and more angry and wish I were at home. However, he returns at a quarter to 8, has his supper and promptly goes to sleep on the sofa. Could shake him, and could throw things at him, but do neither. Instead I sit and brood silently. When his mother has gone to bed, he comes to me and says Am I Fed Up with him, so say Yes, Today I am, Very. So he says, with a little hesitation, Don't I Love Him Any More, and I reply coldly Not Very Much At the Moment, so he goes and sits down. Think he sounds a little upset when he says goodnight to his mother, but harden my heart and tell myself that it will do him good. Will have to make myself hard and casual and indifferent, I think. These things seem to pay far more than affection.

Sunday, December 19th: Don't feel at all easy in mind when I wake up this morn, after last night, and wonder whether Freddie will bother to waken me or whether he'll just go straight downstairs, With Independence. However, after a time he ambles in and says Have I Slept Well. Says he had a nightmare and not much sleep at all. Asks me in all innocence why I was so sulky and peeved, so tell him, and he says he was not out of the house many minutes, and that what he said at lunchtime was meant as a joke. Says that the real trouble is that he is Not a Lady's Man, but tell him that I think it is just a Question of Manners – and this shakes him a little, I think. Tells me again that he loves me very much and other things. At breakfast he even hands me things and pours out a cup of tea, so evidently the remark about manners went home! Am very surprised. Tells me also that he'll take me for a walk this morn, but a man comes to see him about new vests, so it is too late.

After supper Freddie says he won't neglect me again. Says he has enjoyed being with me – to which I snort, so he tells me not to be cynical, and that he means it, and thinks I'm the sweetest girl in the world etc. Tells me again that he couldn't live without me, and that he doesn't mean to live without me.

Thursday, December 23rd: We bestow a silver napkin-ring on Connie, and she gives us each an address book, and with mutual good wishes we part. A whole fortnight's holiday, whoopee! Have my hair washed and set, then to the flicks with Barbara to see submarine flick – *We Dive At Dawn*. Sit behind a Loving Couple, head on each other's shoulders and arms entwined etc. It is Amy and the Navy! Recognise her at once. She is staggered and confounded, though not nonplussed, when she turns round and sees us.

Note from Freddie saying he has arrived back safely, but little else. Says he hopes we'll spend next Christmas together. I wonder! Omit to write to him for the second day, as I think it might do him good.

Friday, December 24th – Christmas Eve: Swanee drops in. Asks, of course, how Freddie is and I tell her the tale of last weekend. She is shocked and indignant and says She Wouldn't Have That, and that men don't improve on acquaintance, but get gradually worse. True, too true! (Of some men, anyhow.)

Saturday, December 25th – Christmas Day: Letter from Fred. He can't get away now until 5th Jan. Says he's still a bit worried about the weekend (I should think so too!) and has not forgiven himself yet for neglecting me so badly on Saturday. He didn't mean to, he says, and is most sorry about it, and wishes we could have this weekend together to make up for it. But the trouble is, it wouldn't. Last weekend made a Great Impression on me, and I haven't been able to push it aside. Besides, it's no use doing so. It aroused too many questions.

Anyway, if there is to be any cooling off, I intend to be the one to do it this time. Once in a lifetime is enough – for me, at any rate.

Am not feeling too affectionate towards him, even though it is Xmas and I should. But it would be silly to go on in the same old way when all it produces is an utter Lack of Consideration and Selfishness. He's utterly selfish, and I'm not being mean either. I've known it for a long time. Reply therefore saying that I enjoyed the weekend but not as much as I have sometimes before and that Perhaps I Expected Too Much (though don't mean this. Am being mildly sarcastic but don't think he'll notice).

Go to Amy's for tea. Have trifle and strawberries – and a Christmas cake with currants in! Luscious. Her new young man, an Australian sub-lieutenant – Ken – is very much at home and seems very nice.

Thursday, December 30th: Two letters from Freddie. He wishes that we were together. He says, very primly, 'As I seem to have disappointed you very much last time we were together I am very anxious to make amends.' He's done nothing but work this Xmas, poor soul. He says, 'I had been feeling that perhaps you didn't love me very much after all. I am longing to see you, my darling.' He was also amused, he says, by my description of Amy's Ken – aimed at him, as I think he must know.

Go to the club with Mother, Auntie N and Joyce to cut sandwiches for the New Year's Eve 'do'. Have two glasses of cider and feel lightheaded.

Friday, December 31st: Ends permed this morn. Letter from Freddie, who wasn't going to write, as he had just done 12 hours' duty, but he found my Sorrowful Note (as he calls it) awaiting him – in which I said I hadn't heard from him. He says, 'Try to have a little more confidence in me next time you don't hear from me for a while. You may rest assured that I shall always write to you when circumstances permit. You should know by this time that I love you my darling.'

1944

Monday, January 3rd: Freddie arrives just after 2, but refuses to go to Barbara's to tea. Mother and I go alone to Mrs Gee's and I return about 7, but Mother and Dad don't come back until after midnight. Very nice to see Freddie again.

Friday, January 14th: Freddie returns to Peplow but hopes to get over again next week for two days. Nice. Have not said much about his leave because of actual incident there was little, but we had a lovely time – a great improvement on the last time together. Freddie seemed much nicer and less self-centred. Discussed several things, and Freddie said much to make me happy. Hard to be cool to him when he is so nice, but I suppose I'll have to try, when he comes again, according to Amy and the Modern Psychology.

Wednesday, January 19th: Freddie is here when I get home at 4. It is a pouring wet day, so he comes in his little hat which I like very much. (Like his big one too.) Amy comes along at teatime, and stays for the evening, so Freddie teaches (or tries to teach) Mother, Amy and me the rudiments of Bridge. He is suffering with a stiff back and neck.

Friday, January 21st: Mrs T and Amy come to supper. Mrs T talks to Mother about nothing but Ken all the evening. Freddie and I sit up talking until after 1 o'clock. He tells me I'm Cold, and not affectionate, and serious-minded, except for a Light Frivolity!

Saturday, February 5th: Have my hair set this morn, then off to Derby straight after lunch to meet Freddie. He arrives just before 3, nearly dead after night duty. Go to see about an engagement ring, but the shop is closed.* Have the evening indoors. Freddie says he's disappointed about the ring. Mother goes to the Whist Drive.

Wednesday, February 9th: Set out for Coalville, but am on one of the buses with the Awful Gas Contraption tacked on to the rear, and so we are late and I miss my connection at Ashby and have to return.

Saturday, February 12th: A day with a surprise ... Go to meet Freddie at Whatstandwell, and he tells me that he has bought something for me. On the way home he produces it – it is an Engagement Ring! Very sweet indeed, with three diamonds. Show his mother when we arrive and she thinks it is lovely too. Keep looking at it all evening. It is a bit big though and keeps slipping round. Try putting cotton round but it looks rather poverty-stricken and unsightly.

Sunday, February 13th: Late getting up, after the excitement of yesterday. Go to show Freddie's relatives at the farm before going home. Mother is about ¾ hour before she sees the ring, and my father says He Would Never Have Noticed.

Monday, February 14th: Surprise visit from Swanee, who is Very Excited by the news. Mr Wheat announces that he Shall Have It Ready for me This Summer (meaning the orange blossom he has been threatening me with ever since I knew him), and that he Shall Come To the Church! He's looking ahead. Connie sees the ring almost at once and says coyly Must She Congratulate Me? Ring up Freddie but discover he has chopped the end of his thumb off and fainted. Oh dear!

---

*The diary has not mentioned a marriage proposal or a decision to buy an engagement ring.

Tuesday, February 15th: Auntie Nell views the ring and likes it very much. George rings me up and is very nice. He says Freddie's Got One of the Best . . . Oh dear! Tell him he's making me blush. Get a contrivance for my ring from Dinnis's and it is now a lovely fit and feels much more as though it belongs to me.

Ring up Freddie's mother and find that Freddie is still at home – going back tomorrow. Thumb still very painful.

Saturday, February 19th: Letter from Freddie, doubtful about coming today, and saying Don't Meet Him In Case he doesn't come. However, prepare for him, but keep reminding myself that I don't think he'll come. Very cold day. Meet two buses and am just preparing to go and meet a third when Freddie arrives looking rather pale and tired, I think, but am very glad to see him. His thumb is still in a Raw State.

Sunday, February 20th: Up late, and we don't go out at all. View Freddie's thumb – a terrible mess, though going on satisfactorily it seems. Must have been, and still be, terrifically painful.

Monday, February 21st: Dad's 60th birthday. Up late again and spend the afternoon indoors, then we go to the Empire to see *Anthony Adverse* – which I saw about 6 years ago! Freddie's thumb hurts at night. I do feel sorry about it.

Monday, March 6th: Letter from Swanee, very lively and breezy. She has been to see *Madame Butterfly* recently and remarks: 'How very accommodating these women are who take their own life! The men are free to flap their wings again. That's not my policy, domestic or foreign.' She goes on to say: 'My husband, alias Geoff, has had a month's leave in Tunis, and has been round the Bey's palace, but didn't see the ladies of the harem.'

Spend the evening indoors ironing and mending. Feel anew

Pangs of Dismay for the last state of my underwear is Worse Than the First.

Thursday, March 9th: Sally forth to meet the bus which I've calculated Freddie will be on, but find it coming in with No Freddie, so am just waiting to go and meet the next when in he walks. Very very nice to see him again, and he brings me 2 oranges and a bar of chocolate – which little thought and action make me feel very touched, and I think it Awfully Sweet of him. Don't go out anywhere but just sit by the fire until about midnight.

Friday, March 10th: Oh brevity! Freddie returns to Peplow this morn, but hopes to get over again next Wed.

Saturday, March 11th: Keep a rendezvous with Hilda this morning, and we cruise round the shops, scanning and criticising and occasionally making a small purchase. I go hopefully into Smith & Hollis after an underset that has captivated me – pink crêpe-de-chine with white spots, but on being told that it is Rather Expensive (nearly £6) I change my mind, but it makes the 17s. 11d. Utility ones look very Utility. However buy a Utility blue and white striped blouse for £1 0s. 10d. and also (at long last!) two pairs of stockings.

Sunday, March 12th: I scan my wardrobe hopefully for Something Nice to Wear, but can find naught, so have to don an old and moth-eaten bluish-grey dress, which is Hoary with Age. No prospect of having much new either, to cheer me up. Write to Freddie before tea – though needlessly. Fear this may tend to spoil him so must be careful not to keep up this positive shower of letters. Still, felt I'd like to write. He was very very nice the last time he came over.

Wednesday, March 15th: The Ides of March, but no Grim Thing befalls. Instead, the reverse. Freddie comes for two days' leave. Spend the evening indoors – Freddie very very nice. But he doesn't like my new Utility blouse. Says he could have given me a shirt to have made a better one.

Saturday, March 18th: Don't get up too early because my father is operating in the chimney and bringing down loads of soot. However, the time soon comes for Freddie to be on his way, so go to the station and see him off. Leave his sandwiches in the paper shop. The time does seem to have gone quickly. Go in search of wool for pullover for Freddie and knit a bit more of his sock after neglecting it sadly.

Monday, March 20th: My financial position today shows so great a deterioration that I am forced to borrow £1 4*s.* 6*d.* And this because I lavishly expend £1 5*s.* on 4 pillow cases. Am in direst poverty.

Wednesday, March 22nd: Doctor calls to see Mother and says Well I've Taken the Step then, but tell him Not Quite. Asks in a very quizzy and nosey fashion when IT is to be, but when I tell him I Don't Know he says Keep Him Guessing, He'll Value Me More. Inclined to agree with these wise words.

A shock this morn. Advance towards the postman fully expecting a letter from the erring Freddie, but instead find one from Dougie in my outstretched hand. Gaze at it with mixed feelings. He is in Renfrewshire and says the letter will come as a surprise, but he'd like to know how I am getting on, and will Quite Understand if I don't answer, because He's to Blame for Everything. (Am very puzzled by this.) He is Waiting For Things to happen, he says, and that's one reason why he'd like a letter from me if I can find time. He is now a dispatch rider. He

Shudders to Think what I will say when I get the letter, because he knows I can't be Keen On Writing to him. But he concludes that whether I write or not, he wishes me All the Very Best of Luck Always.

Auntie Nell says 'Poor chap' and Amy 'Poor old Dougie' when told of this. My father says that he 'Wasn't A Bad Sort, Doug.' Agree. He certainly wasn't.

Sunday, March 26th: Hear the PM on the news at night – not frightfully interesting and nothing new. Just a review, with a Pat on the Back for the Government and a Hurt Word to its critics.

Monday, March 27th: Hilda T's Bert is back in England again, after his 3 years abroad. Haven't seen her but she told Mother the news had made her tummy whirl (?!). Nearly hooted; she's so sedate.

Friday, March 31st: Letters from Freddie and Hilda. Hilda hardly had any sleep last weekend. She was so excited, she says, that it was Most Uncomfortable. Tut!

Tuesday, April 4th: Freddie arrives and comes for the night on his way home for his leave, but am deterred from meeting him off the bus by the unfortunate and tragic fact that my stockings can be found nowhere, and remain a mysterious loss. Have only one other pair, which I am saving for Easter.

Wednesday, April 5th: Staggering news! Note from Hilda to say that Bert has adopted Commando tactics and has presented her with a special licence, so they are to be married on Saturday. Am very pleased.

Tuesday, April 11th: Parcel from Doug containing 12 bars of chocolate and sweets, with a note saying that I haven't replied to his last letter but he would like me to have the chocolate etc for Easter. Oh dear!

Thursday, April 13th: Rather wet. The Vicar calls this afternoon and is introduced to Freddie. We go to the Empire at night for want of something to do, but it gives Freddie a headache. He rings up the aerodrome and discovers that it will be all right to stay till Saturday, but all leave is cancelled for at least 6 months. Oh dear! Blow the invasion! To bed fairly early.

Tuesday, April 18th: Glorious evening, so to tennis. Discuss the RAF and their Morals, or Lack Of. Have some good singles.

Saturday, April 22nd: To Alderwasley. Most lovely day. Travel from Derby with Suspiciously Nosey Person who asks if I have any Inside Information about when the Second Front is going to start. Must think I'm Montgomery's aide-de-camp or Churchill's private secretary, or some Influential Being in the Ministry of Information. Says he thinks it's all A Matter of Bluff, but I disagree.

Trek down to the station to meet Freddie, hoping he won't have been prevented from coming at the last minute. Am just rounding the bend to the station when he comes off, and greets me with the remark that I am Nearly Late, and goes on to launch an attack on my Maroon Ankle Socks. However he's very nice after this.

Monday, May 1st: Put Mother to bed for 6 weeks with a fatted heart.

Wednesday, May 24th: Half-holiday for Empire Day. Unfortunately, Freddie reads something in an old diary of mine about himself which hurts him very much – and me too. Wouldn't hurt him for the world, so feel very upset about it, and wish those wretched trashy tripey stupid diaries were in Hanover. Freddie exceptionally nice too – can't remember him ever being nicer to me. Which makes me feel worse than ever. Try to make up for it, but fear that the thought of what he read will recur. Oh dear! Hate to hurt him – I love him too much. Tells me he will always love me and that he needs me. Says it is time we were married.

Thursday, May 25th: Feel very miserable after Freddie has gone back. Write to him in an effort to make myself feel better.

Saturday, May 27th: Glorious hot day, with a lovely letter from Fr who says that if I stopped loving him there'd be nothing left.

Whit Monday, May 29th: My poor old neglected diary! It gets no attention these rushed days. Maybe it's as well!

Wednesday, May 31st: Despite my fears and pessimism, Freddie manages to get over, and I meet him on the station at Derby and we proceed to Alderwasley. Hot again but with a freshening breeze. Do a bit of gardening after tea, then it starts to rain.

Friday, June 2nd: Freddie goes back alas and alack! We catch the 20 to 10 train to Derby, and I leave it at Burton. He says he will apply for leave to get married when he gets back. Howbeit, with things as they are, I am not unduly optimistic.

Tuesday, June 6th: A day of dither. We have invaded Normandy, and landings have been going on successfully since early morning. Oh dear! Sit around listening for news and poring over the paper.

Note from Freddie again, also the Budget, containing good wishes for Freddie and me on our engagement.

Wednesday, June 7th: Reach the Advanced Age of 30 today. Receive letters from Freddie and his mother. Freddie says that my love is the most important thing in his life now, and that his dearest wish is that we shall be spending my next birthday together, and by that time we shall really belong to each other. Do little on this my birthday. Go to Miss Joyce's to have blue dress fitted. Wonder if it will be my wedding frock? Wish I had something really fetching.

Thursday, June 8th: Wondering all day if Freddie will be able to make it, but when I get in at teatime I find him at home, much to my joy and relief. Lovely to see him. He goes to bed for an hour after tea. Up till about 12.

Saturday, June 10th: See Freddie off again, woe is me! He says shall we fix our wedding day when he comes next week, if Mother is up? Doesn't seem real to me somehow.

Monday, June 12th: Note from Freddie which is very acceptable. Then to the music lecture at night. See Hilda there – Bert is in the second front, she thinks. Forgot to say that I had a letter from Doug last week, written on the 3rd but held up because of the invasion, I expect. I think he is in it. Very pathetic. Says he hasn't heard from me, and that friends forget one at a time like this, but it is always nice to hear from old friends, especially me.

Saturday, June 17th: Catch the 8.48 train to Birmingham, where I have promised to meet Freddie at 11. Am just waiting when I spot him not many yards away deep in converse with a WAAF. Leave them to finish their conversation and this takes some 10 minutes, before he finally looks around and notices me. This makes me slightly and unreasonably peeved.

Sunday, June 18th: Freddie says he's worried because I don't seem very enthusiastic about our getting married. But it is all so indefinite. No use making plans very far ahead these days.

Saturday, June 24th: Lovely hot day. Go to Derby and meet Freddie there. Arrive at Alderwasley just after 5. Decide to get married the second week in August.

Tuesday, June 27th: My 2-piece comes and looks quite nice, except that the coat doesn't fit quite tightly enough. But she's made it beautifully. Think it will have to be the bridal attire. Parade in same.

Saturday, July 1st: Journey with Auntie Nell to Burton to prospect for new hat to go with my two-piece. Mrs Mapp exhibits wonderful flowery model costing a mere 7 guineas. Tell her I wouldn't dream of paying it, and she offers to make similar one, though less beflowered, for a more modest 45/-, so leave it at this. Spend the rest of the morn wondering whether I'll regret this piece of Fancy-work. Also buy low-heeled brown suede shoes and brown fishnet gloves, and have to spend 3 of Mother's coupons. Go to the Ritz to see Bette Davies in *Now, Voyager*. Very good.

Tuesday, July 11th: To Amy's to tea to confer with her about being bridesmaid and to look at her frock. Ivy has offered to lend me her wedding dress and Joyce her veil.

Wednesday, July 12th: Freddie arrives. We fix our wedding day for 19th August – a Saturday.

Sunday, July 16th: Our banns are read out this morn. Feel very dithery.

Friday, July 21st: Freddie arrives. He brings some lovely roses. But he grumbles at the thought of having to see the Vicar, and goes on to tell me of a party he went to last Sunday, when he danced with the WAAF officer I saw him talking to in Birmingham and even walked back with her. She invited him in for coffee, and he and the man Francis, who had also escorted another WAAF officer, accepted. Huh! Feel very peeved. This causes some slight restraint. Know it's silly – or rather, hope it is, but can't help it. Anyway, he's still free to choose. Can still manage without anyone, though I wouldn't like to now. It would shake me a bit, I fear.

Monday, July 24th: Letter from Freddie, to my relief. Had been hoping for one, and this makes me feel a little more settled. Says he has been missing me since he got back (and the WAAF too probably! She's left!). He thought I wasn't quite so happy as usual and asks if I found him a bit dull. But he says he wants me to know that he does love me a terrific amount and always will.

Friday, August 4th: We break up, oh thanks be! Am presented formally in the hall with £3 5s. 6d. from school.

Tuesday, August 15th: Sat will soon be here now! I have my ends permed at 11. Take the certificate to the vicar, then to Miss Joyce's.

Thursday, August 17th: Poor old Vera has to work hard. We bike to Burton this afternoon and I buy headdress of gardenias. Then Freddie comes about 5.30 and we all go to tennis.

Friday, August 18th: What a day! Am worn out. But Freddie, Vera and I go to the flicks at night. Set the tables in the Wesleyan schoolroom. By bedtime am almost prostrate.

Saturday, August 19th: The Great Day! No opportunity to recline and relax in bed before the Ordeal. Up at 7, and tear around. Marjory (of the flowers) delivers letter from herself at 7.15 a.m. beginning 'Good Morning to the Bride'!

A thoroughly wet day but fortunately fine for 2 hours to let us get to church and back. Everything goes smoothly except for slight muddle when George (Best Man) and Freddie chase each other around, because I have forgotten to put George's name on the car list to be picked up – my fault, as my father doesn't hesitate to say. He sits brooding about it, before we set course. And Freddie's folks are late arriving – having had to finish the journey by bus. Howbeit, we get married with all due ceremony. I

Freddie and May on their wedding day

wear Ivy's white wedding dress and Joyce's veil, and Amy, Brenda, Elaine and Jackie waft down the aisle after me. Have quite a decent feed afterwards – ham and tongue, strawberries, loganberries and cherries (bottled), trifles, cakes, salads and whatnot. Bella and Kay come, and Swanee – about 50 altogether, including The Staff, who give us a silver cake basket.

Freddie makes a Small Speech and says this is the Happiest Day of our lives (which touches Auntie Nell very much!) and there are several other speeches, including Vera's. Then we dash off for the Derby bus and have a taxi at Ambergate where the rain is gushing down and it is thundering and lightning. Freddie's mother feels sick when we get there, and Freddie has indigestion in the night. But a lovely day.

Rest of the Week: I suppose I should end my story now with, 'So We Got Married and Lived Happily Ever After.' But that remains to be seen ... Seems queer to think that I am actually married after all I've thought and said on the subject. Can't believe it yet. Little of incident happens during the rest of the week. We go to Derby one day to the flicks, after visiting Freddie's bank at Wirksworth. We also watch the corn-cutting, and Freddie shoots some poor old rabbits. The week is over much too quickly.

Saturday, September 9th: To Derby to see Gielgud, Leslie Banks and Peggy Ashcroft in *Hamlet.* Simply marvellous. A super show.

Saturday, September 16th: Wrote to Doug last night to thank him for the fruit and also to tell him I'm married.

Sunday, September 17th: Little of note, except that the extra hour's summer time is taken off, and the blackout is replaced by a Dim Out. We can take down blackouts and blinds here now.

Monday, September 18th: Very nice letter from Freddie – also letter from Doug ... Oh dear! He says he hasn't heard from me for months, and would like to know how I'm getting on (he won't when he knows!). He is very sorry for himself at the moment – being in bed after a motor bike crash. And he's going to send us some more fruit when he gets home – afraid he won't!

Wednesday, September 20th: Freddie arrives at teatime but for a Very Flying Visit – here today and gone tomorrow in literal truth. We trundle out to the NUT dance at the Rink, but when we get there at 9 p.m. the crowd is thin.

Thursday, September 21st: Freddie returns to Peplow. Am amazed when he gets up before I go to school – an unheard-of thing, but do not attribute this to a desire to Look His Last Upon Me, at this stage.

Saturday, September 23rd: Go to see Bill Swan married. He hasn't altered much. Hear him yodelling 'Pip, Pip', my name from school-days, as he's being photographed outside the chapel afterwards.

Monday, September 25th: Cold day, with a letter from Freddie to say that he hasn't heard from me since he went back. Queer! Not because I haven't fulfilled my wifely duties to him though – although it isn't so much of a duty as a pleasure to write to My Old Man.

Tuesday, September 26th: Greet the Old Man in the flesh today, much to my satisfaction.

Wednesday, September 27th: Think that perhaps Freddie will come with me to the Sale of Work, but oh no! not Freddie! He firmly decrees that Such Places are not for him, so after spending my £2 in about as many minutes on trifles and oddments, we go to the Picturedrome to see *North-West Mounted Police*. Find that I have already seen it.

Mother not too well, so goes back to bed again.

Thursday, September 28th: Freddie goes back once more. Oh dear!

Saturday, September 30th: Mother to stay in bed until Christmas at least! She doesn't look at all well when I come back from Nottingham where I've been with Hilda. Auntie Nell stays the night.

Sunday, October 1st: Awful day. The doctor comes but doesn't think much of Mother – her heart just twice as big as it should be, he says. Up all night with her.

Wednesday, October 4th: Freddie's place at Peplow is being taken over by the Fleet Air Arm, which means a move. Oh dear! I hope he isn't sent far afield. Makes me have a horrible sinking feeling to think about it. I'd miss him now more than I would ever have dreamed possible. Am more than satisfied with my husband, and very much in love with him. After all these years! Freddie exceptionally nice tonight.

Thursday, October 5th: Hate saying goodbye to Freddie again. Come as far as Burton with him, and am home by 12 o'clock. Dad's night up tonight.

Saturday, October 7th: A very welcome letter from Freddie to cheer up an otherwise dull and gloomy day. He says he was nearly frozen in bed and longed to be back with the missus. Good old Freddie! Only wish he had been! He says I get more precious to him every day, which is very comforting.

In all day again. Auntie Nell comes to stay the night but has a bad one – up all the time.

Sunday, October 8th: Miserable, dark, drizzly, depressing day. My father rants and raves about the parading Italians who go by the window in 2s and 3s. He calls them Blooming Articles and asks what those Damn Things are allowed out for – they ought to be behind some Blessed Wire, he says with ferocity. He could easily shoot the lot if he had a gun, he declares.*

Monday, October 9th: Awful day again. Can do no work, but just sit and watch the clock round. Mother very ill. Auntie Frances and Auntie Nell stay the night. Only bright spot a letter from Freddie which I read many times for comfort. He says the days seem like years when he is away, and seem to fly when we are together, and that it is heavenly to think that I belong to him. He wishes we had been married ages ago – and so do I!

Tuesday, October 10th: Mother asleep for most of the day, after a sleeping tablet last night, and seems a bit better as a result, much to our relief. And then Freddie comes too, which further brightens my outlook.

Wednesday, October 11th: Mother not much better, I'm afraid. Beginning to wonder what is going to happen, but can't bear to think of it. A miserable, wet, depressing, gloomy day. The weather seems to intensify the general gloom.

* * *

*There was a camp in the district of Italian prisoners of war, who worked on the farms. Charlie's sour view here was probably owing to his having served on the Italy-Austria Front in support of Italy in the previous war.

Friday, October 27th: Mother died at 8.20 a.m. this morning.

* * *

Sunday, November 19th: Have had no heart to write in my diary, and couldn't bear to write those dreadful words. But they are an unalterable fact.

Freddie during this time has moved to Hixon, a bomber training station near Stafford, but only till Christmas, then he'll be on the move again, which is very sad. At the moment he is fairly handy, and can get over more easily than he has been able to before.

Have had a visit or two from Bella. Still think she's a very good pal, in spite of years of comparative silence. She was very good while Mother was ill. Auntie Frances is here looking after us.

Monday, November 20th: Make up my mind to broach the question of having a week off when Freddie has his leave, to Connie, but as the day goes on I shiver and shake and put off the evil moment. And I trail home with the deed not done. Cowardice, shameful and arrant cowardice! A very nice letter from Freddie who says he is even happier now than when we first married and that it is wonderful being married. This gives me a very warm comfortable feeling for the rest of the day. And he rings up at night. This too is thoughtful of him, and his stock stands very high.

Tuesday, November 21st: Am a craven coward. Shiver and shake yet again at the thought of telling Connie about the week I want, and only at 4 o'clock do I muster enough courage to march to her door and knock. Out comes my request but I am amazed to hear myself asking timorously for A Day Or Two, instead of a Bold Week, which Connie takes literally, and her face clears somewhat. Am paralysed when I realise what I have done, but luckily she takes one look and asks suspiciously do I mean Just One or Two days? However finally agree to ask Barbara H to come in – which will surely give me the week if she does. So bike there on my way home, and she says she will. Very relieved.

Thursday, November 23rd: Auntie Nell and Joyce call. Joyce has bought a ¾ length fur coat – spotted! Am completely dashed by this and ponder with gloom the shabby state of my wardrobe. Have nothing decent to wear. What a war!

Saturday, November 25th: To Derby with Bella – dress-hunting. We are soon reduced to despair. Assistants merely look at Bella and tell her they have Nothing in a 42 hip, so Bella weighs herself and accuses me of putting my foot on the scale when it shows 11 st. I am 8 st 5. I try on pale turquoise dress – very nice, but when I catch a glimpse of the ticket, £18 6s., say with untruth that I don't really like it so will leave it. In fact we leave the shop, in despair. I buy blue dress material, then wonder if I like it.

Saturday, December 2nd: Hair permed this morn. Freddie's leave at long last. Meet him in Derby at 5.30 and we proceed to Alderwasley. Lovely to see him again.

Tuesday, December 5th: To Derby via Wirksworth. Go immediately after lunch and do a bit of shopping, then see *Champagne Charlie* at the Gaumont. Back by 9.30. Freddie has given me £6 to buy a new dress for Christmas. Am overwhelmed and very touched by this. A nice day.

Friday, December 8th: Up betimes and we go to Birmingham shopping. Lunch at Lewis' where we sit with a very breezy naval man. Have enjoyed Freddie's leave. There are still times when it seems unreal that we are married. Then at others it seems the most natural thing in the world. But I think I expect too much for any human man! Anyway I wouldn't like to be married to anyone but Freddie, even though he does sometimes just think only of himself.

Saturday, December 9th: Have my hair set – a needful and very necessary thing. Freddie declares afterwards that my hair is a mess, and that it looked much nicer before, and that I ought to sue the hairdresser. All this very dashing to my self-esteem, which also suffers a severe shock every time I view myself in the mirror and behold a large Cold Spot that stretches from my top lip to the base of my nose and has adorned me for the whole of this week. A Nice Thing to Have on his Leave, says Freddie.

Monday, December 11th: School once more, and I promptly proceed to make two mistakes in my register. Freddie comes to school with me this afternoon. Introduce him to Connie, and see no more of him till 2.20. Am just on the point of deciding that he has gone home without letting me know, when in he rolls, exclaiming that He Couldn't Get Away from Connie. He asks my children some mental questions and tells them pleasantly that they Are Poor, Aren't They? He strolls away at playtime, but I have to slog on till 4 o'clock. Stay in at night and do various oddments. Freddie's leave virtually over now.

Tuesday, December 12th: Letter from Eunice – Eric still surviving the rigours of a Japanese prison camp, and is doing clerical work.

Wednesday, December 13th – Freddie's birthday – his 32nd!: Spend the day clambering upon desks putting up garlands, festoons and other Xmas tokens. And this evening we press on with the Christmas cake. However, sad to relate, the Christmas Cake proves a fiasco. In spite of the most careful mixing and beating and so forth, and frequent pilgrimages to the oven with a candle to watch progress, when we take it out after 3½ hours, it looks quite all right on the top – but alas, the sides! and alack, the bottom! As black as coal, and the whole thing heavy like a lump of lead. Sad! We nearly weep.

Thursday, December 21st: Very touching card from Doug – with thanks for Happy Memories, and best wishes for Future Happiness. He sent to Mother and Dad too.

Friday, December 22nd: Miss Tooth and Bert call about 5.30, and stay till 7 o'clock. Bert follows Hilda in the most docile way, and doesn't seem to mind being taken out at all. Freddie would!

Saturday, December 23rd: This is going to be a very miserable Christmas, I fear. Feel very depressed today. Wish Xmas were over. Have a few nuts, which make things at least *look* a little more Christmassy.

Monday, December 25th – Christmas Day: The most miserable Christmas we have ever spent, I think. Foggy. No letter from Freddie. Am very disappointed. Dad gives me £2 and Auntie F 7/6. Will be glad when Christmas is over.

Wednesday, December 27th: Freddie comes. Lovely to see him again, especially after this miserable Christmas. It *has* seemed long drawn-out.

Sunday, December 31st: The last day of the Old Year. Am not sorry for that.

1945

~

Monday, January 1st 1945 – New Year's Day: And so a New Year begins. Think I'm getting too old to make rash resolutions and to expect too much! Am content now to take things more or less as they come – and to accept the good with thankfulness, and live through the bad with a hope of better things ahead. Anyway, last year was very mixed, and I'm very glad it's over. Freddie once more has to return.

Sunday, January 7th: To Church this morn. Very cold. Finish my ironing after dinner. Spend the evening indoors. Don't like Sundays at all now – quite a relief when Monday comes again.

Thursday, January 11th: My blue dress arrives, but as tight as can be. I daren't breathe. A great disappointment.

Saturday, January 13th: Letter from Freddie – he'll be here tomorrow, all being well and thanks be! Scuttle around in the morning and Hilda comes to tea. We go to the Majestic to see *San Demetrio, London* – a good flick about the Merchant Navy – and with never a woman in it! Quite a relief!

Friday, January 19th: Freddie says his future is still uncertain. Oh dear! It is a worry! Wish we could settle down together in peace.

Wednesday, January 24th: Alas! – Freddie won't be able to come tomorrow, in fact he doesn't know when he'll be able to come at all, as they have to go to their new place, 20 miles the other side of Sheffield, by the 2nd; and have to pack up and take all their equipment with them. What a job! And what a life! Am very disappointed.

Letter from Bella – seems to like housekeeping very much in her flat in Southend. Very tickled by her discreet little PS. A letter also from Amy. She is apparently in her element, with splendid digs, good school, friendly headmaster and staff, and near to Piccadilly! Her mind will be at rest at last.

Sunday, January 28th: After telling me not to expect him, Freddie walks in at teatime, which is a very joyful surprise. Shan't be seeing him again for some time after this visit.

Saturday, February 3rd: Hilda here to tea. We take my father to the flicks to see *The Way Ahead* – very good.

Wednesday, February 7th: Forgot to record about a fortnight ago a letter from Doug to say that his young brother has been killed in action in Italy. It *does* seem awful. Doesn't seem long since he was just a lad frisking about at camp.

Saturday, February 10th: Have quite a nice morn in Burton, though very cold, and buy dress length of Liberty silk, though it is coarse and looks like sacking, at the colossal price of 29/6 a yard. Have qualms before and after buying but hope it will look nice. Catch the 4 o'clock bus to Derby. No sign of Freddie when I get to the station so my faint hopes die. Then when I am in the train, see him strolling along the platform, and am I pleased to see him! He has been in Derby since 3 o'clock so has been to a football match. He *is* a dear and exceptionally nice somehow today.

*

Easter: Freddie has his leave and we have a lovely time together – 2 football matches, *Arsenic and Old Lace* and gardening etc. But it goes very quickly. Think we will be laying the foundations to our family about the end of October! Have a great thirst, and Freddie beseeches me not to drink so much – he's sure the child will be web-footed, or else need a dinghy!

April: Lovely hot spell – glorious weather. Bask in the sunshine.

May: To make up for this oversight we have awful cold spell – brrr! But war news quite good. Old Musso has been shot by the partisans, and Hitler and Goebbels have committed suicide. The Germans in Italy have capitulated. Sounds incredible really, but actually it's a bit of an anti-climax, after hoping for it all these years. Seems a tame end. The rope has been affixed to the flag-pole so now we can fly the flag on VE Day.

Saturday, May 5th: Freddie has the weekend off – we go to Alderwasley. Late for school on Monday morning – dive in at 10.30. Had hoped that VE Day would be announced this week-end. Freddie needn't have gone back then.

Monday, May 7th: VE Day at last announced for tomorrow. Flags appear everywhere, but would be much nicer if the war were *all* over.

Tuesday, May 8th: VE Day. War in Europe over. Broadcasts by Prime Minister at 3 p.m. and the King at 9 p.m. Day falls some-what flat, and feel rather washed out this morning. Auntie Nell and Joyce come to tea and we go to the Thanksgiving Service in church at 7. The church is full.

Wednesday, June 6th: Our street holds its Victory Celebrations – a sumptuous repast in the Wesleyan schoolroom, followed by a fancy dress parade, sports, and a big bonfire, and dancing in the street.

Thursday, June 7th: Reach the hoary age of thirty-one. Freddie very generously sends me £5. Father gives me £5 too, and Auntie F 10s. Vera has already given me Pyrex and Hilda skin food (necessary at my advancing age).

Tuesday, June 12th: Oh, what a poor forlorn thing my diary is these days! I fear it gets pushed very much in the background. An election due too, on 5 July, so election meetings in progress, and speeches on the wireless. Our Member comes on Thursday – must try to be there to give him a cheer. Good old Paul!

The Baby's trousseau isn't progressing very rapidly, sad to say. Am absolutely at sea when I think of prams, cots and what-not. Am a perfect Ignoramus on such matters. Poor little soul – the baby, I mean! Fear it will have to be trundled about in the wheelbarrow in its early stages, and the hand-cart in the later ones. Bill Swan's wife is expecting a baby in December.

Wednesday, June 20th: Nice note from Freddie – He says I grow dearer to him every day, and that he loves me with all his heart.

Thursday, July 5th: Another blank space in my diary! Shame! shame! Arouse my sluggish self however to announce that this is Election Day, and a scorching hot day too. Don't get to the polls till this evening, having taken Auntie Nell on a shopping expedition with me to Birmingham. A fruitless one too! See nothing worth buying. Have to stand all the way back and arrive with blister. Hobble along to put my X for Our Man though don't think for one minute he'll get in.

Thursday, July 26th: Election results announced. A Labour government, I fear, with a sweeping majority. Poor old Emrys-Evans eliminated, sad to say. Attlee Prime Minister and Bevin Foreign Minister.

Friday, July 27th: Finish school today for good, I trow, though Connie thinks I am going back in January, and has induced me to ask for Leave of Absence. Shall see! Holidays prolonged to 5 weeks this year, so shall not be going back at the end of August. Have our arrears of pay and feel like Croesus.

Monday, July 30th: Freddie's leave begins. He has a fortnight, so go to Alderwasley. The first week is lovely. Thoroughly enjoy being with Freddie, though we do little of any import. Do odd jobs in the garden. Slip home together on Friday because I have to go to the clinic, but return early Sat morn. Very hot indeed. However, after this very good start, the second week an anticlimax, and have moments of great boredom, and even wish I were at home. Freddie slips off on his own for most of the day, leaving me alone. Rudely begins his meals without me, and is either out or sits with his nose in a book and is no company at all. Have had much better weeks with Delia or Vera or Bella. Don't think all married couples are like this. Hope not, anyway, or Married Life Generally must be very dull. Home again Fri until Sat but feel done in when we arrive, after queues and buses and the heat.

Monday, August 13th: News has been developing rapidly this 2nd week – Russia has declared war on Japan, and we have developed a new Atomic Bomb – much smaller than most, but terrifically powerful and causing widespread devastation. Have used 2 so far, but expect the Japs will surrender now.

Home, beset by a few doubts. Am beginning to wonder if life with Freddie is going to be just being taken for granted and expected to sit at home until he's ready to notice me. If so, shall either have to subordinate myself to him – which is not at all likely! – or else strike off on my own, and lead my own life. Will not be a mere shadow, or a mere negation of myself, nor yet one of those Devoted, Docile Wives.

Tuesday, August 14th: Awakened at midnight by a disturbance in the street outside, which grows, and learn that Peace has finally been declared. Lie and listen for a while, then come downstairs and switch on the wireless but have missed it all except the tail end of a service. True though. Nearly everyone in the street turns out. They light a bonfire in Ward's Field. Jack Ward comes along in his pyjamas. Concertinas play, bells ring and sirens go, and the noise continues until about 4 a.m. Peeved that I can't join in.

Wednesday, August 15th: VJ Day – the first of two days' holiday. Rains this morning, and I make an apron to bath the baby in. Then go with Auntie Frances to a United Service in the Wesleyan Chapel.

Auntie Nell comes to tea, and we go to the service in church at night, then Renie, Brenda and Cecil call. Show them the baby things and at last evoke a bit of enthusiasm from someone! After supper wander along the street to see the festivities – dancing outside the Empire which is floodlit. But just watching is no fun, so retire to bed before 11 and leave them to it. Once more peeved that I can't join in. Bet Freddie is having a Rare Time – hope to goodness he won't be silly and get drunk.

Thursday, August 16th: Jack is on the way home from Italy – and I forgot to record that Eric has arrived at last on leave. He has been here for nearly a fortnight. So he and Joyce and Auntie Nell come to tea and don't go till 9 o'clock. Brenda and Cecil call too. Feel very much the grass widow when I view these happy pairs.

* * *

Monday, October 1st: October here at last. Large Query: Boy or Girl? and When? Oh dear! Freddie keeps telling me in lofty tones that it will be A Holiday ... Huh!

Sit Quietly At Home – a policy I deplore, but am hoping it won't be for the long term. Howbeit, with a longing eye to the (I hope) Not-Too-Far-Distant Future, I hurl myself with zeal into a Wardrobe Spring Clean, getting ready my Normal Clothes to wear again. Oh blessed day – when I can once more dress as I please, and not have to bend to the dictates of a Cumbrous and Lumbering Figure. Unfortunately, my existing clothes are all old – years and years old! – would dearly love to turf out the lot and start with a new wardrobe. But at the moment my finances look grim, to say the least. Haven't even had my allowance – wish I could simply march to the Post Office with a book and demand payment. Even a small amount per week – drawn impersonally – would be acceptable! As it is, hate the thought of being absolutely and utterly dependent on Freddie. Makes me feel both embarrassed and – well, too Dependent. Cherished my independence dearly, when I had it! I mourn its going.

October 14th–27th: Seem always to skim over these Important Events. During this period am in the Nursing Home! – a little before my time! Baby born at 1 a.m. Monday 15th October. Dr Cochrane had to come at the end and help him on his way, and they had a bit of trouble with his breathing, but all right now, thanks be! And a boy after all. The nurse is very very good, and altogether the fortnight not bad at all. Have Freddie to see me the next day. Baby has gained 10 oz this fortnight.

* * *

January, 1946: A New Year! Me Pore Old Diary, neglected again, shamefully and sadly. Never seem to find a single moment these days to write even a little word. Ah – the days of copious entries, of lengthy heart-searchings, of amorous outpourings. Suffice it to say that by now – touch wood! – Young Duncan has, as the Book says, Formed Regular Habits of Eating and Sleeping (particularly the latter, I rejoice to say). And had we but known, he would have done this from the start, but the poor mite was being underfed, and when he cried he was just clamouring for more. He loves his old bottle. And by now he notices things, and follows us around with his eyes, and tries to talk. Had him christened on January 3rd. Freddie's pal Edgar was his godfather. Baby as good as gold.

May and her son Duncan in 1946

Afterwards

A few months after the scenes greeting the end of the war in West Street, the diary came to a close. When the current volume was full, May did not start another. With her baby, she no longer had the time for 'diarising', especially as she was fairly soon doing stints of teaching supply work. Meanwhile Britain had settled into the long haul of post-war austerity. May's second child, Barbara, was born in 1950. May, Freddie and their children still lived at West Street with Charlie Smith and his sister Frances (who had moved here after May's mother's death). It was now time to leave the overcrowded house and set up the family's first home, on the edge of the town about a mile away.

It was not until April 1960 that May took up her pen again. The occasion was the day of her first driving lesson. Beginning with some characteristically droll description of her motoring progress (success at the second test), she continued to record her daily life for another twenty years. But the account is a different sort of journal compared with that of the war years: jottings and summaries with just occasional extended coverage. Soon after the resumption there is a mention of war diary regular Amy (whose sparkling teaching is still remembered in Swadlincote today). Where Amy taught is not stated, but it is apparent that, in her thirties, she was already a headmistress.

May returned to full-time teaching in the mid-1960s, doing ten more years at Springfield Road Junior School – and finding post-war teaching much more enjoyable than the wearying slog of earlier days. Her marriage to Frederic, whose courtship had for years seemed so unpromising, was in the event long and successful. May did, however, keep the promise that she made to her diary on the day before the end of the war that she would not be 'one of those devoted docile wives'. She cultivated a degree of independence through her friends and interests.

Freddie became deputy head of Castle Gresley School (a secondary modern in the post-war eleven-plus reorganisation) and he was deputy head of South Derbyshire's first comprehensive school, The Pingle, in Swadlincote, presiding (owing to the head's illness) when the local MP (and deputy Prime Minister), George Brown, performed the opening ceremony. He was also chairman of the Burton and South Derbyshire Schools' Football Association.

May and Freddie retired from teaching in the mid-1970s and both had active retirements. Freddie was a keen snooker player and gardener, being especially fond of roses. He died in 1999. May involved herself in the Townswomen's Guild and WRVS, including 'meals on wheels' and baby clinic work, as well as in art – she was an accomplished painter.

The remarkable institution of The Budget continued. Started in 1934, it lasted, inevitably with diminishing numbers, until May's death, aged ninety, in 2004. There is one surviving member, Vera Brown, who lives in Buckinghamshire. At ninety-nine, Vera is still busy, helping with the work of Calibre audio books.

World war did not return in May Marlor's lifetime, but of course there was always war in the news. May lived to see – and deprecate – the Iraq War. How much a theme war will be in future 'ordinary person' diaries we cannot know, but May's diaries show how great is the cost of modern war. And these accounts and observations will, it is hoped, add to the enduring testimony of that British generation which, in the defence of its islands against fascism, faced the abyss, and did so with cheerfulness and humour.

Duncan Marlor
November 2011

May and Freddie with their grandson 1978

Pupil essays in wartime

By chance May Smith's 1940–1941 teaching record book has
survived. It illustrates the effects of war on the content of the classroom curriculum. Essay subjects for the year include 'The house
that was not blacked out' and 'What to do in an air raid'. There was
further war topicality in 'Helping our country', 'Adventures of a
Spitfire', and 'War Weapons Week'. Time-honoured composition
favourites such as 'The autobiography of an old shilling' and 'When
I grow up' were varied by the imagery and reflections of war living.

Rumours

In May Smith's diary we find some of the classic rumours,
including Lord Haw Haw's supposed local knowledge of everyone's area. These widely circulating tales were untrue. The
preposterous story of refugee German Jews signalling to German
planes reflects the hysteria in elements of the press about 'enemy
aliens'. This was the summer of 'parachutist' frenzy, with everyone on the look out for parachuting spies and invaders. The
German parachutist with his folding bicycle, who features in the
South Derbyshire supposed sightings, was a favourite. The report
which the diary quotes on 7 October 1940 of four failed German

invasion attempts is in line with other such stories, some with floating German corpses or human remains on the beach.

The 24 September 1940 rumour about collapsing morale in London is of course untrue. The credibility of bombing reports varied greatly. The diary for 27 June 1940 mentions 'tales in circulation to the effect that Crewe station has been bombed to bits . . .' These were not true. George Orwell's diary for 19 August 1940 observes, 'A feature of the air raids is the extreme credulity of almost everyone about damage done to distant places.'* Reports sometimes contained some truth but were exaggerated or distorted. Mrs Tweed's 4 November 1940 story of fifty-seven dead bodies at a cinema in Birmingham must refer to the bombing of the Carlton Picture House in Sparkbrook, Birmingham, on 25 October 1940. The event did occur, but the actual fatality figure was nineteen.

On the other hand on-the-spot accounts of local bombing could be more accurate than the printed contemporary record, given press censorship for military reasons and because of slanting of coverage in order to keep up morale. May Smith's account of the bombing of Melbourne, a village close to her home, on 11 July 1940, is correct regarding casualties, as the graves in Melbourne cemetery of the eight victims attest. The coverage is valuable because no mention of the fact that the dead were soldiers was permitted in the press. Nor was the indignation at the recent cutting back of the local ARP allowed to be reported.

Evacuees

The evacuation of inner city Birmingham children to South Derbyshire in 1939 had been worked out as a contingency plan

---

*George Orwell, *The Orwell Diaries*, edited by Peter Davison (Penguin Modern Classics, 2010).

before the war. In the evacuation zones all schools were to close immediately on the outbreak and their populations were to share facilities with the schools of the reception areas. Springfield Road was twinned with Saltley's Bloomsbury School, on a 'shift system'. There was an imbalance, because although all the Birmingham teachers turned up (having no option), over half of their pupils were kept back by their families. When the expected bombs did not fall, the majority of the Birmingham evacuees drifted back home, many of them quite quickly. Most of the Birmingham teachers were recalled to conduct 'home study groups', pending the reopening of the schools on the completion of air-raid shelters. At Springfield Road the remaining evacuees were soon absorbed into the local classes.

The events of the summer of 1940 and fears of a German invasion of the south-east coast of England brought more upheaval. May Smith describes being on billeting duty when the Southend evacuees arrived in June 1940, but Springfield Road did not receive a contingent. The next big influx into Swadlincote was the result of the heavy bombing of London and some of the provinces in the latter part of 1940. The return of children from South Derbyshire to Birmingham was thrown into reverse.

After 1941 May's billeting services were not required. November 1942 diary news includes the German army in retreat in North Africa and the return of signposts to the South Derbyshire landscapes. The two circumstances were related: fear of invasion was largely removed by the Allied progress. Many of the Southenders now returned home.

There was one final wave of evacuation to South Derbyshire. It occurred in the latter part of 1944 when Hitler's 'V' missiles were taking a heavy toll in London and south-east England. May Smith's school did not receive any of the new evacuees.

COs

On 12 March 1940 May Smith remarks, 'What notoriety!' She had read a report in her local *Burton Daily Mail* on the latest batch of registrations of called-up men. It was headlined, 'Only one "Conchy"'. This was the family's lodger Mr Skerritt. 'Conchy' was the derisive term often used. Many local authorities, including May Smith's employer Derbyshire County Council, voted to sack conscientious objectors in their employ, despite protests (for example from the Bishop of Derby) that this was a denial of the rights for which Britain was supposed to be fighting. Ted Skerritt was successful at the Midlands Conscientious Objector Tribunal at Derby in making his case on religious grounds to remain on the CO register. But he had a difficult time at work when his stance became known, being 'sent to Coventry' by his workmates. Fortunately the Smiths, though they disagreed with Mr Skerritt's pacifist point of view, respected his personal courage in following his conscience. John Ollerenshaw, who took the diarist to the inter-church 'Group' on 17 May 1940, at which the discussion favoured a pacifist line on the war (to May's silent indignation), is mentioned on 30 April 1943 on leave from the Army bomb disposal service at heavily bombed Plymouth. A number of conscientious objectors served in this way. It was highly dangerous work.

Rationing – and good meals

The diarist's accounts of the wartime eating experience look like paradox. May Smith did not live on a farm, nor despite the joyfully greeted presents from Doug do we hear of any special food supply. Yet her family seems to have enjoyed some good meals, and May regularly worries about whether she is putting on weight. However, impressions can be misleading. The deprivation was in the variety of food available. The basic staples of bread and potatoes were never rationed during the war. On the other hand imported foreign fruit disappeared, and meat, fish, butter, cheese and jam were among the rationed commodities. And May's 'Oh misery!' lament on 11 July 1941 when Doug's twenty eggs were lost in the post needs to be understood in the context of an egg ration of one fresh egg per person per week and one packet of dried egg powder per month. The rationing of sugar seems to have been felt painfully in the Smith family. The white cardboard covers to represent icing on the cake noted at the 1 March 1941 wedding were standard as a result of a ban on icing, though at a wedding in May's family a week later the prohibition was evidently disregarded. There was much improvisation. No doubt May's mother followed the Government's 'Potato Pete' advice on cooking versatility. We do not hear about this because the kitchen was May's mother's preserve.

Along with rationing and shortages went queuing. May Smith's 29 March 1941 morning of joining queues without knowing what was on the end of them seems to have been regular shopping behaviour at this time. This was the worst period of the war for shortages, with the Germans having considerable success in sinking Allied shipping. As in the First World War, both sides used blockades. It is against the background of economic warfare that the free dinner schemes for school children of low-income families were introduced. May, herself a voluntary organiser for a children's charity, was soon converted, after her initial scepticism, to the benefits of the new system. School lunches, an innovation locally, were quickly assimilated into the routine.

SELECT BIBLIOGRAPHY

The home front:

Juliet Gardiner, *Wartime: Britain 1939–1945* (Headline, 2004). The classic and highly readable account of the social history of Britain at war.

Norman Longmate, *How We Lived Then: A History of Everyday Life in the Second World War* (Pimlico, 2002)

The BBC 'The People's War' website www.bbc.co.uk/ww2peopleswar, a wide-ranging collection of personal accounts, includes the reminiscences of Margaret Sanders who was a Southend teacher evacuated to the Swadlincote area with her pupils.

Evacuees:

Mike Brown, *Evacuees* (Sutton Publishing, 2000). The book gives detailed and illustrated coverage of all aspects of evacuation, as well as the history of the various phases. Included is an account of private evacuation. There were many private evacuees, including some at Springfield Road School. The Birmingham evacuee who so delighted May Smith with her recitations in September 1939 would be one of these.

Accounts of evacuation to Derbyshire include:

Pam Hobbs, *Don't Forget to Write* (Ebury Press, 2009). Reminiscences of a Southend to Derbyshire evacuee.

Juliet Blick, *Pass the Parcel: Evacuee 1940–1945* (Norden Books, 2005). Evacuee reminiscences which include south Derbyshire.

Rumours:

James Hayward, *Myths and Legends of the Second World War* (Sutton Publishing, 2003)

Mark Rowe *Don't Panic: Britain Prepares for Invasion 1940* (The History Press, 2010). The author's study possibly explains the origins of the report of German parachutists around Rugby and Leicester which the diary mentions on 1 July 1940. Mark Rowe describes how on 30 June 1940 a low-flying British plane over Worcestershire led to stories about German paratroops, such that the LDV at Stourport rang the church bells; as a result parachutist rumours spread across parts of the Midlands.

The bombing:

Winston G. Ramsey (ed.), *The Blitz Then and Now* (3 volumes) (After the Battle, 1987, 1988, 1990). This is a comprehensive record with explanatory articles. Among crash incidents, the authors list (vol. 2, p. 598) a Junkers 88, flying low with engine failure, which crashed with the loss of all crew on Staffordshire moorland at 1 a.m. on the night of 7/8 May 1941. This appears to be the plane which May Smith mentions as 'crippled and caught in the searchlight'. (The plane's target was Merseyside.) Also listed by Ramsey (vol. 3, p. 47) is the Heinkel 111 which crashed at the village of Lullington to the south of Swadlincote on the night of 24–25 June 1941, the wreckage of which May and Hilda looked for on June 28th. The pilot was killed when his parachute failed to open and the other three crew were taken prisoner.

The British Blitz experience:

Juliet Gardiner, *The Blitz: The British Under Attack* (HarperPress, 2011)

Peter Stansky, *The First Day of the Blitz* (Yale University Press, 2007).

War dead:

The Commonwealth War Graves Commission: www.cwgc.org/ d_of_honour. The CWGC website includes civilian dead. Five fatalities are listed for Swadlincote for the night of 20/21 November 1940.

Wartime teaching:

David Cannadine, Jenny Keating, Nicola Sheldon, *The Right Kind of History: Teaching the Past in Twentieth-Century England* (Palgrave Macmillan, 2011). The authors include many insights into state school life in the period of this diary.

P. H. J. H. Gosden, *Education in the Second World War* (Routledge, 2007)

RAF life:

Brian Kedward, *Angry Skies across the Vale* (B. H. Kedward, 1996). The author gives a detailed account of life during WW2 at Honeybourne and Long Marston airfields, where Frederic Marlor was stationed.

'Polish girl pilot':

The book *Spitfire Women* by Giles Whittell (HarperPress, 2007) sheds some light on the diary mention on 21 May 1943 of Freddie having had a chat with a female Polish pilot. She would be a member of the ATA (Air Transport Auxiliary), which included 166 female pilots. Their job, ferrying planes about, was high risk, and fifteen died. There were four Polish women fliers, all with remarkable personal stories: these are described in this book.

Conscientious Objectors:

Rachel Barker, *Conscience, Government and War: Conscientious Objectors in Britain, 1939–1945* (Routledge, 1982)

Derby and the war:

Clive Hardy and Russ Brown, *Derby at War* (Sutton Publishing, 1998). Details are given of the attack on the Rolls-Royce aircraft engine factory on 27 July 1942, in which there were twenty-three fatalities, in what was Derby's worst loss-of-life incident in the war. Derby, in view of its military importance, escaped relatively lightly in the war, with a total for the war of 74 fatalities. The 'pasting' which was feared never happened. The authors discuss possible reasons for this.

Birmingham and the war:
Carl Chinn, *Brum Undaunted: Birmingham During the Blitz* (Brewin Books, 2005)

ACKNOWLEDGEMENTS

My thanks are given to the many people who have provided help with this book, including especially:

Former pupils of May Smith: Dennis Alcock, Mrs Noreen Illsley (née Parker), Geoffrey Nutt, the late Roy Nutt, Ronald Webb, and the late Gerald Wheat; Joy Holmes, daughter of Mr (Ted) Skerritt, wartime lodger of the diarist's family; Vera Brown and Delia Foulkes-Jones, friends of May Smith; Eric Hill and the late Diane Woodhouse of Birmingham Heartlands Local History Society, Birmingham; the headteachers and staff of Springfield Road School (Swadlincote), Belmont School (Swadlincote), Overseal School, Hartshorne School, and Saint Saviour's School (Saltley); the British Museum Newspaper Library (Colindale); Imperial War Museum (London); Commonwealth War Graves Commission (Maidenhead); Swadlincote Public Library; Derbyshire Record Office, Matlock; Birmingham Central Library's Local History and Archives Departments; Derby Local Studies Library; Sharpe's Pottery Museum, West Street, Swadlincote, and the Magic Attic archive and local history centre, which is situated here, with special thanks to Graham Nutt; David Kynaston, author of *Austerity Britain* and *Family Britain*, for his encouragement and valuable advice; my agent Hannah Westland and Ursula Doyle, Joanna Goldsworthy and Tamsyn Berryman at Virago for their inspirational guidance of the diary to publication; and last but not least my sister, Barbara Joyce, for her encouragement and patient help with family information.

th me, for I have found the
nch I had lost.

ips begin to subside, so
   Kitchen we trek once
under outside, to find
t alive with curious
no have popped out of
es like worms after a
to investigate the extent
damage. We find that
's fffffth window is half
  littered over the pavement,
e the fire engines go
   by at great speed.
that most of the shop.
s along High St. are out,
the bomb has fallen just
   Hastings Rd., in Baker St.,
wing to cottages. We
ately think of the effect
  have on all our friends
   Delia would get the full